The Covenant People of God

The Covenant People of God

Clifford Denton

He has showed you, O man, what is good, and what does the LORD require of you? To act justly and to love mercy and to walk humbly with your God. (Micah 6:8)

First published 2001 by Tishrei International in association with Cambrian Bible College

Typeset by Alison G Cross through co-operation with Prophetic Word Ministries.

Line drawings by Miriam Willey and Mark Williams are reprinted from Tishrei

Printed by CPI, Bristol England

Distributed by Cambrian Bible College, c/o The Orchard, 5 The Street, Gillingham, Beccles, Suffolk NR34 0LH, England. Enquiries relating to Bible Study courses including Certificate, Diploma and Degree programmes should also be directed to this address.

ISBN: 1 901516 10 5 Hard back
1 901516 11 3 Paper back

Contents

Section 3
Halakhah
Part 1: A Walk with God

Part 2: One Covenant Community

Part 3: Character and Purpose

Part 4: Be Filled with the Holy Spirit

Appendix

Introduction

The history of mankind is short - just a few thousand years. The beginning of the story is in our Bibles. God created the heavens and the earth and all that is in them. He made man from the dust of the earth and breathed life into him. He made mankind for fellowship with Himself - to walk with Him. The history of the world is about the fall of man from this fellowship and God's plan of recovery. Men and women exercise their God-given free will to walk with God or walk away from God. God's plan takes account of mankind's free will to choose but He has made it possible for us to regain that walk with Him. The central issue of this plan is redemption through the shed blood and sacrifice of the Son of God, who is also the Son of Man, who before going to the Cross prayed: "Now this is eternal life: that they may know you, the only true God, and Jesus Christ, whom you have sent." (John 17:3) To know God like a pure bride should know her husband, more and more intimately, is God's purpose for His redeemed community.

God showed mankind His purpose and set out His requirements through His Covenant. He taught us His ways through his Torah. He does not compromise, yet still enables mankind to walk in friendship with Him, through the workings of His Spirit.

The end of the story is declared in the Bible ahead of time. There will be one united redeemed covenant community restored as one man in fellowship with God forever. This one covenant community is drawn from all nations. There is a hebraic identity within the background to the Scriptures intended to form our character. In the Last Days this will be re-emphasised as many Jews will be saved by faith in Yeshua (Jesus) restored to the covenant family among the many who have been saved from among the Gentile nations (Romans 11). We are already in this era of restoration to the true roots of our faith as the one covenant family is being prepared like a bride would be prepared for the return of the bridegroom.

This book is a compilation of papers written over recent years. In the book I have emphasised the fact of there being one covenant community with one teaching and one purpose - to walk (halakh) together with God. I have introduced some of the major Hebrew words (Yeshua for Jesus, Torah for teaching, Halakhah for walking with God) in order to contribute a little to the restoration of hebraic terms in a Church that has drifted too far into Greek philosophical ideas in its scriptural interpretation. I have tried particularly to be sensitive and clear in my use of these terms in the balance of God's teaching through the whole of Scripture. The whole of Scripture is the teaching of God. However, I generally use the word Torah as applying specifically to the foundation of all Bible teaching laid in the first five books of the Bible, so freeing these books from the word law which I use specifically in relation to the clear legal instructions and their interpretation given to Moses at Sinai. The "Law of Moses" is therefore a subset of Torah, and can also apply to the authoritative interpretation of what was given through Moses in the Wilderness years. In this way we can see that grace always came before law, the life of faith always being higher than ritual legalism, setting the scene for our prime call into a walk by faith in fellowship with God by the power of His Spirit.

It is my hope that this book will contribute to the restoration, not so much of a Hebrew framework to our lives as to a true and meaningful walk with the living God. This is why Yeshua HaMashiach (Jesus the Messiah) came to earth to die as a sacrifice for our sins and to rise again to lead us into eternal life. Let the Lord God lead you into this relationship more deeply as you read through the pages. You are strongly advised to take time to read each section looking up the relevant Scriptures and answering the questions which are posed at the end of sections. The sections can be studied alone or used as a stimulus for family or group study. Use each section as a stimulus for prayer and meditation, listening to God for yourself.

Clifford Denton
Spring 2001

Foreword

It is rare to find practical and useful information in one volume. 'The Covenant People of God' provides both. Herein, Dr. F. Clifford Denton provides practical and useful information about the most important issue facing God's believing community today - walking with God.

Walking with God is an important issue yet very little is written to help those seeking 'how' to walk with a 'consuming fire' (Deuteronomy 4:24). Adam and Eve lost their walk with God due to sin (Genesis 3:8) while Enoch walked with God and 'was no more because God took him' (Genesis 5:24). Sin causes man to 'hide' from walking with God while obedience 'restores' it to those who please God (Hebrews 11:5). Peter and Andrew wanted to please God through obedience. Jesus said to them, 'Follow Me.' 'At once they left their nets and followed (walked with) him' (Matthew 4:20).

In 'The Covenant People of God,' Dr. Denton makes the same request to all currently seeking a walk with God. He wants everyone's walk with Jesus Christ to produce the same result as it did with the two who walked with Jesus to Emmaus. He wants minds opened to understand the Scriptures! Luke 24:44-45 says, 'He said to them, 'This is what I told you while I was still with you. Everything must be fulfilled that is written about me in the Law of Moses, the Prophets and the Psalms.' Then he opened their minds so they could understand the Scriptures.'

Following an excellent presentation of 'Who are we?' (how the covenants fit together as one) and 'Torah, the teaching of God,' 'The Covenant People of God' provides the reader a practical section called 'Halakhah' (walking with God). This book teaches how to walk with God.

'The Covenant People of God' is written, I believe, to the 'Joshua Generation.' The 'Joshua Generation' are those who will welcome

Jesus, our Messiah, back to this earth. It helps prepare God's people for this historically anticipated event. 'The Spirit and the bride say, 'Come!' And let him who hears say, 'Come!' Whoever is thirsty, let him come; and whoever wishes, let him take the free gift of the water of life. ... He who testifies to these things says, 'Yes, I am coming soon.' Amen. Come. Lord Jesus' (Revelation 22:17, 20).

Karl D. Coke, Ph. D.

Section 1

Covenant

God's Covenant with mankind has one supreme purpose - to gather one united people together in restored relationship with Himself. As we move towards the day when the Lord Jesus will return, we who are called into this fellowship must understand who we are as this one covenant family. This can be done by considering how all the steps of the covenant plan fit together.

The worldwide covenant community must solve its identity crisis and learn to live together as one new man.

Who are we?

The Covenant people: An overview

Readings Ephesians 2:12-22, Romans 11:17.

There is one and only one body of believers who make up the family of God. By physical line of descent all human beings can trace their ancestry back to Adam, where family life began. If it were not for the Fall, the one family of God would be identical with the family of Adam. After the fall there was a need to draw together, out of all mankind, a new family from all the descendants of Adam. Almighty God did not abandon His plan to have a family drawn from among the descendants of Adam, and all the continuing history of the world has been for the purpose of drawing together that one family. The primary need, over all the generations of salvation history, has been to overcome the power of sin. In so doing, God made the needs of mankind known so that the call of God would be met by willing response from those who would become members of the one new body. Membership of the family of God is through faith and there is one and only one provision for forgiveness of sin and that is through the shed blood of God's one and only Son, Jesus Christ (Yeshua HaMashiach). The need for reconciliation with God began at the Fall, it was made possible through Jesus (Yeshua) and the final picture is shown in the Book of Revelation (Revelation 7) where we see a picture of the whole family of God gathered around the Throne, drawn from all the Tribes of Israel and all the Tribes of the earth. Out of the broken and dispersed family of Adam, members of the family of God are united through faith in Jesus (Yeshua) into this new family, which spans all of history.

Having outlined these basic truths relating to the plan of salvation there needs to be a review of just who the one family of

God is. There have been a number of key steps along the way, when God has revealed His plan and outworked His purposes among the families of mankind, the physical descendants of Adam. Because there have been a number of steps over history, it is possible to lose sight of the one plan for the one united family of God, and perhaps think that the various stages have been separate and distinct plans, instead of the one overall plan. For example, the Tribes of Israel were chosen within the central part of God's plan before the Gospel message went out across the whole world. After the full revelation of the Son of God and after His sacrifice for sin a new era began, but this was not the beginning of the family of God. Instead it was the time when, as outlined in Romans 11, those saved from among the Gentile nations were brought into membership of the *already existing* family. The end of the picture is when God brings in, among the end time harvests, those who will be saved from the physical descendants of Israel, grafted into the Olive Tree beside those grafted in from the nations of the world. We must not lose the picture of the one family as we consider the phases of salvation history, a family finally made up of Jews and Gentiles with equality, in that all have been saved from their sin through the sacrifice of the Son of God and who are saved on account of their faith. The one historic body goes back to the beginning of time. All who come to God the Father with the same saving faith, whether looking forward to Jesus (Yeshua) or back, are members of this one body.

The central key to understanding the way Almighty God has gathered His family is to consider how He has made covenants through history and to consider how these covenants have led progressively to the fulfilment of the overall purpose of God, to gather a family typified by faith. There is one plan embedded in all these covenants that is finally enabled through the sacrifice of Jesus (Yeshua). The New Covenant, through the shed blood of Jesus (Yeshua) whereby the principles of Torah are written on the heart of believers, is the means of gathering the one family. It is not a new covenant in the sense of replacing all that went before, but of enabling the plan of salvation which was also the goal of other aspects of God's covenants. If we read Chapter 11 of the Book of

Hebrews we find men of faith going back to the beginning of time who were saved by faith, including for example, Abel, Enoch, Abraham, Isaac, Jacob, David, Gideon and all who lived by faith. Members of the one family of God join with those mentioned in Hebrews 11 and all who have lived by faith from the beginning of time.

The principal of covenant goes back into ancient times. The Hebrew word for *covenant* is *B'rit*, a word whose root can be associated with eating or dining, pointing to customs which were used to signify the sealing of a covenant. The shedding of blood is associated with the making or cutting of a covenant (See Genesis 15:8-10). This could point to the penalty for breaking the covenant, as well as the high cost of sealing the covenant. Though agreement is intended between the two parties of a covenant it is not an agreement between equal partners. The originator of the covenant establishes the conditions for both sides. The conditions are made clear to the lower party (for example, Deuteronomy 28) and the obligations of both parties to the other are made clear. The covenant is confirmed by an oath (for example, Genesis 26:28, Deuteronomy 29:9-20). Almighty God has made covenants throughout salvation history, confirming them with irrevocable oaths. The overall purpose was to reverse the separation of mankind from Himself that began with Adam and Eve. Out of all mankind He has been drawing together a family based on His Covenants and sealed by His Oath. The progress of these covenants and oaths enables us to understand who we are. The point to be born in mind always is that there is one and only one plan for the establishing of one redeemed family.

Just as we all have a common ancestor in Adam, so we all have a common ancestor in Noah. At the time of Noah, God made a covenant, which would ensure that all of mankind could survive through the provision of food. Thus mankind could be preserved while the rest of the plan of salvation was developed. God committed Himself to providing food for mankind as long as the earth would exist. The next step was a covenant with Abraham. Within this covenant was the promise of a physical family that would inherit their own land. Later revelation shows that Abraham's family were primarily to be the family of faith, so we can see that the provision of the Promised Land for Israel was within the context of preparing a people for living by faith. If we review these two steps we see that through both Abraham and Noah were essential steps of provision within a background of a deeper plan of salvation. The later covenant with Moses brought revelation of God's righteous requirements for His covenant people. Later we learn that the righteous requirements of Torah are not taken away, but that the chief goal in terms of the plan of salvation was to reveal sin, pointing to the life of faith. The covenant with Moses was within the framework of the covenant with Abraham. It was not a new plan. Similarly the covenant with David was that a King would come from His seed, ensuring that the Saviour of the world would restore the Kingdom to Almighty God. The various covenants thus pointed towards a final fulfilment in Jesus (Yeshua) and this was enabled through the covenant, made with Jeremiah, concerning the Torah becoming a spiritual manifestation to be written on the hearts of the covenant people, who would live by faith. The interaction of all of God's covenant plans, sealed by oaths, pointed to one recovery plan and one family of faith.

There has been an identity crisis in the Church for hundreds of years, whereby it was thought that a new plan was begun with the incarnation of the Son of God, and whereby the failure of Israel made it necessary for a new body called the Church. There are many issues to consider if this is to be given full treatment, but it is now time to review the full plan that Almighty God has developed throughout history. He is gathering one body and this body has members going back to the beginning of time, drawing into one family those who live by faith. Believers from Gentile nations have been drawn in alongside the rest, and many from Israel have and will be drawn into this same family towards the end of time. There is one plan and one family, and there is equality within this family whether we come into it first or last.

Who are we?

A People of Faith

Reading: Hebrews 11.

Almighty God created people with free will. He also created them to live in fellowship with Him. Thus there is a condition relating to free will that must characterise the covenant community of God; we must learn to exercise our free will to conform to God's own will. This reverses the curse of the Fall, when fellowship with God was lost. The Fall came when Adam and Eve disobeyed God. Behind this disobedience, however, were other factors. The chief one was that they had failed to trust God. God had told them what to do but without a full explanation of why, so they were meant to trust Him. This they failed to do. The plan of salvation restores this trusting relationship between God and His people, which was lost through the disobedience of Adam and Eve. The understanding of this goes beyond human logic into the area of the spiritual gift called faith, which God Himself gives us. There is a free-will response on our part to God's call into His fellowship as we affirm that we will respond to God's plan to build our faith. Since we are to be redeemed from the sinful world resulting from the Fall, God requires a sacrifice for our sin in order to gain entry into this relationship by faith. This sacrifice was His only Son Jesus (Yeshua). It is through faith in Him and the power of His shed blood that we can be restored into fellowship with the Father. In every generation, the call to restored fellowship has been through faith in God's own provision for sin through His one and only Son. This is the trusting relationship that typifies the covenant community.

There is One God and it is to Him we are restored. He is the same One God with whom all His children are reconciled throughout all generations through faith. This principle is not new. It goes back through all history, as we see from Hebrews chapter 11. Abraham, with whom the central covenant was made, is the principal human example of how to live according to saving faith. It was said of him, 'that faith was reckoned to Abraham for righteousness.' (Romans 4:9) In many places of Scripture we are shown that Abraham is our father of faith, according to the truth of Hebrews 11:6, that it is only faith that pleases God. We realise, however, that such faith also reversed the character of disobedience that caused the fall of Adam and Eve when we read, 'Abraham obeyed my voice, and kept my charge, my commandments, my statutes, and my laws.' (Genesis 26:5) In the restored fellowship based on faith and trust in God, within which there is a covering for the weakness of the flesh to sin, Abraham also showed that this must result in obedience. The covenant community of God is typified by these overlapping principles. First, there is to be saving faith, and then the fruit of the restored relationship with Father God, is obedience.

An important principle within all of this is to recognise, particularly through meditation on Hebrews 11, that the covenant community contains those who were called and who responded to God according to these covenant principles *from the beginning of time*. This emphasises the important principle that those of us who join the covenant community, in any generation, join this one ancient body (the Olive Tree of Romans 11), going back to the beginning of time, and the same principles of membership of this family of God apply to all, whether from Israel or from any other nation.

Hebrews chapter 11 mentions many powerful examples of those who learned to please God through faith. All of these men and women preceded the incarnation of Jesus (Yeshua), demonstrating that God was building His one covenant community throughout all of history. His provision of the sacrifice of His one and only Son, which we understand more fully than those who preceded His incarnation, was nevertheless the object of their own faith throughout all generations. For example, Paul illustrates the principle of Jesus (Yeshua) being with His people before His incarnation as the object of their faith, when he shows how the Children of Israel lived in His presence (spiritually): 'Did all eat the same spiritual meat; and did all drink the same spiritual drink: for they drank of that spiritual Rock that followed them: and that Rock was Christ.' (1 Corinthians 10: 3-4) John also refers to the grace of God through Jesus (Yeshua) that was always above the Law of Moses, '*For the law was given by Moses, but grace and truth came by Jesus Christ.*' (John 1:17) The principle of grace through Jesus (Yeshua) encompassed all that the Father did both before and after the incarnation of Jesus (Yeshua). To consider these same principles of grace and salvation through faith throughout all history helps us to realise who we are in this generation, when we are called into the one covenant family. We join all those who went before. We enter the family by the same principles of faith in God's provision, now more clearly understood than before, but no less true for those saved thousands of years ago than for us. Across all of history, there is one covenant community restored into fellowship with the Father through faith.

We do not have a record of how many people there are throughout all the generations since the Fall who responded to the call to the life of faith. The Father knows who these are, but it is not necessary for us to know. There may be many more than we realise. However, we do have records in Scripture of those whom the Father would use to teach us important truths about the call to fellowship with Him through the life of faith. The list in Hebrews chapter 11 should inspire us to go back and look at some of those who preceded us into the Olive Tree of faith, going back to the beginning of time.

Abel, for example, teaches us about acceptable offerings to God. He speaks to our heart about the faith that must accompany sacrifice if it is to please God. This principle is perfectly revealed through the faith that we must have in the sacrifice of Jesus (Yeshua) to whom His own sacrifice pointed. Abel's faith, at heart level, was in accord with the faith that we must have in the Son of God, who laid down His life for us.

Enoch teaches us about a walk with the Father that should grow out of our faith in Him. Throughout all history, no-one else has been commended for their walk of faith like Enoch, before or after the incarnation of Jesus (Yeshua). Note how God's plan of salvation was to be given to those who could walk by faith from all the nations. Both Abel and Enoch preceded the special call on the Children of Israel. This is specially shown by Noah, who is the forefather of all people from all nations after the flood, not just Israel.

Through Abraham, God began to reveal more clearly His plan to save many from all nations. He built faith in Abraham and made this a prior condition for fellowship than was the resulting works of obedience. Abraham modelled for us many principles of the life of faith. His greatest test was on Mount Moriah, with his own son on the sacrificial altar, which pointed clearly to the substitute of Jesus (Yeshua) for all the community of faith who aspired to the high heart principles demonstrated through Abraham.

King David is the central figure in the nation of Israel who lived by faith, in harmony with the requirements of the Law of Moses. We understand this from many of the Psalms and also from the history of his life. David points us to the Messiah through the pattern of his life, and he also teaches us about the balanced heart response to the Torah of God through faith.

Just as the writer of the Book of Hebrews indicates in chapter 11, there are many other examples and much more that could be said about the faith of those who are included in Scripture to teach us about the life of faith. The important point we are making here, however, is that there is just one covenant community throughout history. The plan of salvation through faith is a continuous one. We join all who went before us in this life of faith. They are part of our family and we are a part of theirs. The mysteries behind the incarnation of the Son of God may not be easy for us to understand, but we would be wise to accept that there were many whose faith pointed towards His coming even though they did not see with their eyes or read clear Gospel accounts such as we have. Indeed, God has made it that many who preceded the Incarnation had deeper faith than those who came in later generations including our own. May the Lord Himself strengthen our understanding of who we are as members of the one historic body when we join this one people of faith, and give us joy in our membership alongside all who went before.

Who are we?

Children of the One True God

Reading: Deuteronomy 6:4, Malachi 2:10, Mark 12:29-30, Romans 3:29-30, 1 Corinthians 8:6, Ephesians 4:4-6, 1 Timothy 2:5.

At the foundation of our faith as members of the one covenant community spanning all history is the truth that there is One God who created all things. From before the time of Moses this was known. It was known by Adam and Eve. It was known by Enoch and all who have walked by faith since then. It was known by Abraham and his children. After the Fall, the One True and unchanging God revealed Himself in a variety of ways to Adam's fallen race, according to different aspects of His character, as He also brought the Covenants into being, swearing by an unchangeable Oath that He would redeem a family for Himself. His command to Israel through Moses: 'Hear, O Israel: The LORD our God is one LORD: and thou shalt love the LORD thy God with all thine heart, and with all thy soul, and with all thy might.' (Deuteronomy 6:4-5) was an explicit statement of the foundation by which God's community would be built, a truth reflected also in the first of the Ten Commandments. From the beginning of time all who have been redeemed from the curse of the Fall have been brought into a family relationship with One God, the Creator of the universe, the God of Abraham, Isaac and Jacob and the Father of the Lord Jesus Christ (Yeshua HaMashiach). This family relationship is as children to a father. It is the same God and Father of all, whenever we came into this redeemed community of faith.

How could it be otherwise if there is only One True God? Yet it is true to say that when we are careless in the way we perceive the developing plan of history over all generations. There can be a tendency to think that there is one God for the Jews and one for the Gentiles, or a different God for those redeemed before the incarnation of Jesus (Yeshua) than afterwards. Even the most carefully and eloquently stated Christian doctrines can also have the effect of dividing and separating our concepts of God when we do not consider them carefully, unconsciously breaking up our understanding of His unity. For example, the doctrine of the Trinity (Father, Son and Holy Spirit), when expressed by the best theologians can be the best statement of the way the One True God has made Himself known, but can also give some people, consciously or unconsciously, the impression that God is three and not one. Indeed, we can become theorists instead of people of faith, knowing *about* God and not knowing God through relationship. We can study doctrine and not have a relationship with the Father. Indeed, we can impose our views of the plan of salvation on our views of God. If we lose sight of the *one* plan to gather *one* redeemed people of faith through all history we can lose sight of the oneness of God and so develop a view of God divided in history and divided in His character and relationship with His people. We can end up thinking that *we* serve Jesus (Yeshua) while *others* serve Yahweh, for example. The truth is that the plan of redemption for all of God's covenant community is to bring us all into restored relationship with the one God, Yahweh, but to know Him as Father. Redemption is through the Son of God, Jesus (Yeshua), but redemption is to relationship with the Father in whom the Son dwells. We are taught by the Son and we are His disciples, but redemption is to the One true God and Father of us all, who expresses Himself fully in His Son, who is in Him and completely united within Him.

As we recover the true concept of the one redeemed covenant community, a recovery of our understanding of the One True God is also necessary. Whereas Christian doctrines may have originally been developed out of understanding of this one community and of the One True God, it is possible that some people who begin with these doctrines rather than of seeking after relationship with God through their own study of the foundations of our faith, can be lead to misunderstanding of who we are as the children of the One True

God. It is better to study the Scriptures afresh, learning directly from the forefathers of our community beginning in the Book of Genesis and through the revelation of all Scripture as we also walk in living relationship with the One True God as children with our Father. As we rediscover our identity in the one covenant community, so we can learn from the full scope of Scripture what God wants to teach us directly. The redemption that was bought for us through the sacrificial death of Jesus (Yeshua) was built on the truths already set at the foundation of our community. The truth that Jesus (Yeshua) confirmed was already given through Moses as is recorded in Deuteronomy chapter 4. This came to be known as the Shema (the Hebrew word related to the command to 'hear', which also implies understanding). We, like the Children of Israel, must have at the foundation of our faith the understanding that our Father is One God. The concept of the One God is based on the Hebrew word for *one*. This word is *echad*, unity with diverse expression. The covenant people must understand that our Father will reveal various and partial aspects of His character out of His oneness at various times and in various ways. This is why our One God and Father can reveal Himself through the written words of Scripture, which were revealed spiritually into the framework of understanding of men. God has revealed Himself through Scripture, but the Bible is not itself God the Father. Among these revelations are specific, perfect and clear revelations of God's will and His plan through the Prophets. This did not make the Prophets God any more than it makes us who have the Holy Spirit living in us God, but God's Oneness gives Him variety of expression according to what aspect of Himself He is revealing and how He is making Himself known. This is why Isaiah and the author of the Book of Revelation can speak of the sevenfold Spirit of God (Isaiah 11:2, Revelation 3:1). This is why Paul can speak of different manifestations of the Spirit of God as He ministers through us (Romans 12, 1 Corinthians 12, Ephesians 4).

The Son of God was always one with the Father. In this fallen world, it is hard for us to understand how a son can be in complete unity with a father, being a part of him, but that is how it is with God. When the Son of God became incarnate in Jesus (Yeshua), God the

Father fully and completely revealed Himself as never before in any of His other revelations of Himself, including Creation, through Moses and through the Prophets (Hebrews 1:1-4). Jesus (Yeshua) could say that He and the Father are One and also that the Father was greater than He (John 10:30, John 14:28). The Father could create all things through His Son and still be the One greater than the Son, while also revealing Himself fully in the Son. In the wider work of the Father there is the sending of His Spirit to all of His family throughout the earth so that we may be drawn into unity with Him through the unity He has with the Son who abides in the Father.

It is my suggestion that the one redeemed covenant community should seek a renewed understanding of their relationship with the One True God. We are not called into His family to treat Him as a distant God through logical doctrinal expressions of the Christian faith alone, or through the partial revelation of aspects of His many-faceted character. His highest intention for us is not to call Him either Holy Trinity or Yahweh, but to know Him in the secure relationship of child to Father, all of us together, one community, drawn into living unity in the One True and Living God, abiding in Him as we abide through our unity with His Son. A fundamental question is not so much how much we know *about* the One True God, but how united we are with Him as He has revealed Himself to us personally through His many words and ways, through His Creation and most of all through His Son, not in theological terms alone but in relational terms as we are drawn more deeply into fellowship with the One True God and Father of our family of faith.

Out of our relationship with the Father we might also be in a better position to minister in His Name to those from all the nations who do not know Him. Some think that Christians, as we are known, serve three gods. Others think that they themselves serve one god, and others serve many gods. The gods of the nations are known by the ways in which they reveal their character and by what they have revealed of themselves through their relationship with their people. Our God is known to us through our own personal relationship as well as through the general revelation throughout history, pointing always to the full and perfect revelation through Jesus the Messiah.

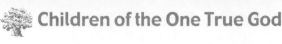

Our ministry must be based not so much on doctrinal arguments, therefore, as on personal relationship. What sort of relationship do those who follow other gods have, compared with our relationship with the One True God, who has become our Father?

Who are we?

All Scripture is our Scripture

Reading: 2 Timothy 3:15-17.

Paul's young friend Timothy is an excellent example to us of the principle of a disciple of Yeshua (Jesus) being grafted into the one Olive Tree, which gives us a picture of the one covenant community. With a Jewish mother and a Greek father, he helps to provide a bridge to our understanding of who we are, and he also helps us to understand how both Jews and Gentiles should use the Scriptures. We can consider him from either his Jewish or Gentile origins. On the Jewish side he was educated from childhood from the *Tanach* ('Old Testament'). These Scriptures had made him 'wise unto salvation', and he had become a disciple of Yeshua HaMashiach fulfilling this truth in his own life. He had seen beyond the superficial interpretation of Scripture to their fulfilment in Yeshua. He had learned, as Paul his teacher had, the way to handle the truths of the *Tanach*. He did not abandon these Scriptures when Messiah was revealed, but continued to use them in a deeper and richer way. While recognising the deep spiritual heart of the *Tanach*, he did not spiritualise them so much as to lose their practical emphasis. This we can see from Paul's reminder:

'All scripture is given by inspiration of God, and is profitable for doctrine, for reproof, for correction, for instruction in righteousness: that the man of God may be perfect, thoroughly furnished unto all good works.' (2 Timothy 3:16-17)

From the Greek side of his birth, we can reflect on how a believer from a Gentile background should be grafted into the Olive Tree. It could be disputed whether the fact that he had a Greek father made him a Gentile, or whether his Jewish mother made him a Jew. Actually, as far as recognising all of Scripture as his inheritance, it does not matter whether he considered his Jewish or Gentile origins. If we consider him as a Gentile converted to the Messianic faith we would assume that it was to his advantage that he had a Jewish mother who tutored him in the Scriptures, so that his grafting into the Olive Tree was so natural. If we consider him from his Jewish background he would continue to use the Scriptures in all their fullness. Whether from his Jewish background or his Greek background he was called into membership of the one covenant community and took all of the Scriptures into his walk as a child of the One True God and disciple of Yeshua.

It is interesting that immediately after the Council of Jerusalem, which clearly showed that there was no requirement for believers from the Gentile world to be circumcised, Paul circumcised his young friend (Acts 16:3). This illustrates the balanced and mature understanding that Paul had of the *Torah*, within the principle of Romans 14:5. It also indicates to us that we all, whether from a Jewish or Gentile background, should have a balanced and mature view of all Scripture. We would benefit from the sort of education in the Scriptures that Timothy had and from the mature and balanced interpretation of Paul (as shown in all his writings).

If we are members of the one and only covenant community, saved by faith in the one Messiah, brought into the fellowship of the One True and Living God, everything that has been revealed is for our growth in all of the Scriptures. There can be a false distinction between what have come to be called the 'Old' Testament and the 'New' Testament. Many believers have an unbalanced approach to the Scriptures because of the fact that they have lost sight of the continuity of God's plan of salvation and so have never learned to study and apply the whole of Scripture to their lives. Just because it is possible to make a wrong application of the *Tanach* ('Old Testament') as the Jews were doing at the time of Yeshua, turning grace and truth into bondage, this does not mean that it is the only way to interpret Scripture. We need to be like Timothy under his mother's and Paul's tuition, seeing both the practical application and the Messianic fulfilment of all Scripture.

This goes beyond a mental appreciation of the way all Scripture has been given to us, to a heart response, which will result in a full and balanced approach to Scripture. We must come into ownership of all that God would teach us from the whole of Scripture. Some of us have been accustomed, even if subconsciously, to not entering fully into our covenant relationship with our historical family and with our Father in Heaven, which has resulted from and weakened our limited view and use of all Scripture, especially the *Tanach*. If we consider *Torah* (the foundational teaching of God) as the first five books of the Bible, as is the tradition of the Jews, we should realise that this is not a Jewish section of Scripture. There were no Jews on this earth until the end of the Book of Genesis. In this first book of the Bible we discover our heritage as children of the One True God and Creator of the universe who calls us to a life of faith. We join the other 'Gentiles' who preceded us whose lives are described in this great book that sets the foundations of all Scriptural truth. We go back before the time of Moses in our study of *Torah*, when we start in Genesis. This also puts in perspective what our Father wants to show us through a mature study of the rest of *Torah*. The detail of the history of the Children of Israel is for our education in the same manner that Timothy was taught. This means that we must seek to discover the true intent of *Torah*, rather than reject *Torah* because others have misinterpreted it or not been able to obey fully its teaching.

The Prophets have a message that applies to the covenant community today. Again, we must discover what this message is. For example, Jeremiah speaks clearly to us concerning the heart condition of mankind when he says: 'The heart is deceitful above all things, and desperately wicked: who can know it?' (Jeremiah 17:9) He and the other Prophets point us through their understanding of *Torah* to the need of our Saviour Yeshua (Jesus), without removing the holy requirements of *Torah*. Yeshua (Jesus) confirmed this, as did Paul in his own teaching. Indeed, it is the teaching of the *Tanach* which itself is founded on *Torah* that reveals the condition of the heart and points us to justification by faith alone. This was always the case, but was not enabled in the fullest sense until what Jeremiah prophesied came to pass through death and resurrection of Yeshua:

'Behold, the days come, saith the LORD, that I will make a new covenant with the house of Israel, and with the house of Judah: not according to the covenant that I made with their fathers in the day that I took them by the hand to bring them out of the land of Egypt; which my covenant they brake, although I was an husband unto them, saith the LORD: but this shall be the covenant that I will make with the house of Israel; After those days, saith the LORD, I will put my law in their inward parts, and write it in their hearts; and will be their God, and they shall be my people.'
(Jeremiah 31:31-33)

The new covenant to enable us to fulfil the righteous requirements of *Torah* through faith and obedience (with covering for our sinful failures which still occur) was for the house of Israel and of Judah and to those grafted into this covenant community (Romans 11). This covenant community has one family history and one set of Scriptures for all. We may need to study more fully and carefully these Scriptures from Genesis to Revelation in order to find true and valid understanding and application, because many believers have not entered fully into their inheritance, due to some neglect and some superficiality or misunderstanding of who we really are as the one covenant people.

There is one covenant people with one set of Scriptures that are given to us all. The Holy Spirit has been sent to us to impart understanding to our hearts and to release us to be the one family of God, in the various ways He will lead us through all the Scriptures according to His plan and purpose for us as individuals, within the one family.

Who are we?

The Covenant people:
Our Covenant through Noah

Reading: Genesis 8:21-9:17.

And the LORD smelled a sweet savour; and the LORD said in his heart, I will not again curse the ground any more for man's sake; for the imagination of man's heart is evil from his youth; neither will I again smite any more every thing living, as I have done. While the earth remaineth, seedtime and harvest, and cold and heat, and summer and winter, and day and night shall not cease.And God blessed Noah and his sons, and said unto them, Be fruitful, and multiply, and replenish the earth. And the fear of you and the dread of you shall be upon every beast of the earth, and upon every fowl of the air, upon all that moveth upon the earth, and upon all the fishes of the sea; into your hand are they delivered. Every moving thing that liveth shall be meat for you; even as the green herb have I given you all things. But flesh with the life thereof, which is the blood thereof, shall ye not eat. And surely your blood of your lives will I require; at the hand of every beast will I require it, and at the hand of man; at the hand of every man's brother will I require the life of man. Whoso sheddeth man's blood, by man shall his blood be shed: for in the image of God made he man. And you, be ye fruitful, and multiply; bring forth abundantly in the earth, and multiply therein. And God spake unto Noah, and to his sons with him, saying, and I, behold, I establish my covenant with you, and with your seed after you; and with every living creature that is with you, of the fowl, of the cattle, and of every beast of the earth with you; from all that go out of the ark, to every beast of the earth. And I will establish my covenant with you; neither shall all flesh be cut off any more by the waters of a flood; neither shall there any more be a flood to destroy the earth. And God said, This is the token of the covenant which I make between me and you and every living creature that is with you, for perpetual generations: I do set my bow in the cloud, and it shall be for a token of a covenant between me and the earth. And it shall come to pass, when I bring a cloud over the earth, that the bow shall be seen in the cloud: and I will remember my covenant, which is between me and you and every living creature of all flesh; and the waters shall no more become a flood to destroy all flesh. And the bow shall be in the cloud; and I will look upon it, that I may remember the everlasting covenant between God and every living creature of all flesh that is upon the earth. And God said unto Noah, This is the token of the covenant, which I have established between me and all flesh that is upon the earth.

The history of mankind began with a family in the Garden of Eden and will end with a redeemed family from all nations. Almighty God swore that He would redeem this family and He is continuing to do this today. Redemption was necessary to save mankind from the curse brought upon the earth due to the disobedience of Adam and Eve. Redemption is from the power of sin. The whole purpose of the continuing history of this universe is for God to complete the plan of redemption. We must consider all Scripture in this context. This means that behind all of God's acts through history lies this one foundational plan, to gather together a restored family, restored from their separation from Him, the power of sin having been overcome. When we consider the various steps that God has taken, we must have this one overall plan in mind.

The covenant that God made with Noah must be considered in the context of judgement of sin. We should also consider the various components of the covenant, their application to our life on this earth and their deeper application to the foundational plan of God to gather one people into everlasting fellowship with Him.

The context of the covenant with Noah is sin and its

consequences. The Flood teaches us dramatically about the wages of sin being death. As well as a pointer to the judgement under which all who sin should come, it is a practical teaching of the price paid by Yeshua for the salvation of God's family. Since the Fall, all mankind without the help of God will continue to live separate from Him because of their continuing sin. The final result for those who live without God's help is permanent separation from Him and exclusion from His family. The consequences of this are to be paralleled by the devastation of the great Flood that covered the whole earth. We see that this is only a picture of the final judgement of God because it is a judgement on flesh and not spirit and God promised never to flood the whole earth again. We also learn that the final judgement of sin will come in a way that is described as eternal fire (Matthew 3:10-12, 5:22, 13:38-43, 25:41). The Flood was not the final judgement, but a warning of the judgement to come, and a pointer to the fact that there is also a plan of salvation. In this plan, God will impute righteousness to those whom He calls into His family, covering their sins and causing them to live by faith.

Noah represents all those saved into this covenant family. Indeed, those saved are both physical and spiritual descendants of Noah, physical by line of birth, spiritual by the principal of righteousness through faith (in the same way that Abraham is our father through faith, and is also a spiritual and physical child of Noah). Noah also points us to the Saviour Yeshua (Jesus), just as the Ark points to our abiding place in Him. He covers us through the power of His shed blood, as the Ark was covered inside and outside with pitch.

The historical account of the Flood has both practical and spiritual applications. Practically, we learn of God the Creator working out His purposes through His creation and within the framework of the continuing life within this creation. Spiritually, we see pointers to the deeper plan of salvation that will bring the covenant family into a new heaven and a new earth one day, when the family is fully gathered and the power of sin is broken forever for that family. The gathering of the one family takes place while we are on this earth.

In practical terms we see that God promised that while the earth remained, there would always be food for us to survive. He also confirmed that mankind was His priority in all creation, giving us dominion over all the earth and allowing us to eat the flesh of animals. He established the sanctity of blood, within this, which points ultimately to the precious blood of the Son of God, but which was also to be a constant reminder of the sanctity of all life including the animals which could be eaten, providing the blood was drained. In short God, having, through the Flood, taught immense truths about the power and consequences of sin that exist in Adam's fallen race, then looked forward to the future of mankind on this earth. We go back to this historical account to consider and constantly remember the truths God showed us so that we might seek Him within the context of the continuing earth for inclusion in the plan of redemption. His acceptance of Noah gives us confidence that we can be saved like Noah. His promise of an earth where there will be provision for our continuing life, despite our tendency to fall into the same sins as those who lived before the Flood, demonstrates that there is a further purpose in the plan of God beyond this physical life.

As we consider these things, we realise that the covenant with Noah does not stand alone. It was a step along the way to the later things that God would do within the plan of salvation. Having set this covenant in place, the plan of redemption moves on to the next step, and the covenant with Noah is related to this next step just as all things on this continuing earth point towards the one plan God has had in mind since the Fall. Having established the fact that this earth, under the hand of God, would continue to sustain life, and that God would hold back further judgement until the end of this earth, we are all free to live our physical life and to seek God for the deeper aspects of His plan for redeeming a covenant family. Though the covenant with Noah precedes that made with Abraham, it is intimately bound into it as it is with all other aspects of the one overall plan.

At face value, when we look at the rainbow we, with God,

remember that we have a promise of continuing life on this earth, with food to sustain us, but what is the purpose of our physical life? That we might be redeemed into God's own family. When we look at the rainbow we should see not only a promise of food and security from a universal flood, we can also see a promise of the Messiah who came to save the covenant community from their sins. The rainbow is God's promise of salvation (physical and spiritual) for all God's people through all history. The covenant with Noah is not an ancient historical document for those who preceded us on this earth, and it is not separate from all God's promises to mankind. It is as relevant to each of God's family as it was to Noah. It is at the foundation of God's overall commitment to mankind. The rainbow reminds us of God's provision, His patience and all that He has promised, including Yeshua Hamashiach (Jesus the Messiah).

Who are we?

The Covenant people: Our Covenant through Abraham

Reading: Genesis 17, Acts 15, Genesis 15:5-20, Genesis 22:15-18, Matthew 3:9, Romans 3:27-4:25.

God's purpose throughout history has been to restore one family for Himself from all nations. Since the Fall, the power of sin in the world has been such that God would have been justified in abandoning any such plan. However, God committed Himself to fulfilling the plan through the principle of covenant and we are secure in the fact that this plan will and has been fulfilled. God swore on Oath that He would fulfil the plan, even though we know that it was at the high cost of the sacrifice of His own Son Yeshua HaMashiach (Jesus Christ) on the Cross.

The covenant was the basis on which God released the Children of Israel from bondage in Egypt:

'And it came to pass in process of time, that the king of Egypt died: and the children of Israel sighed by reason of the bondage, and they cried, and their cry came up unto God by reason of the bondage. And God heard their groaning, and God remembered his covenant with Abraham, with Isaac, and with Jacob. And God looked upon the children of Israel, and God had respect unto them.' (Exodus 2:23-25)

It was also the basis on which Moses could later appeal to God on behalf of the sinful Children of Israel:

'And Moses besought the LORD his God, and said, LORD, why doth thy wrath wax hot against thy people, which thou hast brought forth out of the land of Egypt with great power, and with a mighty hand? Wherefore should the Egyptians speak, and say, for mischief did he bring them out, to slay them in the mountains, and to consume them from the face of the earth? Turn from thy fierce wrath, and repent of this evil against thy people. Remember Abraham, Isaac, and Israel, thy servants, to whom thou swarest by thine own self, and saidst unto them, I will multiply your seed as the stars of heaven, and all this land that I have spoken of will I give unto your seed, and they shall inherit it for ever. And the LORD repented of the evil which he thought to do unto his people.' (Exodus 32:11-14)

It is of great importance that we should all understand our true identity, as did Moses and Abraham, as people of the covenant. This is the basis of our Father's commitment to us, and the basis of our appeal to Him. When we consider the covenant He made with Abraham, we see it as central to the whole plan of salvation. This is the covenant He made on our behalf as well as for the rest of our one family drawn from all nations of the earth. The covenant with Noah is insufficient to take us to the infinite future in fellowship with God, but it is the beginning of the overall covenant plan. In effect there is just one plan and one overall oath in God's mind, but there are steps along the road of history that we should study to realise fully what God has done and who we really are. The covenant is the basis and strength of our relationship with God our Father, giving us confidence to appeal to Him in times of need and giving us understanding which will lead to worship of our Father because of what He has done for us.

Like the covenant with Noah, the covenant with Abraham has characteristics that have application in the framework of the physical world, but it also has background truths relating to the overall plan of salvation. The era that began with Abraham opened the way for God to give specific and timely teaching through the physical descendants of Abraham. We continue to see that the principle of God's choosing who His people are still applies. It is a definite line of descent through Isaac and Jacob, who are to be the people of the covenant and who are to inherit their own land. The physical descendants of Abraham are to confirm their membership of the covenant people through the sign of circumcision of the males. So began the process of God calling one nation to Himself, giving them a land in which to learn to be His own people in order that, eventually, there might be a fuller manifestation of God's covenant to Abraham to bless all nations. Much of this was to be accomplished through the leadership of Moses. Abraham looked forward through eyes of faith to what God would establish.

Abraham may have wondered about how the promise could be fulfilled through physical offspring. We can understand this in relation to the birth of Isaac in his old age. Where were even the physical offspring to come from unless Abraham had a son? Yet, he also realised that the character God was building in him was a character of faith. Abraham is our father of faith in two respects at least. In one respect, he has faith in God for his own walk with God. It is this faith that is accounted to him as righteousness. Obedience, which is also a characteristic of our father Abraham, is a consequence of this saving faith. In the second respect, Abraham held faith for the covenant promise that God would bless many people from all nations through him.

Abraham's children were intended to be like him. First God expected this within the covenant Children of Israel. He gave them a land and leaders to tutor them in His ways. Thus we see that the physical side of God's covenant was for the separation of one nation who would be the means of God's teaching all nations. They not only had the promise of survival according to the covenant with Noah, but they also had the security of their own land where they could respond to God directly as their King and their Father. Nevertheless, when we can consider this in the light of the teaching of Yeshua and the New Testament writers we realise that there was to be more than the privilege of being physical descendants of Abraham that was intended to characterise the covenant community. They were to be like Abraham as living by faith, and this condition was essential for them to be true and complete children of

Abraham and true members of the covenant family gathered for eternity.

The deeper understanding of the covenant with Abraham lies in the context of the greater plan of redemption to reverse the curse of Eden, saving mankind from their sins. The true children of Abraham and inheritors of the spiritual aspects of the covenant are those who live by faith. This condition applies to anyone from any nation who is called and who responds to the call to enter into the family of faith through the shed blood of Yeshua HaMashiach. For Abraham's physical descendants there was a physical mark of the physical side of the covenant through circumcision. The physical descendants could also be spiritual children through circumcision of the heart and through the principles of living by faith, and so they should have taught all who entered into the covenant community of faith from other nations, in God's good time. Indeed, we learn many of our most important lessons as people of faith through the history of the Children of Israel. The Olive Tree of Romans 11, however, is a family characterised by faith and we enter by faith. There is equality in the family, albeit that we join a family that God brought together based on His principles made known to the Children of Israel before other nations. Those from other nations are not called to be like Israel with a physical mark of the covenant from a fleshly point of view, and this is why circumcision of the flesh is not necessary. Without the teaching that God gives us through the history of the Children of Israel, He might have called us into His community in a different way, perhaps as He called them, but it was His plan that we enter by faith and by faith alone, learning essential truths that point us to Messiah from their history, experience and suffering.

When God gave the covenant to Abraham, He had a redeemed community of faith from all nations in mind more than He had in mind the physical line of descent, though that line is still important in the faithfulness of God to His people. We must look beyond the physical if we are to be the covenant community and when we do, we realise that the covenant that God made with Abraham is *our* covenant. We must possess this covenant by faith in our hearts and truly *be* the covenant people. There is a sense in which we carry on the work of Abraham today. Abraham looked forward to Yeshua while we look back, but faith for the fulfilment of all God's plans in redeeming a family is still required of each succeeding generation. We are that generation if we have responded to the call of God to be members of His family through faith, and the covenant is fully ours to live through faith and to hold in faith.

Who are we?

The Covenant people: The Covenant with Moses

Reading: Exodus 20, Deuteronomy 29.

When God made a covenant with Moses and the Children of Israel it was in the context of the overall plan of salvation. The Fall had led to broken fellowship with God. In general, mankind no longer walked with Him or knew Him. The purpose of the overall plan of salvation was to restore this fellowship and it is summed up in Yeshua's prayer recorded in John 17:3 '....**this is life eternal, that they might know thee the only true God, and Jesus Christ, whom thou hast sent.**' The whole sum of salvation history, indeed the whole sum of history, is for that one purpose, to redeem a family to live in close fellowship with God and to walk with Him as Adam and Eve were intended to do in the Garden of Eden. This family, drawn from all nations over all history, is saved through faith and faith alone. Thus we must consider every step within the overall development of God's plan of restoration. This includes the covenant with the Children of Israel, and we must lift our ideas higher and deeper than the immediate focus.

Hebrews Chapter 3 reminds us of the one high goal of God's plan for Israel. Their failure was not based on works but was on account of unbelief. When we consider the many commandments and rules for righteous living brought through Moses, we might think that righteousness for Israel was through strict obedience to these things, whereas the chief principle was always faith. Abraham was the father of Israel and the principle of living by faith had already been shown through Abraham. All Abraham's children were intended to be like him in regard to this principle of living in fellowship with God through faith. Indeed, as well as the rules for living that Moses taught Israel there was recognition of the need for forgiveness from sin. This was within the practices of sacrifice through the shedding of blood at the brazen altar of the Tabernacle and Temple. Israel, even while knowing God's righteous requirements, were nevertheless human beings caught up in this sinful world. They could not be changed through attempted obedience of the external requirements of the Law of Moses. Their need was for covering for sin just as any other of Adam's fallen race. Temporary provision was made through the sacrificial system for what would later be made permanent through the shed blood of Yeshua. Nevertheless, the life of faith was open to all of Israel just as it was to Enoch, Noah and Abraham who went before them. Indeed, the giving of the Law was not for the purpose of eliminating sin but exposing it, so that the path of humility and faith would result. To obey the whole of the requirements of the covenant through Moses required Israel to seek righteousness before God in their community life regulated by the Commandments, but in the overall context of the life of faith.

This is why we read in Deuteronomy 29:13 that the primary purpose of God was that Israel would be His people and He would be their God: '**That he may establish thee to day for a people unto himself, and that he may be unto thee a God, as he hath said unto thee, and as he hath sworn unto thy fathers, to Abraham, to Isaac, and to Jacob.**' This is why Yeshua could sum up the whole of the Law and Prophets as pointing to Himself as the one who would redeem a people into fellowship with God through faith and why the Law and the Prophets hang on two principles, '**Thou shalt love the Lord thy God with all thy heart, and with all thy soul, and with all thy mind. This is the first and great commandment. And the second is like unto it, Thou shalt love thy neighbour as thyself.**' (Matthew 22:37-39) This is why we read of the Children of Israel's walk through the wilderness being typified by the provision by God for all their needs, often provided miraculously. Their walk was primarily to be one of faith where they came to know the One True God through His care for them as a

Father and Husband (metaphors to show how close the relationship with the One True God is intended to be for the redeemed community).

By the time that Yeshua came to earth as the Son of Man, the role of the Law of Moses had become so misunderstood that the interpreters of the Law tended to see it as a road to self-righteousness before God than as a background to the life of faith. They imposed burdens upon the Children of Israel that no people could bear or succeed in keeping, if fellowship with God was to be through full obedience of the law without the balance of faith in God. The Law of Moses should have led to humility and dependence of a fallen people on the grace of God. Though the animal sacrifices of the Tabernacle and Temple were only temporary measures pointing to the time of fulfilment through the sacrifice of Yeshua on the Cross and the release of the Holy Spirit, it was possible to live a life of faith which pleased God in a way that would eventually be perfected for those living by faith through Yeshua. This is why King David could understand the deeper truths and balance of faith and works of the whole of the Torah of God. Even though he committed sins worthy of death (adultery and murder) he could find forgiveness through true repentance (see Psalm 51). The author of Psalm 119 had also seen deeper truths than a call to try to live through self-righteousness in the Torah.

We must not look on the covenant with Moses as a covenant of works, which failed. The failure was always on the part of people who were given the opportunity to live in fellowship with God through faith. There was to be a fulfilment of all that the Law of Moses contained through the sacrifice of Yeshua and the life of the Holy Spirit who would come to live in God's people. This fulfilment reaches down to the deeper meanings and principles of the covenant with Moses. Yeshua fulfilled the sacrifice required for forgiveness according to principles that were already contained in the sacrificial system of the Tabernacle. Yeshua fulfilled all the deeper requirements of the Law in His life, showing the perfect balance between the principles of justice, mercy and faith. He also taught the heart principles to which the practical precepts and commandments pointed. The covenant with Moses was a step along the way to the overall plan of God's redeeming a family of faith to Himself. It is the first step of teaching for a whole nation, after the time of the Patriarchs, who chiefly walked by faith in smaller families and communities. We must see what God did in the context of the whole plan.

The covenant with Moses was in the context of clear principles that are manifestations of God's holy requirements. Through their revelation we begin to understand how a community should live. It might succeed in living in that way if it was not impregnated with sin. It is discovered through this that mankind cannot live to please God without further and deep help, despite the seeming simplicity and beauty of the principles. Thus the covenant with Moses and the Children of Israel is teaching for us all. The Torah principles that are contained in all that Moses brought, have pointers to Messiah and are manifestations of heart principles that we should know. The spiritual truths by which we are to live and which are taught through the principles given to Moses were intended to be manifest on the hearts of God's people, and we learn that this can only be accomplished with the help of God.

The covenant with Moses must be seen as profound teaching along the course of history wherein God worked out His one plan of salvation. We must not consider it as a failed covenant but a covenant that has to be taken in the context of the whole plan. Of itself it did not have the power to save, due to the deeper need of mankind trapped in sin. The New Covenant in the blood of Yeshua would write the principles of the Law of Moses on the heart, while fulfilling the sacrifice for sin once and for all. We must see the principles taught through Moses as pointing to greater and deeper truths which are still relevant to God's community. Salvation was always to be by faith and ultimately it was to be faith in the Son of God, through principles learned through the types and shadows, which still give us an accurate picture of this truth. Beyond salvation, there is the process of sanctification to which the righteous principles of Moses point to deeper heart conditions. We can confirm the fact that righteous living is still relevant, according to the heart principles of the teaching of God begun through Moses, by reference, for example, to Paul's exhortations to the Corinthians (1 Corinthians 10:11). Just as the Laver comes after the Brazen Altar in the Tabernacle, so sanctification follows salvation in the life of faith as we approach closer fellowship with God. The enabling through the Holy Spirit, who writes the general principles of Torah on our hearts, puts the walk of faith and obedience in an achievable framework. As far as the teaching of the covenant with Moses is concerned, it is a reference for our heart's condition, given for us to study and for meditation. It is true that Yeshua has fulfilled all the requirements of Torah, but we must continue to study the Scriptures relating to Him and to our life of faith, which were given as continuing patterns to edify us. Beyond this, our families, communities and nations are part of this ongoing world and the framework of the Commandments (according to the deep understanding that the Holy Spirit can give, beyond the interpretation of the Scribes and Pharisees) give the boundaries of true freedom, which cannot be replaced by humanistic frameworks of government. The covenant community, seeks to be ordered according to God's teaching and to live in fellowship with Him. God's perfect model cannot be replaced by human ideas of empire, so we must continue to study prayerfully the teaching of Moses.

We must not consider Moses in contrast to Yeshua, but find the way God teaches us through Moses in the context of Yeshua. We are not to deny Yeshua and return to a ritual interpretation of Moses, but neither are we to neglect the covenant God made with Moses, as we seek to understand the whole of God's covenant plan. We are to continue to dig deep into eternal truths that are still relevant. The New Covenant through the shed blood of Yeshua enables us to live the life of faith in fulfilment of the teaching through Moses. The covenant community joins the remnant of the House of Israel who achieved this balance, like David the King. We are all members of the one family of faith (Romans 11).

Who are we?

The Covenant people: The Covenant with David

Reading: Psalm 89.

Almighty God established David on the throne of Israel and Judah as a man after His own heart. Through his life we have many lessons which teach us about the coming Messiah. Because of this there is a messianic theme running through the Psalms, pointing accurately and prophetically to fulfilment through Yeshua (Jesus). For example, Psalm 22:1, 22:18, 31:5, 34:20 were fulfilled on the Cross, and other Psalms are fulfilled more generally, including, for example, Psalms 2, 16 and 89. King David's life established a root from which the Messiah would come forth. This was all in the plan of God and a step along the way to the overall fulfilment of His covenant plan.

This plan began before the beginning of time, as did the covenant family. The head of the family, the Son of God, existed before creation. We can assume, therefore, that the completion of that family was in the mind of God before creation. Then within the created order we can discover steps along the way. As we have seen, the covenant with Noah was one step, whereby the continuance of the earth and the survival of people upon the earth would be guaranteed until the family was redeemed. Through Abraham the principle of salvation by faith is understood. Through Moses the righteous requirements of the covenant community were established. Within all these steps there is the tension between sin and righteousness, but it was God's plan to overcome sin and bring righteousness through faith in Him. The need of fallen and sinful mankind is made known through God's Holy Torah (teaching), so that righteousness through faith and the need for substitutionary sacrifice became deeply implanted principles of the covenant community. Each step along the way of fulfilling the one covenant plan must be seen as part of the whole. When we come to the covenant with David, we learn about the part of the plan whereby God Himself will ultimately be the ruler of His own covenant family; He Himself would be King. David is not the Messiah. He sinned along with all mankind, even though his walk with God pointed accurately to the principles which the coming Son of Man would perfect.

It is a profound principle for our meditation to consider that God Himself was to be King of the covenant family, even though Israel wanted their own king just like the other nations (1 Samuel 8) and even though it seemed that God had let them go their own way. His plan was to finally restore Himself as the King of the covenant people through their willing submission. It was a dark day when God said to Samuel, 'They have not rejected thee, but they have rejected me, that I should not reign over them.' (1 Samuel 8:7) The centuries of Israel and Judah living under the rule of an earthly king are laid out clearly in Scripture and the story is interwoven with the other principles of salvation history, fulfilling exactly the warning given through the Prophet Samuel in 1 Samuel 8. Yet the scarlet thread of God's covenant plan was not broken even through this. The contrast between Saul and David is there for us to study so that we learn about the limits of human kingdoms in this sinful world while also establishing a heart desire for a perfected king from the seed of David, building our faith for the coming Messiah. Throughout the history of Israel and Judah, the successes and failures of the whole nation were linked to the ability of their kings to walk with God, again pointing to fulfilment in the coming Messiah, who would perfect this walk with God, upholding the true intent of the Torah of God.

Yet before all this, there was already a covenant promise that would be fulfilled through the line of Judah:

Judah, thou art he whom thy brethren shall praise: thy hand shall be in the neck of thine enemies; thy father's children shall bow down before thee. Judah is a lion's whelp: from the prey, my son, thou art gone up: he stooped down, he couched as a lion, and as an old lion; who shall rouse him up? The sceptre shall not depart from Judah, nor a lawgiver from between his feet, until Shiloh come; and unto him shall the gathering of the people be. Binding his foal unto the vine, and his ass's colt unto the choice vine; he washed his garments in wine, and his clothes in the blood of grapes: his eyes shall be red with wine, and his teeth white with milk. (Genesis 49:8-12)

Here, stated mysteriously but predicted accurately, are pictures of the coming Messiah Yeshua HaMashiach. He would come from the Tribe of Judah. He would be the righteous judge of His people. He would receive true worship from His people. Judah would rule God's people until out of Judah would come the ruler to rule over all of the covenant community. This message is echoed in all the biblical Prophets.

Psalm 89 summarises the covenant promise that was sealed with an oath through David during his reign as the first king in the line of Judah:

I have made a covenant with my chosen, I have sworn unto David my servant, thy seed will I establish for ever, and build up thy throne to all generations. (Psalm 89:3-4)

In this Psalm the principles of David's life and his relationship with God are woven together to speak prophetically about the coming Messiah, the King of the Jews. Despite all the sin of mankind, including that of Judah and King David, the covenant plan to redeem a family of faith was established by Oaths of God that could not be reversed, including the establishing of the important principle that God would again be King.

History shows that the Messiah was later born from the tribe of Judah and even proclaimed king of the Jews by those who crucified

Him (Luke 23:38). Yeshua was born as the Son of Man, being completely human as well as having the completely divine nature of the Son of God, being completely united to the Father. He was and is a human king as well as the Son of God, and through Him, God the Father is King. Paul summarised how the restoration of the Kingdom to the Father will be accomplished through Yeshua when all of salvation and covenant history is fulfilled. This is also echoed in the Book of Revelation:

> ...now is Christ risen from the dead, and become the firstfruits of them that slept. For since by man came death, by man came also the resurrection of the dead. For as in Adam all die, even so in Christ shall all be made alive. But every man in his own order: Christ the firstfruits; afterward they that are Christ's at his coming. Then cometh the end, when he shall have delivered up the king-dom to God, even the Father; when he shall have put down all rule and all authority and power. (1 Corinthians 15:20-24)

> And I heard a loud voice saying in heaven, Now is come salvation, and strength, and the kingdom of our God, and the power of his Christ: for the accuser of our brethren is cast down, which accused them before our God day and night. And they overcame him by the blood of the Lamb, and by the word of their testimo-ny; and they loved not their lives unto the death. (Revelation 12:10-11)

If we consider the whole of history as containing one covenant plan, we can understand how each step is part of the overall plan. The covenant with David ensured that God will be King of His own people at the end, establishing His Kingdom through the Messiah coming from the line of Judah, and then adding to this kingdom family those saved from all nations, in accordance with His covenant with Abraham.

Who are we?

The Covenant people: The Covenant with Jeremiah

Reading: Jeremiah 31.

The Prophets of the Bible have two main themes. They all call the people back to God and to His teaching (Torah), and they all look forward to a better day for the covenant community. Within this there are shadows of understanding that Torah will be fulfilled gloriously one day in the Messianic Kingdom and there is a sense that all of Israel's struggles will come to an end. There are shadows of understanding that though Israel has sinned, there will be a fulfilment whereby they can live at peace with God. Sometimes there is explicit reference to the coming Messiah and sometimes there are types, shadows and metaphors for our meditation to discover deeper truths. There is a continual theme that Israel will not be abandoned by God and that there will be a remnant, a representative group, who will be saved and redeemed. The restoration of Judah after their first exile to Babylon can be seen as pointing to a future restoration after a second exile. This is seen in a number of passages, one of which is in Jeremiah 31. In verse 15, we read of the weeping of Rachel for her children. Matthew quoted this verse as being fulfilled at the time of Yeshua's birth (Matthew 2:17-18). After this passage we read Jeremiah's prophecy concerning the restoration of Judah to her land. Thus we see this as the prophesied return of the Jews after the time of Yeshua and after what turned out to be a near two thousand year second exile. The Land of Israel and the city of Jerusalem point beyond the kingdoms of this world to the eternal Kingdom of God, so that the return from exile prophesied by Jeremiah and other prophets is a restoration not only to the Land of Israel but also to God, in the context of the gathering of all of God's covenant family to salvation through faith. The New Covenant (verses 31 to 34) is in this context.

In Jeremiah 31 we see a number of themes interwoven. We see that the covenant plan for Israel and Judah goes beyond the covenant with Moses, which itself becomes the basis for a deeper plan at heart level, without losing any of its basic principles. We see that those who become the true covenant community of faith, with the law on their hearts, are to be a community drawn from all nations, joining those from Israel and Judah to whom the covenant was given. We see that the Land of Israel, while being given as provision on this earth to the people of Israel, is nevertheless only symbolic of a heavenly kingdom where God is King. We see metaphor from everyday life interweaving with deeper spiritual meaning, as it so often does in the teaching of God. We also see that faith is the key to righteousness while holy living is possible through the deeper principles of the Law of Moses being written on the hearts of the covenant community.

We must study the New Covenant in balance with the other steps of God's covenant, covering all history. It is certainly the greatest part, because it points to the fulfilment of the purposes of God through Yeshua. Like Noah, Yeshua will save those to whom righteousness is accounted. This righteousness is according to faith in Him to restore believers to the Father, through His shed blood on the Cross. This faith is modelled by Abraham, who looked forward to the city without foundations whose builder was God Himself, and who saw beyond the works of man. This was most magnificently expressed in the faith offering of his own son, pointing to faith in the substitute (Yeshua) symbolised by the ram in the thicket (Genesis 22). Moses taught the righteousness of God that reveals the sin of mankind, whose hearts are set on obeying the principles of God's laws. Our righteousness is in Him, who fulfilled all of Torah and whose sacrifice covers all who have faith in Him. He will also restore the Kingdom to God as King of the Jews. We must read Jeremiah 31 carefully. Then we might understand what the writer to the Hebrews meant in chapters 9 and 10, which lead up to the great

Chapter 11 on righteousness through faith. The Old Covenant was that forgiveness would come from the sacrifice of animals in the Temple and Tabernacle. The important issue was that the teaching of Moses would reveal the sin of the people, even in their best attempts to follow God's laws and that this sin had to be removed if the people of God were to continue in fellowship with Him. Israel's failure shows us that something better was required if it were to be lasting. It was not possible for ritual obedience to the laws of Moses to bring the heart of man to the necessary condition. Thus the types and shadows of the Temple and Tabernacle sacrifices had to be lifted to their full revelation in the permanent sacrifice of the Son of God, through whom also came the outpouring of the Holy Spirit so that all of God's covenant community could have the principles of the Torah taken to heart level and so that ritual observance of the laws of Moses was no longer necessary. The Types and Shadows of Pesach (Passover) and Shavuot (Pentecost) were brought to fulfilment through Yeshua and through the outpouring of the Holy Spirit that had been prophesied by Joel.

The New Covenant prophesied by Jeremiah was fulfilled in Yeshua and brought to a climax the whole plan of redemption of God's covenant family. All the other steps were necessary for this one plan. The gravity of sin was shown as well as the awesome judgement of God at the time of Noah, but also a promise was given which ensured the survival of mankind until the whole covenant family is gathered. The life of faith was shown through Abraham, our father and model of saving faith, before the righteous requirements of the covenant community were revealed through Moses. Through Abraham and Moses we have our constant reference points for the righteous requirements of God to be lived within the life of faith. Indeed, forgiveness through substitutionary sacrifice was a full part of the teaching of Moses, but God chose only one small nation, Israel, through whom this would be taught, since the time of fulfilment had not come. We must continue to learn from the history of Israel and Judah the need that we have for a New Covenant which will enable us to live according to the teaching of Moses but with a better and perfect sacrifice for sin (Yeshua) and with a better understanding of the Torah, at heart level rather than through laws written on stone. The fulfilment of all the covenant plan was through Yeshua as prophesied through Jeremiah. This does not change any of the heart principles or intent of any other part of God's overall plan, but enables the plan to be fulfilled. In particular, righteousness through faith was already a principle for the covenant people, for Abraham, Moses and all who would walk by faith through all of history. Jeremiah's covenant, fulfilled through Yeshua, brought all of the teaching and all God's plan to a climax, so that after the time of Yeshua the full teaching, the Gospel (Good News), could go to all nations according to the promise given to Abraham that God's family of faith would be drawn from all nations.

The New Covenant was first given to the house of Israel and the house of Judah (Jeremiah 31:31). The covenant family is rooted in the faith community, which was first built from some of Abraham's physical descendants. The covenant family from all over the world joins those who have lived, are living and will live by faith from Israel and Judah. The family goes across all history. It is not physical descent from Abraham that counts regarding the covenant community, but from the physical descendants have come principles that are to be the teaching of all those who would be saved by faith. The Head of the covenant community is Yeshua the King of the Jews who draws together all of us who live by faith in Him, that faith having been given to us as a gift. This salvation faith is brought by the same Holy Spirit who writes the laws of God on our hearts and into our minds, so that we might also learn to live a Holy life where the teaching of Moses is brought to fulfilment through heart principles instead of legalistic principles. Those of us who are called according to the New Covenant in the blood of Yeshua have the whole of covenant history to consider. We are not simply 'New Testament Christians', as if God finished with one plan and started another; it goes deeper than that. All the steps of covenant history, written and developed across the pages of all Scripture are our inheritance, so that we may properly identify ourselves and live according to the ways God intended, being drawn to the unity of the One New Man in the days leading up to the return of the Messiah.

Who are we?

The Covenant people

Reading: 2 Peter.

Abraham was given the foundational covenant of all Scripture. Through him we learn the major lessons about the life of faith. Through Moses we learn about the righteousness before God of the covenant community, but also that the covenant made with Abraham cannot be fulfilled without the help of God through Yeshua, who fulfilled all our righteousness and established the covenant made with Jeremiah. Hence we who live by faith in the Lord Yeshua are also called to be heirs of the covenant. The covenant made with Abraham was passed on to Isaac and then to Jacob. Then it was held in faith by those who lived by faith through all of salvation history. Finally, the covenant was brought to fulfilment in Yeshua and then the Gospel was sent to all nations. We who are in the covenant family now, have inherited the covenant as Abraham and others before us inherited it. We look forward to the Messiah's return with the same faith and we must possess this covenant by faith at heart level.

It has been important to review all of the key steps of covenant history in order to establish the fact of the one overriding plan of God since before the creation of the world, that is to draw together a family of faith from all nations and across all history. If we are part of this family, we were drawn together by the outworking of the covenant plan through all its steps. The Church did not begin when Peter preached at Pentecost, though an important new era began when the Holy Spirit was given for the final part of the plan and so that some from all nations could now come to faith and belong to the one community. The family of God began before time and is to be characterised by the unity between the Father and His only Son who existed before creation. He is the Head of the community and those who walk with God in a relationship of trust and faith are part of this united body. We can identify some of the members of God's family from the Book of Hebrews. Abel is a member of this community. Enoch is a member. Noah is a member. Abraham is a member, so is Isaac, Jacob, Sarah, Ruth, Rebekhah, Leah, David, the Prophets, Anna, Simeon and many more. This family of faith existed before the Gospel went out from Jerusalem, from those who believed in Yeshua, from among the Jews of His day.

Romans 11 gives a clear picture of this family of faith. Those saved from the Gentile world after the time of Yeshua join an already-existing family. The New Covenant that brought the final step to the overall plan of redeeming this family was given first to Israel and Judah, and some from all the tribes of Israel will be grafted into the Olive Tree. In the end days some of this grafting of Israel and Judah will be done, as those saved from these tribes come alongside the other branches, including those from the Gentile nations.

It may be necessary for some of us to go over and over these principles of the one covenant family of God, first to establish the whole of the historical plan, and then as it were to receive the covenant principles at heart level, possessing them as a personal truth that is spiritually held. This should result in our becoming the covenant community at a richer, deeper and fuller level. This will be important as the days proceed prior to the return of the Messiah. He will come to a purified and united body, which lives a life of faith transcending the denominational boundaries that have been set up between the different Christian sects and between believers in the Gentile world and those from Israel. When we are more fully identified as the covenant community it will have some major effects on the way we live, the expectation we have for the future and the way we study Scripture. Among these might be:

1. a clearer vision of God's plan among the Jews, repenting of the separation of the Church from its Jewish roots and of its anti-

Semitism, that came from a misunderstanding of God's plans for the remnant of Israel.

2. a greater co-operation between Messianic Jews and believers from the Church from the nations. In accordance with Paul's teaching in Romans, there should be a character of the one body of believers that brings jealousy to unbelieving Israel and also there should be a fellowship among believers likened to the branches of the Olive Tree making room for one another. From all believers there should come a seeking after God for an understanding of the One New Man.

3. a greater interest in the Hebraic foundations of our faith. The basic language of the Scriptures is Hebrew and the orientation of the mind of the covenant people is to be more related to the Hebraic background than to the Greek and Roman emphasis that emerged when the true identity of the Church was clouded over.

4. a balanced view of all Scripture and a deeper study from foundations to fulfilment. The basis of all the Scriptures is found in the first five books of the Bible. The themes are developed throughout the Scriptures and fulfilled in the Messiah.

5. a greater emphasis on family life as the foundation of the believing community. This involves many basic themes, including the authority of the head of the home, the education of children in the ways of the Lord and, regarding growth in spiritual wisdom, the way a believing community should be built on the foundation of family life.

6. the role of elders of the believing community. It is time for spiritual authority to be strengthened within the framework of the local community for the purposes of God towards the time of the return of the Messiah.

7. the establishing of a framework of community life which reflects the principles of Scripture as taught by Moses and as fulfilled in Yeshua. There are many practical as well as spiritual

things to consider.

When the principle of covenant is deeply embedded in our hearts, we might realise our deeper identity as covenant people should. It is time to strengthen the one body of believers throughout the world in preparation for the return of the Messiah of the Jews, who also extended His hand to save many from the Gentile nations to fulfil God's promise to Abraham, our father in regard to faith.

Who are we?

The New Covenant in His Blood

Reading: Hebrew 9-10, John 6:53-56.

Hebrews 11 speaks of all who have faith in the One True God and affirms to us that there is one covenant family drawn from all nations over all history, and that the principle that typifies all who are members of this family is that they are people of faith. Yet Hebrews 9 and 10 precedes Hebrews 11. While we must be careful not to miss the foundational issue of saving faith in Hebrews 11, we must also realise that the culmination of all of God's covenant plan over all generations is sealed through the shedding of blood, and that all the types and shadows point to the covenant of faith being through the blood of Yeshua (Jesus).

Bound into this covenant principle are many themes and we should seek to explore them throughout our lifetime. Herein is the central theme of salvation history. Why should it be necessary for the Son of God to shed His blood for the forgiveness of my sins? The humanist would say that there is no logic in this, yet we are reminded of Yeshua's own words: **'Greater love has no one than this, that he lay down his life for his friends.'** (John 15:13) God's love is shown through the fact that His One and only Son's life was given for us, and it is necessary for God's love to be shown to be higher than any other love, or we might follow a false Christ who seemed to have more love than our Saviour. The Son of God showed this love to us in that He endured all the pain and suffering of an ugly death totally for our sakes. No-one can equal or exceed this. The blood in our veins gives us life, so the giving up of life is through the shedding of blood. Life and blood are closely connected in analogy and reality. Indeed, when God became incarnate in

Yeshua, He was fully man, so that the blood of the covenant is indeed human blood, and the life given, while absolutely pure and perfect, was indeed the life of a man. Thus, through meditation on the love of God, we begin to see why the covenant principle had to be sealed in blood.

The covenant is also a matter of life and death. Ever since Adam and Eve, death has reigned over all of God's creation, which was turned over to sin. Restoration from death to life through the covenant requires issues of life and death to be within its principles. Thus again our life is associated with the death and resurrection of our Saviour.

We can, in these ways begin to understand the teaching that developed from the early days of covenant history concerning the association of life with blood, and blood with the covenants of God. If we go back to the beginnings of this teaching we can see how God, through His Torah, intends the types and shadows to give us points for meditation, so that finally we can be deeply rooted in the truth that was fulfilled in Yeshua.

Some of the many passages to study are:

Genesis 4:1-11, in which we see not only the beginnings of true sacrifice but also the relationship of blood with life. We must be careful to see beyond the fact that Abel offered a sacrifice of an animal compared with Cain's fruit of the ground. Later we see that a grain offering was one of the Levitical offerings as well as the animal. Thus, along with the principle of blood and life we should also meditate upon the attitude of offering sacrifice, since God looks on the heart and not just on the offering.

Genesis 9:1-17, in which we see the reaffirmation of the sanctity of life, typified by blood, in the context of the covenant with Noah. We also see the Torah principle of not eating blood with meat. We can assume that beyond teaching about eating healthy, that is Kosher (clean) food, God intended these to be a constant reminder at the meal-table of the sanctity of life, a principle to be deeply ingrained in God's covenant people in their daily lives.

Genesis 15:1-12, where we see that the covenant with Abraham was sealed through the ceremony of shedding the blood of animals.

Genesis 17:9-14, where we see that flesh must be circumcised for God's covenant people, in line with the fact that without the shedding of blood there can be no remission of sins (Hebrews 9:22). From the later teaching on circumcision we see that this was one of the types and shadows pointing to a deeper circumcision of the heart (the heart of flesh that is given to us as a result of the New Covenant in the blood of Yeshua) (Jeremiah 31:31-34)

Exodus 12, where we learn about the power of blood through the Feast of Pesach (Passover), pointing clearly to Yeshua, the fulfilment of the Passover Lamb.

In the Book of Leviticus, there is an ongoing theme of the sanctity of blood. The shedding of blood is essential for the Temple offerings as a constant reminder of the price of sin and the principle of substitution. In the Temple, where blood is offered in profusion, and in the home, where no blood is to be eaten, there is to be an ingrained principle of sacrifice and sanctity, building on the principle that the life is in the blood.

These are just a few examples, but when we come to the New Covenant in the Blood of Yeshua, we should be able to build on deep but clear principles from the earlier Scriptures, showing that forgiveness of sin is only achieved through the shed blood of Yeshua. We should not be like the earliest disciples, who did not understand it when He said:

'I tell you the truth, unless you eat the flesh of the Son of Man and drink his blood, you have no life in you. Whoever eats my flesh and drinks my blood has eternal life, and I will raise him up at the last day. For my flesh is real food and my blood is real drink. Whoever eats my flesh and drinks my blood remains in me, and I in him.' (John 6:53-56)

We should be prepared and not surprised by the theme of true life and forgiveness of sin coming to us through faith in Him and in the power of His sacrificed life (shed blood). We should be among those who understand how the New Covenant through His blood fulfils the types of the Old Covenant, which was the temporary means of forgiveness of sins through the substitution of the life of animals as Temple sacrifices, as fully explored in the Book of Hebrews, understanding too what Yeshua meant regarding this being the constant meditation through the sharing of the wine at our fellowship memorial meals:

'This cup is the new covenant in my blood, which is poured out for you.' (Luke 22:20)

The central pivot of our response to God as His covenant people is the life of faith, and the central issue that must be deep in our hearts and minds is the fulfilment of all that the Father requires through His life poured out for us, and His blood shed for us. It is time for the covenant people of God to have a completely balanced perspective on who we are, responding to and studying the whole of Scripture while fully understanding the fulfilment of all covenant principles through the shed blood of the Lord Yeshua, while living our life with these principles motivating us from the very depths of our beings. The New Covenant in contrast with the Old Covenant is not a comparison of the Old Testament with the New, but a fulfilment of all the teaching that begins in the earlier books of the Bible, a sealing and completion of all that is taught through the life, sacrificial death and resurrection of Yeshua.

Who are we?

The Power of the Covenant

Reading: 1 Corinthians 15: 51 – 56, Genesis 6: 13 – 18, Lamentations, Matthew 27, Ezekiel 16, Romans 11.

The purpose of studying who we are as the covenant people of God goes beyond getting our ideas straight so that we have a logical basis for interpreting Scripture. The main purpose is that we truly take our place within the covenant family, with our hearts deeply transformed through what God has done for us.

1 Corinthians 15 expresses what has been done for us. The sting of death has been removed. Knowledge of God's Torah shows us the holy lifestyle that makes His people worthy of fellowship with him, but because of our fallen nature, we realise our daily failure even with our hearts set on living according to God's teaching. Thus we are humbled and our need is revealed since we know that sin leads to separation from God, as with Adam and Eve at the beginning of time. Repentance leads to faith in Yeshua HaMashiach (Jesus the Messiah) and the sting of death is removed for all that seek to live by this saving faith.

Yet even this principle can be theoretical if we do not constantly meditate to the full on what has been done for us through the covenant of God sealed by an irreversible Oath. We need to go over and over these things, searching the Scriptures from beginning to end, and not being content until our hearts are profoundly changed.

The power of sin that leads to death is shown through the Great Flood at the time of Noah. We must, however, realise that sin did not end with the flood. Indeed, we might conjecture that the sin in the world today is no less than the sin prior to the flood but, because of the covenant, God does not turn us over to the same wrath as befell those who perished at the time of Noah. Indeed, the account of Noah after the flood shows that he was not sinless, but was considered righteous because of God's imputing righteousness to Him through faith, a faith finally fulfilled in Yeshua. It was through the covenant that Noah was saved, and this also pointed to our salvation, salvation, salvation from wrath symbolised by the devastating flood that covered the whole earth. In other words, we too deserved to perish in the same manner as those at the time of the flood, but have been saved in the same manner as was Noah, through the faithfulness of God to us through His covenant plan.

Another profound meditation on the power of sin is found in the Book of Lamentations, written by Jeremiah because of the fall of Jerusalem and Judah. Deuteronomy 28 gives an accurate prediction of the cost of disobedience to the terms of the covenant made with Israel, and Lamentations is the sad reflection on what actually happened. Yet the power of the covenant is to reverse this exile of God's people. The prophets always looked ahead to the day when the fulfilment of the covenant would be possible for Israel and Judah, knowing the faithfulness of God even in the paradox of the exile of His own people. The ultimate power of the covenant is to reverse the horror of the exile, which had resulted in the deep mourning of Psalm 137.

By the rivers of Babylon we sat and wept when we remembered Zion.
There on the poplars we hung our harps
For there our captors asked as for songs, our tormentors demand-
ed songs of joy; they said, 'Sing us one of the songs of Zion'
How can we sing the songs of the LORD while in a foreign land?
If I forget you, O Jerusalem may my right hand forget its skill.
May my tongue cling to the roof of my mouth if I do not remem-
ber you, if I do not consider Jerusalem my highest joy.

Even in the midst of the depth of sorrow of banishment from the land, Jeremiah's heart found a prayer of faith:

So I say, 'My splendor is gone and all that I had hoped from the LORD
I remember my affliction and my wandering, the bitterness and the gall.
I well remember them, and my soul is downcast within me.
Yet this I call to mind and therefore I have hope:
Because of the Lord's great love we are not consumed, for his compassions never fail,
They are new every morning: great is your faithfulness.
I say to myself, 'The LORD is my portion; therefore I will wait for him.' (Lamentations 3: 18 – 24)

The power of the covenant is to humble the heart of God's people, to increase their faith even in perplexing and painful circumstances and to finish the plan of salvation. The power of the covenant is greater than the power of sin to destroy, yet even the lamentations of Jeremiah for the exile and even the devastation of the flood are but symbols compared with the true cost of sin. The true cost was the sacrifice of the Son of God. In His crucifixion we see at one and the same time the full penalty for our sin and also the power of the covenant fulfilled in the sacrifice of the Son of God on the Cross to overcome the power of sin. God's faithfulness was sealed in an irreversible oath and that oath was fulfilled even to the death of His Son.

We would be wise, as it were, to sit where they have sat who went before us. This we can accomplish through meditation on the principles of sin, death and restoration through the covenant woven through the Bible and through the experiences of the Children of Israel. Perhaps God will help us, giving us visions and inspiration of other kinds. Ezekiel saw the suffering of the exiles, understood the judgement of God and yet also saw ahead, as did the other prophets, to the plan of salvation being finally accomplished. Ezekiel 16 seems at first sight to be a revelation of the gross sin of Israel which led to exile, and such it is, but that is not all. First the prophet speaks of the terrible sins of the nation in down-to-earth language. These are sins that seem to bring irreversible punishment, for that is what they deserve. God does not compromise His understand and expression of the wickedness of the people, in betraying Him to become like a wife who has become a prostitute. Yet, He then draws a contrast with what He will finally do, despite gross sin among His people, which is worse than the nations around:

> *This is what the Sovereign LORD says: I will deal with you as you deserve, because you have despised my oath by breaking the covenant. Yet I will remember the covenant I made with you in the days of your youth, and I will establish an everlasting covenant with you. Then you will remember your ways and be ashamed when you receive your sisters, both those who are older than you and those who are younger. I will give them to you as daughters, but not on the basis of my covenant with you. So I will establish my covenant with you, and you will know that I am the LORD. Then, when I make atonement for you for all you have done, you will remember and be ashamed and never again open your mouth because of your humiliation, declares the Sovereign LORD.*
> *(Ezekiel 16: 59 – 63)*

God will remember His covenant and the oath that sealed it, to the end of time. For the faithful remnant of Israel and Judah and all who join this family through faith from all nations, according to the fulfilment of the New Covenant of Jeremiah 31, sealed in the Blood of Yeshua HaMashiach, there lies a reversal of all the curse of sin, shown so clearly through the pages of the Bible. Romans 11 stands as a prophecy that will be, and is being, fulfilled for Israel as also we come branch by branch into the one Olive Tree. The power of the covenant is to us as real as it has been for sinful Israel and Judah, destroying the power of death that hung over us until Yeshua saved us and breathed His spirit into us. Surely we should study and pray concerning this, until the principles are deep within us, we who are the covenant people of God. Then let us bow down in worship to the One who fulfilled all the types, shadows and promises of God's eternal covenant. He did it so that we might be saved for eternal life.

היכלים
להחכמך
אל-הישועה

ומנעוריך
ידעת את-
כתבי הקודש

Miriam

FROM A CHILD YOU HAVE KNOWN THE
SCRIPTURES
WHICH ARE ABLE TO
MAKE YOU WISE TO SALVATION.

Section 2

Torah: God's foundational teaching for His one covenant community

If there is one covenant community, then there is also one set of Scriptures given to that covenant community. We must learn to deepen our foundations of faith and practical living through understanding how the Scriptures fit together. The foundations of Torah (the teaching of God) are set in the first five books of the Bible, emphasised by the Old Testament Prophets and in the Writings of the Old Testament (Tanakh), fulfilled in the life and ministry of Yeshua HaMashiach (Jesus the Messiah) and explored through the New Testament Writings. All major truths begin in the first five books of the Bible developing and interweaving their way through all of Scripture. Our day by day study of all of God's teaching should be built on these firm foundations.

As we meditate upon the truths that we discover as we follow the patterns through Scripture, we should find ourselves deeper into the truth whereby we should live and closer to the Lord through whom all things came.

Torah

Introduction

Think not that I am come to destroy the Law, or the prophets: I am not come to destroy, but to fulfil. (Matthew 5:17)

The central issue of all history is the plan of Salvation. Mankind fell in the Garden of Eden and world history since then has been about the plan of recovery. All that God has said and done relates to this. Central to the plan of Salvation is the Covenant that God made with Abraham. He has sworn an Oath that cannot be revoked, that He will redeem a family to Himself from all nations, and as Yeshua (Jesus) prayed (John 17). the purpose of God is that we might know Him and His Son Yeshua. This is why Yeshua came. All of God's teaching pointed to Him. Everything in all history and in all creation is centred on Him, the means by which God's Covenant is to be fulfilled.

In our day, the central issue is preparation for His return and the completion of all that has been promised. For us, the application of all God has taught points to this, as do all the circumstances of the world in which we live.

The purpose of this section of the book is to encourage disciples of the Lord Jesus (Yeshua) to seek the depth and width of all God's teaching with this in mind. The concept of Torah as the whole teaching plan of God is reclaimed into its fullness relating to Messianic belief, taking us back to the roots of our faith whose foundations are set in the Book of Genesis. If the central theme of all Scripture is borne in mind, then the concept of Torah will be considered in the correct balance, incorporating both practical and spiritual truths. With Messiah in focus, all that God has taught will also be in focus, including the place of Jerusalem and of Israel, the Feasts and Shabbat (the Sabbath Day), Abraham and Mount Moriah, Moses and Horeb, the Children of Israel, the Tabernacle and Temple, the Flood, indeed all of God's work in creation and among His people and among all nations. Behind these and other major points of teaching, is the outworking of God's plan of Salvation and our practical and spiritual involvement in it. Above all, perhaps, we have the pattern of family and community life that Torah indicates.

God is gathering His family in these last days, and He is calling us back to the roots of our faith so that we together, a body of believers in Yeshua HaMashiach (Jesus the Messiah) redeemed from all nations, Jew and Greek, can prepare for His coming.

It is wise to note that these studies are for disciples of the Lord Jesus the Messiah (Yeshua HaMashiach), who already live by faith in Him. Therefore, there is very little discussion on the negative aspects of the Gospel message concerning the eternal separation from God for those who do not accept the free gift of Salvation and to whom, therefore, these studies are not specifically directed.

Torah

The Teaching of God

The word *Torah* originates from the Hebrew language and means teaching or instruction. While it is appropriate for disciples of Yeshua HaMashiach (Jesus the Messiah) to use this term in its correct sense, unfortunately it has been neglected by Christians for many years. One of the reasons for this neglect is that Judaism has given the term a narrow definition within a legalistic framework. It was originally the term used to refer to the foundational teaching of Scripture, based on the teaching of the first five Books. While this is appropriate, in Jewish tradition there have developed other more restrictive shades of meaning to the term *Torah*. There is a strong tendency in Judaism to use the term to refer specifically and sometimes exclusively to the teaching that was brought through Moses at Mount Sinai. Unfortunately, this narrower concept of *Torah* can lead to a legalistic approach to the teaching of Scripture that ends in bondage. It is this legalistic approach that has caused many Christians to turn away from the concept of *Torah*, instead of maintaining its use in the original wider sense of its meaning, as the foundational teaching of God, including the life of faith as well as the 'Law of Moses.' However, if we clear away the misunderstandings associated with the term *Torah*, it is far more appropriate than the term 'Law' which has replaced it in Christian tradition.

Judaism has a tradition that Moses gave both the written *Torah* (the first five books of the Bible) and the Oral *Torah*. The Oral *Torah* is considered to be the spoken instructions of Moses which were interpretations of the written *Torah* into principles of everyday life. The Oral *Torah* was itself written down by the Jewish authorities by about 200 AD, so that the teaching would not be lost due to the dispersion of the Jews after the destruction of Jerusalem in 70 AD. The written version of the Oral *Torah* is called the Mishnah. The two versions of the Talmud (those written in Babylon and in Jerusalem) contain the Mishnah and further teaching and commentary based on the Mishnah. Because of this, the Talmud has become a main reference point within Judaism for how a Jew should conduct his life. The result is that *Torah* to the Jews is now a term that relates to the interpretation of the teaching of Moses into a code of conduct for everyday life, based on the Talmud. When the teaching comes from the Talmud, however, it can be dry and legalistic and so the revelation of *Torah* becomes extremely limited. We can see that this restricted view of *Torah* was not intended, when we study Yeshua's stern condemnation of certain teachers of the 'law' (*Torah*) (See, for example, Matthew 23). Yeshua Himself used the term *Torah* in its correct sense, as the foundational teaching of Scripture, pointing to Him, and we should carry on that tradition, rather than consider *Torah* as being a legalistic approach to Scripture, and thereby neglecting its deeper and wider meaning.

Because Christianity neglected much of its relationship to Judaism in the early centuries after the dispersion of the Jews, partly on account of a rejection of their interpretation of Scripture, but for other reasons too, many links to the Hebraic concepts in Scripture were also neglected. As well as a growth of Greek and Roman influence in Christianity which followed, translations of the Scriptures into other languages introduced words in these languages that added shades of meaning to the original ideas of Scripture. In English, the word *law* has generally replaced the word *Torah*, carrying with it the concept of dos and don'ts, rights and wrongs, with punishment for transgression. While it is true that Moses taught much concerning the legal framework of God's holy commandments, the context of the whole teaching of God was much wider than Roman or English law, so if the foundational teaching of the Tanakh (Old Testament) is seen only in the framework of 'law', then Christianity, as well as Judaism, is deprived of its true foundations. In seeking to correct one error, another error crept into Christianity, which has caused some neglect of the foundational teaching of Scripture, specifically that which is in the first five books of the Bible.

Thus, there can be errors in both Judaism and Christianity concerning the use of the Tanakh (Old Testament). Both Jews and Christians can misunderstand what the true foundations of Scripture are. Jews can live in the bondage of legalism, while Christians can neglect the foundational teaching almost entirely, as an overreaction to legalism. In so doing, the word *Torah* can be misapplied or misunderstood, while it is, in fact, a very appropriate word if used correctly.

The Hebrew root of the word *Torah* is *Yarah*, which is linked to the idea of casting out something in the right direction or on a right course, like an accurately propelled arrow from a bow. It carries the meaning of directing, guiding or instructing on a right course of action. Thus, the word *Torah* means teaching for a true course in life. When applied to Scripture, therefore, *Torah* means the foundational teaching of God. By contrast, the Hebrew word for sin is *Chata*, which can also be related to the shooting of an arrow, but falling short or missing the mark. Thus, the word *Torah* is a very appropriate biblical concept for God's teaching, given to help us know and achieve all His purposes, while sin is the falling short of the standards of God's teaching.

If we only interpret *Torah* in a legalistic framework, as if God has shown us what He requires and has left us to live out His requirements in a ritualistic way, fearful of failure, we have not fully understood what God's teaching is. If we see *Torah* only in terms of 'law', whether Jews or Christians, we have not set the *Torah* foundations firmly. While God's holy principles are awesome, the need of mankind for a Saviour is central to the foundations of true *Torah*. The teaching goes wider by far than legalism. Indeed, if we take the first five books as the foundations of *Torah*, then we find that there are many basic issues whose foundational teaching is established there. Having set these foundations in place, the whole of Scripture becomes deeper, firmer and more meaningful.

Thus, it is appropriate for believers in Yeshua HaMashiach

(Jesus Christ) to recover the concept of *Torah*, freeing it of any narrowness which leads to bondage, widening the view of the whole teaching of God and restoring the firm foundations of all Scripture. This does not mean that the Tanakh (Old Testament) replaces the New Testament, but that all Scriptures are studied from their foundations to their fulfilment. Paul taught (Romans 10:4) that the Messiah is the Telos (the aim) of *Torah*. Thus all Bible teaching (*Torah*) points to Him. The Messiah did not come to abolish the *Torah* but to bring it into its fullness (Matthew 5:17-20). Yeshua in His teaching and exposition of *Torah* directed His followers to approach the commandments with a view to their essence, which He summed up in the 'golden rule' (Matthew 7:12). In this spirit, the Apostolic writers expounded the New Covenant in terms of the Great Commandment (Romans 13:10, Galatians 5:14, James 2:8). If we approach the whole of *Torah*, including the specific commandments, with this in mind, our whole approach to Scripture, our life of faith and our knowledge of Messiah should become well-founded and mature in all ways. In this sense, it is appropriate for disciples of Yeshua HaMashiach to reclaim the concept of *Torah*, studying Scripture from the foundations set in the first five books of the Bible, whose teaching is the foundation of the Prophets and Writings, fulfilled in and by Yeshua, and proclaimed and expounded by the Apostolic writers. With this view of *Torah*, we realise that in the Scriptures is a revelation of God and His ways that all people should study from the foundations to fullest understanding. The practical teaching takes us deep into the spiritual truths. With a knowledge of God and His call to a holy life in fellowship with Him, we learn of the limitations of our practical obedience due to sin. We have a complete teaching for ourselves as individuals, for our families and communities and for our nations. In practical terms we have teaching which directs us on the good path of life which pleases God, but through our conviction of sin as we attempt to walk this good path, we are pointed more profoundly to our Saviour, Yeshua HaMashiach (Jesus Christ). From foundations to fulfilment, *Torah* is all that the world needs to lead us to the Saviour in all humility and repentance. With the signs of His return all around us, purposeful study and application of *Torah* will put all of history in perspective, where the outworking of God's Covenant plan is the central theme. If the nations understood this as it was intended to be understood, the whole world would be making preparations for the return of the Messiah, seeking to live according to the practical and spiritual truths that are embedded in *Torah*, until He comes to complete the redemption of all who truly believe and are counted as His disciples, releasing us finally from the bondage of sin that remains in this fallen world, and which wars against the holy principles of *Torah*. Messiah is truly the goal of *Torah*.

For Study and Meditation: Study the references given in this section and consider the way we should use the term *Torah*. Read Psalm 119 and consider the author's attitude to the teaching of God (*Torah*) which has its foundations in the first five books of the Bible.

Torah

Fulfilment not Replacement

In Matthew 5:17, we read that Yeshua said:

Think not that I am come to destroy the law, or the prophets: I am not come to destroy, but to fulfil.

Elsewhere, He said:

These are the words which I spake unto you, while I was yet with you, that all things must be fulfilled, which were written in the law of Moses, and in the prophets, and in the psalms, concerning me. (Luke 24:44)

In both of these passages we have the word which is translated 'law'. Because the translations of the New Testament go back to Greek rather than Hebrew manuscripts we must always look behind the word 'law' to see what it refers to. Because we know that the Scriptures at the time of Yeshua were in three sections (the *Torah*, the Prophets and the Writings, making up what is called the Tanakh), the first of these sections being the five books that Moses wrote, we can assume that both Luke and Matthew were drawing reference to these divisions, so that on both these occasions Yeshua was referring to the *Torah* in its widest sense, to what we have in our translations as 'law'.

When we study passages such as those above, we can form a sound view of Yeshua's attitude to *Torah*. In saying that He did not come to destroy, He was using rabbinical terminology showing that He did not come to give wrong interpretation of *Torah*. In saying that He had come to fulfil, He was saying that He had come to rightly interpret *Torah*. Thus, His teaching was founded on the correct interpretation of *Torah*. He was perfectly at home teaching in the Synagogues, teaching from the Scriptures, but giving the fullest sense to the meaning, unlike others who attempted to teach, but who taught without full authority and meaning. For example, it was said of Him in the Synagogue at Capernaum:

They were astonished at his doctrine: for he taught them as one that had authority, and not as the scribes.' (Mark 1:22)

Yeshua's fulfilment of Scripture was not in word alone. His whole life and His very being were fulfilments. He was the Word made flesh (John 1:14), the full manifestation of God, incorporating the heart of the *Torah* in His very being. In all that He was and did, He revealed the fullness of *Torah* and all that the Prophets and the Writings of the Tanakh foretold.

This fact is important as we consider how to approach the reading of Scripture. The New Testament was written after the time of Yeshua and bears witness to His fulfilment of what we call the Old Testament, which is also known as the Tanakh and which was the complete set of Scriptures at the time of Yeshua. He points us back to the Tanakh, but with greater understanding. It must also be said that the Holy Spirit has been sent to the Church since the time of Yeshua to make all of our studies more meaningful, and to enable the *Torah* to be written on our heart. Nevertheless, the root and foundation of all the teaching that Yeshua brought and fulfilled was in the Tanakh and was, as we shall see, specifically within the context of the first five books of the Bible, the *Torah*.

Luke 11:39-54 contains a record of one of Yeshua's powerful encounters with the teachers of *Torah*. He revealed the fact that they knew how to interpret the superficial aspects of *Torah* but failed to have the deeper understanding. Indeed, they failed to have the deeper understanding as part of their inner character. He did not say that *Torah* had changed, only that it had been misunderstood and interpreted superficially.

What we, as Yeshua's disciples, should understand from this is that we should not consider *Torah* as being replaced, or changed, but that we should continue to use it as foundational teaching, in the light of Yeshua. We should not abandon *Torah*, but study and teach it correctly. We read the *Torah* in the light of Yeshua by the power of the Holy Spirit who works in us. We also begin with *Torah* in order to study Scripture from the foundations upwards. We lay the foundations in order to understand and know Yeshua more fully. We, who live by the Spirit of God, have the advantage over the Scribes and Pharisees whom Yeshua condemned. We can read the same Scriptures as they did and find life and meaning. The Scriptures, at their heart, point us to Yeshua and to the lifestyle of His disciples. In this sense, *Torah* is as important to us as it was to Yeshua, and at least as important as it was to the interpreters of the *Torah* in Yeshua's day. We study Scripture from where they did, from foundations upwards, but with the foreknowledge of their fulfilment in Yeshua.

For Study and Meditation: Study Matthew 5, 6 and 7 and consider how we should be familiar with the first five books of the Bible to set the foundations of Bible teaching. Refer also to Luke 24:13-35 and 2 Timothy 3:16-17.

Torah

What Torah contains

While *Torah* has a wide meaning relating to the whole teaching of God, we will use the term in the way Yeshua did, as the foundational teaching of all Scripture discovered in the first five books of the Bible. We will free it of narrow legalism and endeavour to discover the whole scope of its meaning. Truths about Yeshua will be discovered rather than neglected and we will deepen our understanding of His fulfilment, as well as the way we should live our lives.

We each have a certain way of thinking. The background to our life, including our education system, establishes certain things that we assume to be true and then everything else is biased by these foundational ideas. Our way of reading Scripture is biased by certain ways of thinking that may have been influenced by others, and it may take time to be confident in starting at the beginning of the Bible to set the foundations of all Bible teaching. Once we do this, however, we will realise that the early books contain foundational teaching on many issues and that this foundational teaching affects not only the way we study the rest of Scripture, but the way we understand Messiah and the way we live our lives.

All of the teaching of the Bible begins in these early chapters. Most of the words that are important for us to understand in other places, are used for the first time in these chapters, and we will only understand them fully if we draw reference to their first usage. The same goes for our understanding of many concepts, including those that give us an understanding of God and of ourselves. Priorities are set in place in these early books, which are then developed right through Scripture.

There is no reliable reference point for the beginning of history other than the first Chapter of Genesis. Far from being ancient history, it is recent history, which also establishes the priority of history when related to the plan of Salvation and the end of the world. The priority of family is written deeply into these early books, whether it be through the first family of Adam and Eve or through the family of Abraham, or the Covenant family of Israel. We learn more about God Himself than anywhere else in all Scripture and we learn about the nature of mankind. Much of the foundational teaching on these and many other themes are in Genesis, the first book, which covers the history of mankind before Moses and before Israel became the Covenant nation. We learn about the life of faith through the life of Abraham, before we learn of the teaching that God gave through Moses. We also learn of the everlasting Covenant given to Abraham and the swearing of an Oath by God Himself. All these things, in their deepest sense point to Yeshua HaMashiach, but the foundations of Scripture are set deeply in these first five books, called appropriately the *Torah*.

The list is almost endless as to what *Torah* contains. When ones eyes are opened, there are many themes that begin here and intertwine with other themes in a rich tapestry that goes on developing like unbroken threads throughout the whole of Scripture. One can read *Torah* over and over again and each time widen one's view of what it contains and deepen one's understanding of what it says. The first important step of discovery is to realise that *Torah* is much wider than what God brought through Moses to Israel. Secondly, all of the teaching of these five books must be held in balance. Moses is to be understood in terms of the faith of Abraham, and both Moses and Abraham point to Messiah. Not one jot or tittle is to be neglected. Those who have neglected *Torah* study, thinking that Yeshua replaced it with new teaching, may need to start at the beginning and study these first five books as if for the first time, in a serious attitude.

On first reading, some of the major themes will be apparent, confirming the wide range of topics in which foundations are set, including for example:

The account of Creation.
The nature and rise of sin.
The rise of the nations and the increase of sin.
The Great Flood.
The call of Abraham.
The Covenant with Abraham.
The renewed Covenant with succeeding generations (Isaac, Jacob, the Children of Israel).
The beginnings of the Twelve Tribes of Israel.
The hard labour in Egypt.
The deliverance from Egypt.
The wilderness journey.
The giving of the written Law of Moses.
The Feasts of the Lord.
The Tabernacle.
The Levitical Priesthood.
The arrival in the Promised Land.

Further reading will then establish some of the deeper priorities of *Torah*. Pictures of Messiah begin to form, as well as the way history's priority is mankind's need of a Saviour. The beginnings of time give clues to the end of time, including the short time-span of history and the judgement of God in the Flood pointing to the last great judgement. The priority of family and family relationships is shown. The way a society could live with God as its King becomes apparent. The awesomeness of God's unbreakable Covenant is revealed, giving us a sense of the Sovereign purposes of God and mankind's utter need of Him. The depth of the life of faith is also most fully founded in the teaching of these first five books. Once orientated to the teaching of these books, reference points can be found whereby truths develop progressively through the whole of Scripture and a pattern of effective cross-referencing can develop into mature and deep Bible study.

It is seen that there is far more to *Torah* than dos and don'ts. God reveals His character to us as we read the chapters of *Torah*.

Alongside this, the character of mankind is also revealed. We see a reflection of ourselves and our need for God and His Salvation. This is why James likened our study of *Torah* (the perfect law that gives freedom) to looking in a mirror to see ourselves (James 1:22-24). We can study the life of Abraham in detail and see the patterns and principles of the life of faith that is intended for all of us. We can consider the history of the Children of Israel and see pictures of ourselves and the way our nations both need God and war against God. All these things God has given us in His teaching programme, lived out through the lives of His people and recorded for us in the foundational books of Scripture.

We can see pictures of Yeshua through these writings too. Indeed, far from being diverted from Him as the foundation and fulfilment of *Torah*, by reading these foundational books we can gain maturity in our understanding of Him being there before Creation and through all history. These continuous and unbreakable truths are threaded through all history and begin in the books of *Torah*. The replacement of Isaac on Mount Moriah by a Ram (Genesis 22) is a picture of Messiah as a substitute for those who are saved from the penalty of their sins. He is also to be discovered in and through the Feasts of the Lord and in the perfect picture contained in the Tabernacle. The plan of salvation is there in picture form too, interwoven with a perfect display of the fall of mankind and the need for a Saviour.

Torah contains all these things and many more. There are some points that are more obvious than others, but the more veiled and subtle points of teaching come to light during times of continual and prayerful study. Every word, every letter, every paragraph breathes something of the teaching of God and points to fulfilment in Yeshua. *Torah* reveals the call to faith and the character of God in whom we have faith. *Torah* contains the foundations of our understanding of God's sovereignty and human responsibility. The balance of these things has perplexed many believers over many years, yet the patterns are to be discovered in *Torah*. Indeed, neglect of *Torah* will give us incomplete understanding of the foundations of our faith. By studying *Torah* we enter our Hebrew heritage and come alongside the patriarchs of our faith. Our faith is put into context and becomes dynamic (a walk) rather than a static theory for a Greek philosophical mindset. We find ourselves drawn into the everlasting Covenant of God, fulfilled completely in and through Yeshua, but established in us as we find a balanced walk of faith with all God's people, based on the foundational studies of His teaching - *Torah*.

For Study and Meditation: Study Genesis 22 and Leviticus 23 as examples of *Torah* study that teach us about God the Father, ourselves, the life of faith, Yeshua and the practices of *Torah*. Then make a general review of the content of the whole of *Torah*, taking this to mean the first five books of the Bible. Do you agree that the whole of Creation, all of our life in our world and society, all of our family life and all of history take on fuller meaning when they are understood through the foundational principles of *Torah?* Reflect on the balance that *Torah* gives us of the life of faith within the context of the revelations that were given to Moses to teach to the Israelites in the wilderness.

Torah

The whole of Scripture is founded on Torah

Once we have studied the first five books of the Bible and realised how all major truths of Scripture begin there, we can continue to develop a way of thinking based on this. We can go from depth to depth of understanding. We can trace pathways of truth that weave their way through all Scripture. Familiarity with all the books of the Bible helps us to trace these paths. Truths interweave their paths through verses and chapters of the Bible. The more we study Scripture in this way the more we find that all Scripture is Messianic. Yeshua is before, within and beyond all Scripture. When He was manifest in the flesh, the full revelation of Him took place, but He was before Creation, within the Covenant with Abraham, with the Children of Israel in the wilderness and in the Land and within the words of the Prophets and Writings. All things were made by Him and for Him. Studying *Torah* with the perspective of faith coming before the Law of Moses, we also realise that this was always to be the priority of a walk with God and that the coming of Yeshua in the flesh, His sacrificial death, His resurrection, the giving of the Holy Spirit were to enable us to become the people of God that all Scripture points to, ourselves fulfilling *Torah* and *Halakhah* in harmony with the original purposes of God laid down from Creation onwards.

With a detailed study of the contents of the first five books of the Bible it is possible to study how the rest of the Bible (both the 'New' and the 'Old' Testaments) is linked to these books. First, we form a way of thinking by establishing the foundations of our faith and then we move forward to deeper and deeper understanding. This is the pursuit of a lifetime. Because Yeshua (Jesus) is the fulfilment of all the Scriptures, there are many Bible teachers who believe that we should only teach fulfilment and so ignore foundations. Having led a person to Salvation in Him, they consider that it is unnecessary to go back to the foundations. Thereby, many Christians lack the deeper rooting that is possible. They seem to come into a different Covenant than the one offered to Israel, the physical descendants of Abraham. This has contributed to the separation of Christianity from its true biblical roots and has led to Christians who are, to a large extent, detached from the Covenant community. It has led to Greek philosophy replacing Hebraic faith. When we study Scripture from its foundations, in the light of our Salvation in Yeshua, we become more rooted in our ancient heritage alongside all the Covenant community. This is beyond a physical thing. It is a spiritual experience.

When Israel grew as a nation in the Promised Land, the requirements of *Torah* had been established. If they had lived as the community that God intended then all that was in *Torah* would have been fulfilled, including the blessings set out in Deuteronomy 28. It is clearer to those of us who have understood the fulfilment in Yeshua that there was bound to be failure, but even this was predicted in *Torah* (Deuteronomy 31 and 32). The fact is that there are hidden depths to *Torah* and we are still discovering them today.

The story of Israel is the story of a people who are seeking to obey *Torah*. The *Writings*, including even Job and Song of Songs, assume a knowledge of the character of God as revealed in *Torah*. Without the truths and teaching of *Torah*, the *Writings* have no foundation or reference point. The Psalms, for example, reflect the perfection of *Torah* and the struggles in this life on account of our knowledge of God and our sinful nature. When we look behind the *Writings* we see the struggle of the Covenant people of God to walk with Him in all holiness. Failure to have faith is more the key to understanding the failure of this walk than is failure in living the holy principles of the Law, when one reads the history of Israel in the light of Yeshua and the further *Writings* of the New Testament. The Psalms, at their highest level, point to fulfilment in Yeshua and to praise to God for His great love and blessings. God put *Torah* into perspective through the chosen nation of Israel. The revelation of the purposes of *Torah* are developed through this nation, while the foundational teaching is set in the first five books of the Bible. It is a valuable exercise to study the *Writings* of the Tanakh (Old Testament) and confirm that what they reveal is a development of the foundational truths of *Torah*.

Similarly, it is an important and valuable exercise to read the Prophets to discover the way their message is completely founded on the *Torah*. The Prophets were sent to Israel and Judah specifically on account of transgressions of *Torah*. If *Torah* were lived in all its fullness, Israel and Judah would have lived in harmony and fellowship with God, not only because of their obedience to the principles of holy living outlined through Moses in the wilderness, but mainly because of their repentant lifestyle, for which provision was always made in the sacrificial system, which was a shadow of the sacrifice of Yeshua. The holy requirements of *Torah* did not change with Yeshua, but the walk of faith was made possible in a way that Israel, in general did not achieve. They separated themselves from God through sin, that sin being chiefly to do with lack of faith. If they had lived in faith they would have lived closer to God and fulfilled the deeper understanding of the Law instead of becoming superficial and shallow, even self-righteous. When the Prophets spoke of the deeper issues of justice and mercy they were calling Israel and Judah to a deeper walk with God. A correct reading of the Prophets reveals the fact that their message depended entirely on a true and balanced interpretation of *Torah*. Without the foundation of this true understanding of *Torah* the Prophets had no basis for their message. They called the Covenant community to repent and live according to the true meaning of *Torah*. They brought a message of judgement according to the principles of *Torah*, and they also brought a message of hope, according to the way God would fulfil the unbreakable Oath that He made to Abraham, and would one day be fulfilled in and through Yeshua.

Yeshua's message did not replace the foundational teaching of the first five books of the Bible, but brought them to full and true meaning. He had no other reference for His teaching. It seemed different because it was the full, true and deep teaching that had not been fully understood before. His life was the manifestation of *Torah*'s principles and Covenant promises. To understand Yeshua fully, it is wise to build on the foundation of the Scriptures that went before. It is then our task in discipleship to teach the true meaning of *Torah*, and build on these foundations. Nothing that Yeshua said, when correctly interpreted, would point us in any other direction. The New Testament is the account of His fulfilment of *Torah*. He fulfilled it in His life and character and He showed us the deeper meanings of *Torah* through His teaching (for example, the Sermon on the Mount, Matthew 5-7). The revelation of Yeshua begins in the *Torah* and is also found in the Psalms (and other *Writings*) and the Prophets (Yeshua explained this on the Road to Emmaus, Luke 24:13-35).

The Acts of the Apostles and the teaching of the Apostles in the New Testament Writings, including all of Paul's teaching in his Epistles, is an account of how the fulfilled *Torah* message was carried into the world. Indeed, the New Testament refers directly and consistently to the *Torah*. It is not intended to be a replacement for *Torah* nor even a complete commentary. The New Testament provides a framework for the full understanding of *Torah*, but this does not replace a complete study of *Torah* itself, both to set the framework and foundation for the New Testament and to bring to light all that it contains in the light of the New Testament teaching. The Book of Hebrews is a masterpiece of exposition of fulfilled sacrifice in Yeshua, to which the types and shadows of the Levitical Priesthood pointed, but to which the prior framework of the Priesthood of Melchizedech more fully pointed. The mysteries and preparations are within the *Torah* of the 'Old' Testament. When the *Torah* foundations are set firmly, we can understand Paul more clearly. He puts the right perspective on what we read in *Torah* rather than seeking to abolish it. Paul, following Yeshua, interprets *Torah* as it was always intended to be understood, and so points us back to these essential foundations without seeking to remove them. Hence, we must realise that all of the New Testament as well as the Old Testament depends on the true foundations of *Torah*. Fulfilled *Torah* is demonstrated and taught in the 'New' Testament, building on and interpreting all that went before. The depth of the New Testament is seen in its relationship with *Torah*, and study of the New Testament should begin in the depth and width of *Torah*.

For Study and Meditation: Since the whole Bible has strong foundations in *Torah*, how might we study the Bible from a fulfilled *Torah* perspective? Should Bible students ensure that they are familiar with the first five books of the Bible as a major priority?

Study the Epistle to the Hebrews and consider whether this is an explanation of how *Torah* is fulfilled in and through Yeshua.

Torah

Torah is both practical and spiritual

Torah has many layers. At the most superficial level, it has practical aspects that relate to the everyday lives of God's people. At a deeper level, we find spiritual truths. Practical aspects of *Torah* usually lead to these spiritual truths, and often both the spiritual and the practical apply simultaneously. At its deepest level, *Torah* points to Messiah in a variety of ways. *Torah* is in complete harmony with the deepest purposes of God. Indeed, not only is *Torah* a matter of the heart for the mature believer, we can discover the heart of God at the depths of *Torah*. As it says in Psalm 42 Verses 7-8:

> *Deep calleth unto deep at the noise of thy waterspouts: all thy waves and thy billows are gone over me. Yet the LORD will command his lovingkindness in the daytime, and in the night his song shall be with me, and my prayer unto the God of my life.*

This is the heart of *Torah* discovered by the writer of Psalm 119. The practices of *Torah* lead to the spiritual heart of *Torah*, which leads to God's heart itself. This was the intention from the start, and God's people were not intended to remain in the shallows of ritual observance.

Torah is practical.

There are two important ways in which *Torah* is practical. The first is that we learn the way to live our lives and order our communities from the commandments passed down through Moses. The Ten Commandments are the foundation stones of this teaching, but there are also other practical dos and don'ts. The Jewish Rabbis have listed 613 commandments (Mitzvot) in *Torah* and teach that they form the basis of the Jewish way of life. It is said that there are 248 positive commandments, corresponding to the number of parts of the human body, and 365 negative commandments, corresponding to the number of days of the year. Though this idea falls well short of the full extent of the practical benefits of *Torah*, it is a useful aid to remembering that one should do good with every part of the body and remember every day not to sin.

Judaism turned these commandments into ritual which took away some of their intent. Yeshua warned about this in His day (see Luke 11:37-54, for example), and these commandments are performed by many people, without correct motive or clear understanding, to this day. Nevertheless, practical obedience to the commandments of *Torah* should be ingrained into the lives of all believers. Since they are part of God's teaching (*Torah*) we can expect them to bring us freedom and not bondage if we understand them and apply them correctly.

The second way in which *Torah* is practical is in the way God uses practical activities to reinforce and demonstrate deeper truths. Good teachers use visual and practical aids in their teaching programme, and God is the perfect teacher. God's people should have a Hebraic nature, which is demonstrated in their lifestyle as well as their way of thinking. This could be contrasted with the Greek philosophical way which is mainly concerned with the mind. We are not expected to be people who think about the teaching of God and simply form ideas. Neither are we expected to only know *about* God. We are expected to know Him personally and experientially, as well as know about Him. We are expected to be doers, practical people. This is found in *Torah*. For example, God did not just ask us to think about the plan of Salvation; He gave us the yearly cycle of Feasts which are a pattern of the plan of Salvation (Leviticus 23). Every element of the Feasts of the Lord is a teaching aid used by God. God's teaching is practical in every way. Similarly, Yeshua did not ask us to remember Him without a practical activity; He gave us a new meaning to the Bread and Wine of the Passover Meal and said,

Do this in remembrance of Me. (Luke 23:19)

When we practice *Torah* we remember *Torah* better and also experience the presence of God in our midst.

God knows that we need constant and practical reminders even of the most precious truths. Sadly, most, if not all, human beings are both negligent and forgetful. We can test this through the experience of our own lives. This is also the witness of *Torah*, where we see that God's own people constantly drifted from the true path, even when He had done mighty works among them.

Torah is spiritual.

There are two important mistakes related to Torah. The first is to neglect the practical value of *Torah*. This can result from a misreading of the New Testament, thinking that it completely replaces the Old Testament. With this view, the Old Testament is considered as ancient history applying to the ancient people of Israel alone, with no remaining practical value. The Old Testament can be considered to have only allegorical meaning, in which the Bible stories convey mysterious ideas, with spiritual meaning rather than teaching relevant practices of continuing value.

The second mistake is to consider *Torah* as having no spiritual value. In this case, everything is interpreted only practically and literally. While the first mistake encourages false spirituality, the second mistake can lead to the same kind of legalism the religious leaders had imposed on the people of Yeshua's day. In this way, *Torah* is likely to be turned into a book of rules for practical application, which falls short of the deeper intent.

Many people live with an uncertainty about the extent of Torah's practical value and others are uncertain of its spiritual value. The fact is that *Torah* is very practical and the way of life that it offers contains God's own design for individual, family and community life.

The fact that it is impossible for human beings to attain the perfection shown in the practical requirements does not lessen the fact that *Torah* has immense practical value. Having accepted this fact, we can also benefit from the spiritual nature of *Torah*.

The depth of the spiritual value of *Torah* can only be discovered through meditating on *Torah* in all its fullness. The writer of Psalm 119 knew both the practical and spiritual value of obeying God's Commandments when he said such things as,

Oh, how I love your Torah! I meditate on it all day long. (Psalm 119:97)

His meditations gave him knowledge of God and drew Him close to God. He was given wisdom beyond the scope of the literal interpretation of God's commandments. He knew God personally, and he knew the life of faith through his spiritual walk with God. Indeed, his meditations led him to understand the deeper meanings of the Commandments. The spiritual value of *Torah* is in our fellowship with God, leading us to worship and praise. We can also find deeper practical significance for the commandments themselves, as the practical and spiritual natures of *Torah* interact.

As an example, we might consider the Sabbath (Shabbat). The practical observance of Shabbat has great benefit in our cycle of life. Rest from work gives us opportunities for recreation, time with our family and an opportunity to strengthen our bodies for the next week. It also has spiritual benefits in that God has promised to bless us as we seek Him on Shabbat. Within the practice of Shabbat are meditations on the deeper meaning of Shabbat, which point to the final fulfilment when Yeshua brings in His Messianic Kingdom, a time of rest and peace (true shalom). Shabbat carries both practical and spiritual meaning and acceptance of this can enhance both our practical and spiritual lives.

Another example comes from the Biblical injunction to drain the blood from our meat before we eat it (koshering, or cleansing our meat). This is a commandment from God and has practical benefits concerning health. It is also connected with our appreciation of the source of true life. Blood represents life and we are not to have lives like the animals that we eat, while also remembering that their lives are given so that our bodies can be nourished, our life in exchange for theirs. There are many practical ideas connected with this commandment. There are also deeper spiritual meanings which we can discover from our meditations. The flesh of an animal is given to us as something of this world which we need to sustain us, but the blood is a reminder of the life of this world from which we are delivered. We are to be pilgrims in this world, partaking what we need to survive, but without partaking of anything unholy from its life. The principle is that Yeshua's disciples are to be *in* the world but not *of* the world comes up again and again in the New Testament and is simply the deeper meaning and point of meditation for us when we eat our meat drained of its blood. Surely it was God's intention to teach us to be in the world but not of it in every way and to meditate upon this truth constantly with a practical reminder (draining the blood from our meat), a practice which also involves healthy eating and respect for the death of the animals that feed us. Deeper meditation is on the life of Yeshua that we should receive, whose flesh and blood we should eat (See John 6:53). At the Council of Jerusalem (Acts 15), it was decided that abstention from blood was to be taught among the new congregations. In this context it can be argued that the main purpose of the four injunctions from the Council were to keep believers from spiritual idolatry. Thus, the practice of draining meat of its blood has deeply significant truths behind it, ultimately leading a believer to take on the life of Yeshua and flee from idolatry. In this way, practical interpretations of *Torah* are the beginning of spiritual truths that come to light from constant meditation.

A third example, of the many that could be chosen, could be the commandment to put a parapet around the roof of a house for the safety of those walking on the roof (Deuteronomy 22:8). For those of us who do not have flat roofs, this might seem to be a commandment with no meaning today. Yet, meditation on the commandment leads to the spirit of the commandment, the care for the safety and well-being of others. Such a principle leads on to rules for society far beyond the literal command (but including it, of course). It can lead to every health and safety practice in our home and in our places of work.

Perhaps the most profound example of all is within the deeper meaning of family life, particularly the relationship between a husband and wife. The Scriptures are full of this theme, from Genesis (the giving of Eve to Adam) to Revelation (where Yeshua returns to claim His bride). Family life is the place where many *Torah* principles are put into practice, and just as Paul showed in Ephesians 5, all these relate to the deeper spiritual truth of the relationship between Yeshua and His Church. Indeed, all that we do in this life prepares us for this relationship.

Oh, how I love your Torah! I meditate on it all day long. (Psalm 119:97)

For Study and Meditation: Should the Christian lifestyle reflect both the practical commandments of *Torah* and the deeper spiritual meanings? How can this be brought about? Should we expect different practical manifestations of the principles of *Torah* depending on circumstances and need (such as a fire extinguisher and parapet representing the same heart principle of *Torah*)?

Study Exodus 20 and Leviticus 23.

Torah

The Completeness and Holiness of Torah

Whatever our understanding and application of *Torah* might be, all of the Bible writers agree that it is composed of teaching that comes directly from God and this teaching has been passed down to us clearly and without error. God chose to intervene in the lives of fallen human beings and to reveal perfect truths and perfect paths for life. There is no other fully recorded and ordered source of perfect communication from the Most Holy God than that which we find in Scripture, of which *Torah* is at the foundation.

Yeshua said that all the *Torah* and the Prophets hang an two commandments:

Love the Lord your God with all your heart and with all your soul and with all your mind and love your neighbour as yourself.
(Matthew 22:37-40)

Thus all the teachings of God should be understood as manifestations of these two Great Commandments. The Ten Commandments give a panoramic view of the way these two Commandments apply in further detail, from the highest view of God down to the infinite care in regard to one's neighbour. The other Commandments demonstrate detailed applications of these Great Commandments to various parts of daily life.

Taken together the *Torah* contains all aspects of life, of individual relationship with God and the way life should be lived, through to family and community life. If we consider the *Torah* as only 613 Commandments then this limits them. Each of these 613 Commandments is a doorway into areas of practical life covering, in total, the complete scope of human life. Meditation upon *Torah* will provide openings to understanding and fellowship with God for every part of life.

Torah is perfect, complete and Holy. The whole of *Torah* holds together as a complete plan for human life, each part depending on the other parts for the perfect plan to be fulfilled. All of *Torah* must be kept, or sin and corruption will have entered a family or nation through one or other doorway. The lesson that we learn from the Children of Israel, however, is that this is impossible to attain. This is why *Torah* reveals our sin. We might try to attain all that *Torah* offers but we will always fail in some area. It is our goal to live our lives as far as possible according to the perfection of *Torah*, but also to recognise, in humility, that we will fall short of perfection. We should try to improve our understanding and practice of God's teaching but we will full short of perfection, always. Nevertheless we should set our hearts and minds on maturing step by step, but reaching into the full scope and depth of *Torah* rather than seeking what amounts to superficiality, narrowness and even self-righteousness.

For Study and Meditation: Is it possible for a nation in the world today to be governed by the Commandments of *Torah?* Is it possible to go some way towards this? In what ways can this be achieved?

Study James 2:2-13

Torah

Faith not Works

Our failure to obey *Torah* and our need for forgiveness through the atoning sacrifice of Yeshua makes it clear that it is not on account of our good works that we will please God. This means that while we set our heart on obedience to the life that *Torah* reveals, it is faith in Yeshua and His atoning sacrifice that pleases God.

The Apostle Paul is very clear in his teaching that this is the case. He often makes this point so strongly that he seems to be telling us not to bother with the Commandments of God because of our imperfection. Paul's teaching makes it clear that the Commandments brought through Moses are not the main point of *Torah*. It is the life of faith that counts and this was always so. The life of Abraham is given as our example. Abraham's life of faith and the way he grew in faith is a foundational part of *Torah*. It is contained in the Book of Genesis. Paul reminds us that the life of faith was emphasised in *Torah* before the Commandments were brought through Moses.

Our *Torah* studies, therefore, are to lead us to a life of faith in Yeshua as we also seek to live lives which reflect the Commandments of God. If we are seeking to be *Torah* observant, following the prompting of the Holy Spirit, then we will also be conscious of our sins and the need of a Saviour. If we are not *Torah* observant then we will not have any measure of our sin. We may improve our *Torah* lifestyle, and that is good, but there will never be room for self-righteousness, only more room for our Saviour Yeshua.

This is a good reason why we should consider our studies as *Torah* studies rather than studies of the Law of Moses. The Law achieves its main goal of revealing sin, while the whole of *Torah* encompasses the life of faith within the context of the Law of Moses. The Covenant that God made with Israel at Mount Sinai was in the context of the Covenant with Abraham, which incorporated the life of faith above all things, looking ahead with faith to the way God would Himself fulfil the Covenant promises. The New Covenant of the Law written on the heart was God's provision for our fulfilling this life of faith in the context of the deeper spiritual truths of *Torah*.

Yeshua's disciples are encouraged to ensure that *Torah* is central to their lives. If this is the case then consciousness of how far short we fall of *Torah* will be revealed. We will see parallels from our own lives in the lives of the people of ancient Israel and we will realise the almost impossible task of living in accordance with all God's requirements. Yet we will not give up. Our failure should spur us on to do better and it will also humble us. In our failure, we need not be burdened, however, if our heart is fully centred on the Lord.

There has only ever been one person who committed no sin. This was Yeshua Himself. He was the living embodiment of *Torah*. Every action in His life demonstrated the meaning and practical outworking of *Torah*, and in His death He fulfilled the sacrifices to which the written *Torah* pointed. The Epistle to the Hebrews speaks of the *Torah* containing shadows of things that were to come (Hebrews 10). The sacrifices of the Levitical priesthood were a shadow of the plan set up in Heaven for the perfect, permanent and final sacrifice of Yeshua.

Torah always made provision for the failure of God's people to obey the Commandments completely, but only when Yeshua gave Himself as our sacrifice was it possible for us to be free of the burden of our failure (our sin).

Because of Yeshua's sacrifice we are free to grow to maturity without condemnation for our failures to obey the perfect *Torah*.

This is the central theme of all of *Torah*.

For Study and Meditation: How can a disciple of Yeshua live a life of faith and good works? How would sin be revealed if we were not seeking to obey the Commandments of God?

What should our approach be to the following of *Torah* now that Yeshua's sacrifice has made atonement for our sins?

Study Matthew 9:9-13, Hebrews 10 and 11, James 2:14-25, Revelation 2 and 3, Romans 3 and 4.

Torah

Fulfilled Torah Studies

Some people may be concerned that when their Bible studies have *Torah* as the foundation they will drift into legalism or Judaising. They may be concerned that *Torah* not Yeshua becomes the centre of their studies. There is a risk that *Torah* can be misused, of course, but the danger lies in trying to achieve righteousness through works of the law as opposed to deepening the life of faith. *Torah* studies done properly will lead to pure revelations of Yeshua. He is at the heart of *Torah*, and *Torah* studies should lead to the deepest of revelations of Yeshua.

A disciple of Yeshua who only studies the New Testament will miss this depth. Indeed, It will be discovered that the New Testament is not a complete exposition of *Torah*. It contains only a limited number of references to the deeper meanings of *Torah*. An example of this is where Paul shows that a fulfilment of the practice of not muzzling an ox as it treads the grain (Deuteronomy 25:4) is in the payment of ministers of the Gospel (1 Corinthians 9:9-10, 1 Timothy 5:18). Where, however, are deeper understandings of other aspects of *Torah* such as the teaching on economics? They are not to be found in the New Testament because we were intended to study *Torah* for ourselves. Leviticus 25, for example, gives a wonderful view of the partnership between men and God that is possible in establishing a right economical structure, but there is no mention of this in the New Testament. Nor is there a mention of the higher meaning of eating meat without blood, or parapets around roofs. All of this can only be obtained through *Torah* study, through which the Holy Spirit sheds light of understanding just as He did for

Paul.

If *Torah* study is simply a secondary issue compared with study of the New Testament revelation, then there is likely to be a legalistic approach. This is because we are likely to miss the depths of meaning of *Torah* and settle for ritual obedience to the Commandments which seem to be important to us. We might, for example, realise that we could follow the Ten Commandments but not really get to the depth of meaning, and so end up applying them entirely legalistically, when they were intended to be manifestations of the great injunctions to love God and our neighbour, willingly, rather than through ritual.

When we are confident about the fact that Yeshua is right at the heart of *Torah*, we are ready to study the fulfilment in Yeshua, with *Torah* as foundation. Indeed, we will find that Yeshua is truly at the foundation of our faith through our deepest meditations on *Torah*. For this approach to work we must be familiar with the whole of Scripture, so that cross-references will automatically come to mind when *Torah* is studied.

For Study and Meditation: Study the Tabernacle as a perfect picture of an abiding place in Yeshua. The Feasts of the Lord are a perfect pattern of the plan of salvation. See if you can detect the way the types and shadows point to Yeshua.

Study Exodus 25 to 40, John 15, Leviticus 23.

Torah

Willing Obedience

Torah was given to ancient Israel. It was God's teaching programme and it contained the requirements for His people and His promises to His people. It has even been likened to a Ketubah or marriage agreement between God and His people. It contained commandments to order the community and it contained teaching on the life of faith. The phrase, 'The righteous will live by his faith', was first recorded by the prophet Habakkuk (Habakkuk 2:4). The full revelation of what this means was given when Yeshua died for the sins of the world and then the message was available to all mankind that through faith in Yeshua there was forgiveness of sins and reconciliation with God the Father. Because of the high and holy principles of Torah, the lesson we learn from ancient Israel is that transgression of Torah is inevitable in this fallen world and so sin is revealed through our attempts to obey Torah. Hence we find the great need of a Saviour. The most important lesson of Torah is that it points to Yeshua HaMashiach, on whom our life of faith is founded.

Now, with the full revelation of Yeshua, we realise that the life of faith is the clear objective of Torah. The teaching programme is still perfect, but it is offered to all God's people for willing obedience rather than ritualistic observance. The Holy Spirit has been sent as our teacher to lead us into all truth. Our goal is to grow to maturity and to willingly follow Torah within the context of humility and the life of faith in Yeshua. Torah can still be the mainstay of family life and even lead to the ordering of our nations, but faith in Yeshua is the central component, which also frees us into willing obedience rather than ritual observance of the Commandments. Nevertheless sin is still defined as falling short of Torah for all people in the world, and we will pay the penalty for that sin if we do not have faith in Yeshua. Disciples of Yeshua are free of the burden of condemnation for transgression of *Torah*, while we continue to allow the Holy Spirit to enable us to be lights to the world and salt to society through the life of Yeshua which *Torah* offers. In Acts Chapter 15 we read that there were only four requirements for Gentile converts. These are considered to be the Noahide laws given for all humanity, well before the Commandments given to Moses (Genesis 9). These are to be taught to all believers as the Council of Jerusalem decided and nothing else is to be a burden. This does not remove the holiness of God's other teaching. The spirit of the Council of Jerusalem was to promote willing obedience. However, it is expected that we will grow to understand the depth of *Torah* as we come to maturity, and that we will willingly obey this teaching of God, in the light of Yeshua's fulfilment. The injunctions of the Council of Jerusalem were chiefly for us to abstain from the things that could be a vehicle for spiritual adultery - following false gods. This is a clear necessity for those whose chief command is to love and walk in fellowship with the One True God.

Guarded against deception, we then go on to maturity, discovering what that maturity is as we grow, and finding that there is a narrowing road which keeps in balance the practical lifestyle of believers who are to be a light of the world, and the deep principles of the life of faith. There are some clear points of obedience early in the faith, particularly the Ten Commandments, and then we should study *Torah* and let the Holy Spirit prompt us step by step into willing obedience of all that God requires. We must remember always not to presume what these requirements might be and particularly to realise that we will not please God with superficial religiosity which amounts to shallow fleshly obedience of the Law. The leaders of the Children of Israel failed because of this.

For Study and Meditation: How can we ensure that we grow to maturity in our *Torah* observance, while living the life of faith?

Torah

Word and Spirit

God's promise through Jeremiah was that the *Torah* would be written on the hearts of God's people (Jeremiah 31:33). Yeshua also spoke of the need to be born of the Spirit of God (John 3). The Holy Spirit of God is both the teacher of Yeshua's disciples and the One who brings about a transformation of the heart to understand and willingly obey *Torah*. Thus the pattern of *Torah* studies is to be a prayerful and meditative walk with the Holy Spirit of God, who will Himself lead believers into the deeper meanings, *Torah* study will be dry and legalistic without the Holy Spirit's regeneration and fellowship, but with the Holy Spirit there will be a walk of faith and a leading into truth and wisdom. The Holy Spirit will use the *Torah* as it was planned long ago, as a means of true teaching leading to a life of faith and good works.

For Study and Meditation: Can we consider the written *Torah* as our work-book and the Holy Spirit as our teacher, so that our *Torah* studies will be full of life and revelation of Yeshua and His will for our lives? Is this an inheritance intended for disciples of Yeshua?

Read Romans 8, Colossians 3:16, Ephesians 5:18.

Torah

The Torah Cycle

There are two cycles of reading of the *Torah* which Synagogues use. The first five books of the Bible are divided into portions (Parashot) which are read throughout the year, week by week. One cycle takes three years and the other one year. It is beneficial for disciples of Yeshua to follow one of these cycles. One advantage is that *Torah* readings progress through the year in step with the cycle of the Feasts of the Lord. This is of great benefit, and is also a point of unity between Jews and Christians.

It is possible for Church congregations to base their Bible Studies on this cycle and for family Bible Studies to follow this sequence. It will be discovered that there are new depths to discover year after year. These studies will also help believers to adopt a *Torah* lifestyle that is based on the life of faith and the practical applications of *Torah*. Their understanding of Yeshua will be increased, and they will have relevant perceptions of the world around, being guarded against deception and being able to interpret current events from a Biblical perspective. They will also discover that their understanding of the New Testament will increase. The study of the revelation of Yeshua HaMashiach will be increased and not neglected. Paul's teaching will be put in perspective too.

The list of readings for the one-year cycle is given on the following pages, and an indication of how threads of truth can be traced through the whole Bible, starting with these readings, is given later in this book. It will be found that the whole Bible can be studied in greater depth starting with portions from *Torah*. If, in addition, the Bible student is careful to ensure that the whole Bible is read in parallel with the daily and weekly portions, a guard will be placed on limiting the reading of Scripture to selected passages. This can be accomplished by carefully recording the passages of Scripture as they are read and devising a plan whereby the entire Bible is read in a given period. If there is also sensitivity to the leading of the Holy Spirit in selecting passages day by day, there will be a balance between routine and inspired reading.

For Study and Meditation: Do you think that Yeshua and the early Apostles intended us to study the Bible from a *Torah* perspective?

Torah

Torah and Haftarah Portions from Yearly Cycle

References are from the Hebrew Bible (these may differ slightly from the translations). The name of a portion (Parasha) is taken from the first few words of the reading. A Calendar can be obtained from a suitable Jewish publisher to fit the readings with dates for each year if readings are done to coincide with the synagogues. Tradition has it that the Haftarahs came into existence when Jews were forbidden to read the *Torah* at the time of Antiochos Epiphanes. They chose parallel readings from the Prophets to highlight key themes from the *Torah* Portions.

1. Bereshit (In the Beginning) Genesis 1:1-6:8, Isaiah 42:5-43:11
2. Noach (Noah) Genesis 6:9-11:32, Isaiah 54:1-55:5
3. Lech L'cha (Go out) Genesis 12:1-17:27, Isaiah 40:27-41:16
4. Vayera (And appeared) Genesis 18:1-22:24, 2 Kings 4:1-37
5. Chaye Sarah (Sarah's life) Genesis 23:1-25:18, 1 Kings 1:1-31
6. Toldot (Generations) Genesis 25:19-28:9, Malachi 1:1-2:7
7. Vayetze (And went out) Genesis 28:10-32:3, Hosea 12:13-14:10
8. Vayishlach (And he sent) Genesis 32:4-36:43, Hosea 11:7-12:12
9. Vayeshev (And he dwelt) Genesis 37:1-40:23, Amos 2:6-3:8
10. Mikketz (At the end) Genesis 41:1-44:17, 1 Kings 3:15-4:1, Zechariah 2:14-4:7
11. Vayigash (And came near) Genesis 44:18-47:27, Ezekiel 37:15-28
12. Vayechi (And he lived) Genesis 47:28-50:26, 1 Kings 2:1-12
13. Shemot (Names) Exodus 1:1-6:1, Isaiah 27:6-28:13; 29:22-23
14. Va'era (And I appeared) Exodus 6:2-9:35, Ezekiel 28:25-29:21
15. Bo (Come) Exodus 10:1-13:16, Jeremiah 46:13-28
16. Beshallach (When he sent) Exodus 13:17-17:16, Judges 4:4-5:31

17. Yitro (Jethro) Exodus 18:1-20:23, Isaiah 6:1-7:6; 9:5-6
18. Mishpatim (Judgements) Exodus 21:1-24:18; 30:11-16, Jeremiah 34:8-22; 33:25-26
19. Terumah (Heave Offering) Exodus 25:1-27:19, 1 Kings 5:26-6:13
20. Tetzaveh (You shall command) Exodus 27:20-30:10, Ezekiel 43:10-27
21. Ki Tissa (When you take) Exodus 30:11-34:35, 1 Kings 18:1-39
22. Vaykhel (And assembled) Exodus 35:1-38:20, 1 Kings 7:40-50
23. Pekude (Accounts) Exodus 38:21-40:38, 1 Kings 7:51-8:21
24. Vayikra (And he called) Leviticus 1:1-5:26, Isaiah 43:21-44:23
25. Tzav (Command) Leviticus 6:1-8:36, Jeremiah 7:21-8:3; 9:22-23
26. Shemini (Eighth) Leviticus 9:1-11:47, 2 Samuel 6:1-7:17
27. Tazria (Conceived) Leviticus 12:1-13:59, 2 Kings 4:42-5:19
28. Metzora (Leper) Leviticus 14:1-15:33, 2 Kings 7:3-20
29. Achare Mot (After the death) Leviticus 16:1-18:30, Ezekiel 22:1-19
30. Kedoshim (Holy) Leviticus 19:1-20:27, Amos 9:7-15
31. Emor (Say) Leviticus 21:1-24:23, Ezekiel 44:15-31
32. Behar (On the mountain) Leviticus 25:1-26:2, Jeremiah 32:6-27
33. Bekhukotai (In my statutes) Leviticus 26:3-27:34, Jeremiah 16:19-17:14
34. Bemidbar (In the wilderness) Numbers 1:1-4:20, Hosea 2:1-22
35. Naso (Make an accounting) Numbers 4:21-7:89, Judges 13:2-25
36. Behaalot'Cha (When you set up) Numbers 8:1-12:16, Zechariah 2:14-4:7
37. Shelach L'Cha (Send thou) Numbers 13:1-15:41,Joshua 2:1-24
38. Korach (Korah) Numbers 16:1-18:32, 1 Samuel 11:14-12:22
39. Hukat (Statute) Numbers 19:1-22:1, Judges 11:1-33
40. Balak (Balak) Numbers 22:2-25:9, Micah 5:6-6:8
41. Pinchas (Phineas) Numbers 25:10-30:1, 1 Kings 18:46-19:21
42. Mattot (Tribes) Numbers 30:2-32:42, Jeremiah 1:1-2:3
43. Masee (Journeys) Numbers 33:1-36:13, Jeremiah 2:4-28; 3:4
44. Devarim (Words) Deuteronomy 1:1-3:22, Isaiah 1:1-27
45. Va'etchanan (And I besought) Deuteronomy 3:23-7:11, Isaiah 40:1-26

46. Ekev (Because) Deuteronomy 7:12-11:25, Isaiah 49:14-51:3 47. Re'eh (Behold) Deuteronomy 11:26-16:17, Isaiah 54:11-55:5 48. Shoftim (Judges) Deuteronomy 16:18-21:9, Isaiah 51:12-52:12

49. Ki Tetze (When you go) Deuteronomy 21:10-25:19, Isaiah 54:1-10

50. Ki Tavo (When you come) Deuteronomy 26:1-29:8, Isaiah 60:1-22

51. Nitzavim (You are standing) Deuteronomy 29:9-30:20, Isaiah 61:10-63:9

52. Vayelech (And he went) Deuteronomy 31:1-30, Isaiah 55:6-56:8

53. Haazinu (Give ear) Deuteronomy 32:1-52, 2 Samuel 22:1-51

54. Vezot Haberachah (And this is the blessing) Deuteronomy 33:1-34:12, Joshua 1:1-18

There are additional readings for the Feasts of the Lord, including Sukkot (Tabernacles) Leviticus 22:26-23:44, Numbers 29:12-16, Zechariah 14, 1 Kings 8:1-21

Pesach (Passover) Exodus 12:21-51, Numbers 28:16-25, Joshua 3:5-7; 5:2-6:27, Exodus 13:17-15:26,Numbers 28:19-25, 2 Samuel 22, Deuteronomy 14:22-16:17, Isaiah 10:32-12:6

Shavuot (Pentecost) Exodus 19:1-20:23, Numbers 28:26-31, Ezekiel 1:1-28; 3 :12, Deuteronomy 15:19-16:17, Habakkuk 2:20-3:19

Note that there are 54 readings rather than 52. In some weeks of the year, two portions are read.

Torah

Oh, How I Love Your Torah
An Old Violin – A Parable

Imagine the best of violins, played by the best of violinists, playing the best of heavenly music, echoing the worship of the heart, a Hebrew melody played in a minor key, conveying sadness and joy intermingled. The sort of music in which the high notes linger in the mind for some time. The emotions are stirred by such music as it rises like incense towards the throne of Heaven.

There was once a man who had a young son. He desired that his son should love him and be at one with him in every way. The way that the son could please his father would be to play beautiful music; music that spoke of the order and discipline of the boy's life but which was free and expressive of the love in his heart. The father gave the son a violin, an excellent model, on which it was possible to play the sweetest of music, and he desired that one day his son might play the violin for him.

The father's business kept him away from home and so he gave instructions to the boy to practise regularly. Because he knew that children need to be encouraged and be shown the right way as they are growing up, until they reach maturity, he wrote out some basic rules for the boy to follow in his practices. He explained how, if these rules were followed, the boy would be trained in how to play the violin and to prepare beautiful music that the father could enjoy one day. It was the intention that eventually the boy would understand the principles behind the rules and he would grow to maturity whereby the desire to play the wonderful music for the purpose of showing love to his father would be a natural thing. Indeed, the father hoped that the day would come when both he and his son would enjoy the music together.

The man put servants in charge of his household and instructed them about the rules and about the violin. At first the boy practised on his violin and made good progress, but later there were distractions in his life and he did not practise as he had done previously. The violin played no sweet music, but only a scratchy noise. The servants enforced the rules for playing, but there was no pleasure for them or for the boy. Indeed, the rules seemed to be punishments instead of a means of pleasure resulting from disciplined practice. They seemed to curse rather than to bless. It came to the point where the boy rebelled more and more and there was no pleasure. This made the servants, who feared the father, enforce the rules harshly but without true understanding.

When the father heard about this he was both sad and angry, and this brought a division between him and his young son, but he had a remedy. There was another son, one like his father in every way, full of love, the very essence of his father's being, understanding his father's ways and, among other things, a great teacher. He sent him to the younger son and told him what to do. The older son arrived and soon brought peace to the household. He told the boy that he deserved punishment but that the father could forgive him. Indeed, the boy was not to live with the fear of punishment any more from the father or the servants. Whenever there was difficulty with the violin playing and whenever he went wrong, he was to write to him and explain, and the older son would go and plead with the father on his behalf, even paying the necessary debt for him if damage had occurred to the expensive equipment, and he would also make sure that no punishments came from the servants. He was so troubled by the rift between the father and the younger son that he even said, 'You know, you are like the apple of your father's eye. I will do anything to make it possible for you to please him. What is my own life worth if our family is not reconciled? I will give my own life for this to happen. I will go to father on your behalf and always seek reconciliation. Believe in me.'

From that time on, the boy was to be free to learn without the fear of condemnation. The servants were instructed that the learning was to be in freedom and the older son even sent someone, like himself, to help in the household, someone who, like him, was an excellent teacher. He would not compromise the instructions that the father had left but would train through friendship and encouragement, as long as the boy chose to listen to his teaching. The boy was to learn to play the violin at an appropriate pace and to enjoy what he was doing, without fear.

When the older son went away it went well for a while. The violin came out regularly and the practices were good, so that sweet music was beginning to come from the violin. The father heard of this and was pleased and imagined the day when high and sweet lingering strains of music from a perfectly tuned and played violin would reach his ears. But then things began to go wrong. First, a string became broken. It was the string that played the bass notes, allowing deep thoughtful meditative notes, the sort of notes than when played give the sombre tones to balance the higher melodies. Without the deeper notes, the music was more superficial, lacking heart. It had been these more sombre undertones that had reminded the boy of his older brother who had been so sincere and moving in his commitment to him, stirring in him a sense of thankfulness and even worship for the sacrifice that his brother had given for him. The higher notes alone seemed like the more superficial aspects of life, which were meaningless when detached from the reminder of his brother and through his brother, the reminder of his loving father.

There was also no fear of punishment now and so one thing led to another and instead of devoting his time to playing the violin in a way that would please his father, he began to explore his new freedom. He found that he could also ignore his teacher and go back to what he thought were the pleasures of life. He forgot the need for disciplined practice on the violin and lost all vision of being an accomplished player. Knowing a new freedom, he misunderstood it to such an extent that he considered the violin and the instructions to be old and incapable of producing pleasure. He did not even consider the fact that his father wanted to hear sweet music from the violin one day, and would even be pleased to hear good attempts at playing when the attitude was right. He did not understand what the older son had said. Without the reminder through the bass notes which were missing because of the broken string, the playing was superficial and lacked true meaning. He did not seek to repair the string and did not listen to the one who had been sent to help. He even despised both the violin and the rules for playing and practising. He smashed the violin and tore up the rules to demonstrate, as he thought, that he was completely free.

Is this what the Church is doing with the Torah of God?

Torah

The Love of God in the Torah of God

The Ten Commandments are a breathtaking summary of the principles of love, when understood in both Word and Spirit. No other philosophy or religion can achieve this perfect principle of love. This should compel us to achieve all that is intended through these commandments. We should study them, expound them and live them with all our heart, soul, mind and strength.

They are principles of love because they are the perfect representation of the greatest message of *Torah*. This is found in Deuteronomy 6:5, which is the foundation of the Shema (the Hebrew for hear. The Shema is spoken frequently in synagogues as a constant reminder to Jews to believe in and obey the One True God), and Leviticus 19:18. This was confirmed by Yeshua. In Matthew 22:34-40, it is recorded that He was asked to state the greatest commandment in the *Torah*. He replied:

Thou shalt love the Lord thy God with all thy heart, and with all thy soul, and with all thy mind. This is the first and great commandment. And the second is like unto it, Thou shalt love thy neighbour as thyself. On these two commandments hang all the law and the prophets.

This principle of love, then, is the summary of all that God intended through all He taught mankind. The principles may be stated simply, but they are profound in their meaning. We can take a lifetime to learn what they mean, seeking, with the help of the Holy Spirit, to obey them. We should treasure highly any teaching that helps us to understand and obey this goal of love. We should look carefully at all that God has said with this in mind, beginning with the most significant teaching.

When Mount Sinai shook and the people standing before it trembled, God gave one of the most significant pronouncements of all time. He gave Moses commandments on stone, which were eventually to be written on our hearts. On stone they were legal and hard. On our hearts they should be spiritual and tender. The same words in two different frameworks are immovable in either framework but when they are written on our hearts they lead us to obedience through free will.

How then do these commandments provide a summary or framework for the principles of love contained in the two Great Commandments? By simply reading them (Exodus 20), prayerfully, with this question in mind, the Holy Spirit can take the opportunity to show each of us individually something of the truth. That can be the start of our discovery.

A study of the first and last commandments gives us an important contrast. The first commandment causes us to look heavenwards to Almighty God, considering just who He is (and surely our attention is towards a perfect Father, not an unapproachable taskmaster!). Our undivided love should naturally be as immovable as His wonderful character. The last of the Ten Commandments is on the horizontal plane, where we should not even desire the possessions of our neighbours, let alone steal or mishandle them. This is a highly sensitive manifestation of our love to our neighbours, treating them as they should be treated in love and in a way that we would want them to treat us. Thus, from the heights of profound love to God, in the first commandment, the Ten Commandments move us through to the finest details and expressions of love towards one another. In the tenth commandment, love itself is defined within the framework of these commandments. If we read them casually, we will miss their deep truths. For example, the second commandment seems to reveal a God bent on punishment, but this punishment is not for those of us who love Him! For us, whose God He is, there is perfect love to a thousand generations!

Thus, we see from the first, moving progressively forward through to the last commandment, step by step, precept by precept, the Ten Commandments present a perfect panorama of the Greatest Commandment to love, starting with the love of God and moving down to principles that result from love towards our neighbour. They are like a colourful spectrum, where the whole range of colours of the one pure white light are spread before us, from the highest heavenly perspective to a most sensitive earthly perspective. They even remind us of the Word of God made flesh in Yeshua, coming down from the heights of Heaven to the low place on earth through love.

In the spectrum of commandments, our family relationships are included, the basis on which a stable and loving society can be built (honouring father and mother, no adultery). In between the commands with the heavenly perspective, comes the fourth commandment referring to the Sabbath Day. The Sabbath Day is the perfect link between things of earth and things of Heaven, from individual rest, through family times and celebrations, to community life and worship, to honouring God the Creator and Deliverer, Saviour, Father, Friend and Sustainer, to holding high the *Torah*, to growing in maturity, love and truth. Perhaps the Sabbath Day is also the means of bringing together the earthly and heavenly perspectives of love and is placed there between the two sets of Commandments for that purpose. It is the command that binds the whole picture together and is truly there for our benefit, ultimately pointing to our abiding together in Yeshua, our Peace.

Just as the Ten Commandments reveal the greatest of all commandments, so *Torah* in all its fullness brings various manifestations of these same Commandments.

Torah

At the Heart of Torah is the Love of God

The Law was given through Moses: grace and truth through Jesus Christ (John 1:17)

He forgave us all our sins, having cancelled the written code, with its regulations, that was against us and that was opposed to us; he took it away, nailing it to the cross (Colossians 2:13-14)

The first of these verses gives us a link between law and grace and between love and law. There is no more precious or important theme than the love of God. When we consider this theme everything else is put into the background. It must be stressed, however, that law and love are compatible. Through the law of God we find the love of God and find that His love is higher than His law and that through His love came His law. We discover this through constant meditation on the whole of *Torah*. By meditating on the whole of *Torah*, holding its principles ever before us, asking God to teach us and causing us to grow in stature, we discover the relationships between all He has taught and all He has done. In particular, our experience and understanding of the love of God is enriched by our meditations on the law of God, through our attempts and failures, our recognition of and worship of the Lord who paid the penalty for our failures, and also our growth in Him to full maturity is highlighted through these meditations. Without these truths held in balance, we have not understood the whole of Scripture.

God's love is deeper than our deepest considerations of the *Torah*'s external requirements, however, and we could be in danger of missing this point because of the complexity of the study on the

Torah alone. We could, as a consequence, be classed among those who bring bondage through legalistic teaching. Yet there is no-one like the God of Israel. To know Him is to love Him, for He is Love. No other god can be compared with Him. This is to be at the heart of all our studies, and unless we realise it, we have not properly discovered the true root of our faith.

We can use our academic abilities to interpret *Torah* and our scholarship to understand Scripture. We can regulate our lives by the high demands of the law of God, but we will have missed the main point if we do not end with a deep revelation of God's love. This is love that is above human reason. This love must be experienced as well as understood. The love of the God of Israel for His people is an intimate personal love.

The Scripture from John 1:17 links our consideration of the love of God with our considerations of the law of God. We must keep in mind the relationship between law and love when we meditate on either one of these themes separately. The Scripture does not mean that first came the law and then came grace and truth. It does not speak of a sequence of events, but speaks of priority. Law, grace and truth were all there at the same time, but grace and truth were deeper and higher than the Law as much as Yeshua (Jesus) the Messiah takes the highest place above Moses. Thus when Moses was given the law there were higher principles at work than simply the provision of regulations for God's people on earth. Yeshua was there with the Father in Heaven at the time of Moses. He was not yet incarnate, but He was there with the Father, full of grace and truth. This grace and truth from the loving heart of God brought the whole *Torah*. This same grace and truth was behind everything that God has done through all history and was finally revealed in Yeshua HaMashiach on earth, to demonstrate the fulfilment of *Torah* and release us from the punishments of the law through the atoning sacrifice of Yeshua.

This is what the second passage quoted above, from Colossians 2:13-14, means when it speaks of the written code that was against us being nailed to the cross. As we learn to walk with the Lord, discovering how to please Him and to obey Him, anything in the written *Torah* or anything recorded that stood against us has been removed. We are free to grow without condemnation for our failures as we learn. This means that a follower of Yeshua who is growing in faith in the power of the Holy Spirit is not punished for failure to obey the whole of *Torah*. We are free to grow in stature as the people of God, because we are not punished as we fail. Also, the writing that was against us because of our failures before we knew the laws of God and records in Heaven of punishments that we deserved, have also been cancelled. This is the message for believers. Unbelievers still stand under the curse of the law because the law is perfect in its requirements and death is the consequence of disobedience. Believers need not die, because they have accepted Yeshua's sacrificial death on their behalf. This is the depth of grace and truth that we are considering. By emphasising the high, holy and righteous principles of the law, we must warn believers that grace is not a licence for lawlessness. This being done, however, the love of God is high above all of this. His high principles are made known, yet He forgives us for our shortcomings of the past and we press forward to learn to follow His ways more fully. This love is greater than all our understanding of the structures and applications of the principles of the law. How can we fully understand the love of God if we do not consider all of His ways and all that has been revealed? We must meditate on the Old Testament as well as the New Testament. It is wrong to consider the Old Testament as revealing a judgmental God while the New Testament reveals a loving God. This was an early heresy in the Church and is rising up in some branches of the Church today. God has not changed. If we scan the pages of the Bible with our minds focussed on the love of God we will find evidence everywhere. It is possible to read the Bible meditating on the law of God as if this were the main theme. It is also possible to read the same passages meditating on the love of God, a simultaneous and even more important theme. We need to discover these things by daily meditation. The love of God brought the law of God. The law of God demonstrates the love of God. We can review some of the essential ideas.

When Adam sinned and distanced himself from God, he broke the loving fellowship with God and, as a consequence, with all of the human race. God need not have allowed future generations even to come into existence, and He could have put an end to His Creation there and then. But He allowed future generations to be born, sinful and rebellious as they would always be.

Not one nation that has come since Adam has been without sin. Not one person in any nation except Jesus the Messiah has been without sin. Instead of leaving every nation blindly to die in their sins, God implemented a recovery plan for all who will enter into that plan.

God showed the terrible consequences of sin through His judgement at the Flood at the time of Noah, yet He also made a binding Covenant that would result in His own Son bearing the punishment of sin that even rose up again after Noah and continues through all generations.

God showed the terrible nature of sin by teaching the chosen nation (Israel) about His holy principles. He showed what pleases Him through all of *Torah*. This privileged knowledge could have been made known to the whole world through Israel, and is now made known through the Scriptures and through the Gospel message. Yet even knowing the principles that would bring true life and blessing, mankind falls short constantly. Yet God does not and did not abandon us. The whole history of the world shows mankind going its wicked and selfish way, yet God did not abandon us.

On Mount Moriah, the whole nation of Israel was in effect under Abraham's knife. If Isaac's life was taken there would be no physical offspring coming from him. Yet God did not allow Isaac to be sacrificed, while knowing that the whole nation of Israel would eventually be born and that the nation would be sinful in every generation. What pain this causes to a Righteous and Holy God! Yet He finally sent His own Son, as a substitute, to bear the penalty for all this sin, so that all who believe would be saved. He includes anyone from any nation, Jew or Gentile, in this plan of Salvation.

Not only does God save us through His Son, but He sends His Holy Spirit to live in us that we too might know the love of God in us as a practical experience. Indeed, we can now obey the deepest commands of the *Torah*, to love the Lord our God with all our heart, soul, mind and strength and to love our neighbour as ourselves because of the Holy Spirit's life within us. This is no distant God. This is a God who gives everything, even to those who choose to fight against His unconditional love and who deserve nothing. Yet He does not condemn us for any of our actions. We simply condemn ourselves by not letting Him show His love to us. Whatever our sins have been, we can be forgiven and restored through faith in Yeshua (Jesus), and that faith is a gift in itself.

The *Torah* reveals the path of holiness and it reveals the sin of falling short. We can know our desperate condition and the necessary penalty for our trespass, but God demonstrates that His love overcomes all of our need, pays our penalty and does not abandon us. The Law is uncompromising in its demands, but God's love transcends these demands without compromise. God could have done far less and still shown His love, but He showed His complete love by giving His own Son who willingly died for us, and by giving Himself to us through the Holy Spirit. If He had done less, we would still have known His love, but He established the plan of Salvation so that it would cost Him dearly. He made it so that there was no other way and in doing so He freed those of us who believe completely, by completely giving Himself for us, even to the death on the Cross.

This is a snapshot of the love of God, which is above all of our other considerations and indeed is the whole goal of *Torah*. It is the truest and deepest theme of the whole Bible. It is the heart of the teaching and the reason for *Torah*. It is revealed in every word and line of all of the Scriptures when we read aright, and perceive the hidden treasures of all that the Scriptures contain. If we miss this we have missed the purpose of our study of the Scriptures and our quest to discover our Jewish/Hebraic/Biblical roots. Deep down in the roots of our faith we discover the lifesource of our existence, the love of God, which echoes across history and is the reason for that history ever being allowed to come about.

> *Greater love has no man than this, that a man lay down his life for his friends. (John 15:13)*

At the heart of the *Torah* is the love of God.

It may seem unnecessary to write this in the context of a study of the roots of *Torah* and of the Christian faith. This is a teaching that all Christians and Messianic believers should know anyway. It is the foundation to their belief. We might think that a study of the root of our faith should reveal teaching that emphasises issues that we don't know so well. This is true. There is also the possibility, however, that in emphasising these other issues we will forget the basic teaching. *Torah* is fascinating at other levels and indeed has applications at other levels relevant to everyday life. If we remain only in these other levels, however, we could be side-tracked into philosophies and fascinations and forget the central theme of Scripture. So let it be emphasised here and ensure it remains at the heart of our further studies, which will indeed enrich and deepen the background to our faith in the coming days. There are many topics but all of them are evidence of the love of God. We perceive this love in all of our considerations of the God of Israel and His Son, the Jewish Messiah. The Law, the Prophets, the Psalms, the Messianic expectations in the Bible or extra-biblical sources, the archaeological finds, the Feasts of the Lord, the agony of the Cross and the emptiness of the Tomb, all remind us of this one great theme.

Torah

Essays on the Fulfilment of Torah
No 1: The Life is in the Blood

Through many examples, we can demonstrate how the deep *Torah* foundations of our faith lead to meaningful interpretations and links with the New Testament. What the Psalmist said can be true for us:

Oh, how I love your Torah! I meditate on it all day long. (Psalm 119:97)

Of course, we need to understand what Yeshua meant when He said that He fulfilled *Torah*. He did not abrogate it but showed the higher meaning both in His personal life and ministry, His very being, and also in the intent of *Torah*. *Torah*, it can be argued, therefore, is still an important source of reference. Once this perspective is opened up there are a multitude of topics to consider. Most important are the types and shadows of Messiah, not that we should worship them instead of Him, but that we should set a framework of understanding for His fulfilment. All biblical doctrine begins in *Torah*. Here we find the model of the life of faith, as well as the commandments which were received at Sinai. All of *Torah* was eventually to be written on the hearts of believers, within the framework of the two main commandments to love the Lord with all our heart and our neighbour as ourselves.

Torah reaches a higher plane when written on our hearts. The physical manifestations outlined in the early books of the Bible are able to bear both spiritual and physical fruit. Meditation upon *Torah* is a profitable exercise wherein the Holy Spirit can enrich and deepen our understanding of what was originally written. This meditation may be over several years, which illustrates how constant we must be in our search for truth. The example I have chosen for this essay illustrates the point, because it took a full seven years for me to discover a higher meaning for the injunction that blood should be drained from meat prior to eating it (Leviticus 19:26). I began with attempted obedience to the physical command. The physical practice, became a reminder to meditate on the Scriptures that were linked to it. I began to understand the deeper meanings straight away, but it was only after seven years that the Holy Spirit gave me the final step of revelation up to this point.

The injunction of Leviticus 19:26 was important enough to be taken up by the prophet Ezekiel when he brought warnings to Israel (Ezekiel 33:25). This teaching has been so strong among Jews, to this day, that it has led to many of the kosher regulations. It is also highlighted at the Council of Jerusalem (Acts 15:20) as an important issue for all believers. From the context of Leviticus and Ezekiel it appears that the eating of blood is linked to idolatry. There were pagan customs which attracted people to try to take on the character of animals through the eating of their blood. This is associated with the phrase, 'The life is in the blood' (Leviticus 17:11). Moreover, the blood sacrifices to pagan gods led to idolatry. God required that none of His people should take any part in such practices and required sacrifice only to Himself on altars built for the purpose. The injunctions of Acts 15 continue to emphasise the need to keep clear of blood in any way which would lead to idolatry. Koshering of meat may well have physical benefits, but it was also, and perhaps primarily, part of the safeguard against spiritual adultery.

It is interesting that when Yeshua taught that His followers should eat His flesh and drink His blood (John 6:53-58) they barely understood what He was saying. Focussing on the practice of koshering meat in the physical sense alone left them short of full understanding, so much so that many departed from Him. Yet at this time He was bringing a higher teaching. He was referring to the spiritual meaning of eating flesh and drinking blood, the principle that we should have in mind whenever we share the bread and wine at the communion table. The negative teaching of abstaining from all blood was a reminder not to be engaged in idolatry of any kind, leaving no doorway for spiritual adultery, which would give false spirits rights to plant their life into us. The positive teaching of Yeshua was that we must take His life and His alone, the only safe blood to drink, meaning the only safe source of life to be found. Useful as the physical practices of koshering meat are, their higher intent was to point to Yeshua, and our life in Him. Meat and blood, of themselves, are limited in their meaning if we do not live according to the principles which they embody.

For me the final point of revelation came only after those seven years of meditating on these principles. In summary, I learned that the koshering of meat is a reminder of the principle that we should live in this world but not be of this world (John 17:11-15). Just as meat is a source of nourishment that is necessary for this life, so we should live in this world taking what is necessary and safe for life, but keeping away from the seductive life that the world offers and the ways in which the spirits abroad in this world would take us. The world has many spiritual seductions, not all of which are so obvious as the pagan practices of old. All our affairs must be clear of the ways of the world. Even the Church can fall into worldly ways, particularly in these days of rising humanism. The ways of the world that Yeshua warned us against are linked to spiritual powers. Draining the blood from our meat is simply a religious practice if we do not see it as symbolic of the injunction not to follow after any wordly ways, but only after the life of faith in Yeshua, feeding on Him in all ways, following only His life and inspiration.

Torah

Essays on the Fulfilment of Torah
No 2: Living Torah

If we agree that *Torah* is relevant to the Messianic Community there are a number of key questions that require an answer. The first one, in my view, is – 'What is *Torah*?' This may seem a trivial question at first. It is obvious to all of us what *Torah* is, surely. Unfortunately, we fall into the trap of thinking that our own implicit definition of *Torah* is the same as everybody else's. This is not so, and this is probably why we find people distancing themselves from us the moment we use the term, because they think that we mean what someone else meant and which they did not like. Indeed, to some *Torah* would lead to exactly the same things that Paul had to confront with the judaisers. We must be careful to give more explicit definition to *Torah* which is perfectly in line with New Covenant faith and which does not deny the foundations of the Scriptures in the earlier part of the Bible.

A thought came to me recently. Why, I thought, do the Gospel accounts read so differently from the teachings of the Apostles (for instance Paul's teaching in Romans and Galatians). One significant key is in the fact that in the Gospels we stand in awe, witnessing the life and teaching of the Lord Yeshua (Jesus) in whom and through whom *Torah* is made completely manifest and unified. *Torah* springs to life in and through Him. By contrast those of us who, like Paul, try to explain how the full revelation of Scripture can be understood and applied, need to approach it piecemeal, one idea after another. *Torah* cannot be defined in one statement like it can be fulfilled in one person. It has many faces to its identity and the best we can do, short of living it out ourselves, is to set down different aspects of its identity one after the other – a number of issues all to be held in balance. I think it is a useful exercise to set out these ideas and refine and polish them bit by it. Here is a part of my list.

1. *Torah* is God's teaching or instruction.
2. *Torah* does contain 'law', but it also contains other things.
3. *Torah* is all of God's teaching so it encompasses the whole of Scripture ('New' and 'Old' Testaments), but all of Scripture finds its foundational principles in the first five books of the Bible. Hence we can safely refer to the first five books as *Torah*, providing we approach them in a Midrashic manner, exploring all the links across Scripture, particularly in Yeshua's fulfilment.
4. Yeshua is the goal of *Torah*, in that all of God's teaching has Him as the purpose.
5. Yeshua came into a world of *Torah* observance (that observance being according to Rabbinic tradition). He came to correct rather than replace, and we can imply from this that a *Torah* foundation for the life of believers is His goal. He came to teach the true heart of *Torah* and fulfil in His life, sacrificial death and resurrection, all that *Torah* pointed to. We should now live in a fulfilled *Torah* community life and our goal is to understand what that is.
6. Yeshua's and Paul's teaching assume a *Torah* consciousness which emerges from constant study.
7. The heart principles of *Torah* are love of God and of our neighbour. Everything is linked to these central issues and a manifestation of them.
8. *Torah* contains far more than the 'law of Moses'. It begins with a knowledge of the Creator of the Universe. It emphasises the life of Faith. It explores the accurate types and shadows pointing to Yeshua. It puts family and community central to life. It shows the path to holiness.
9. The principles of *Torah* are practical and spiritual. The practical mitzvot have meaning in themselves and are also perfect examples of heart principles which can be generalised. Through spiritual rebirth, these principles can be made manifest on the heart of believers so that the practical applications of given

principles can be broadened.

10. *Torah* is lifeless without the Holy Spirit's interpretation on our hearts.

11. *Torah* reveals sin and the need for a Saviour. It always did. If we are not *Torah* conscious we will not be conscious of our need for a Saviour. *Torah*, interpreted correctly, leads to the life of faith.

12. All societies need rules. God has shown the perfect combination in His *Torah*. Even Gentile nations can benefit from framing their laws according to the heart principles of *Torah*.

13. There is a difference between salvation and sanctification. Salvation is through the atoning blood of Yeshua and cannot be gained through works of the *Torah*, but sanctification comes through persevering with the principles of *Torah*, seeing that they are spiritually applied to our hearts as we are led on to holiness.

14. *Torah* is many layered. There can and should be external forms of observance, but also a constant, meditative seeking after the depths of meaning. Yeshua is the perfect model and His teaching demonstrates that unless *Torah* is on the heart it will be only at a surface level. The history of Israel demonstrates that *Torah* does not penetrate from the outside in, but only by the Holy Spirit's enabling can it reach the heart and then come from the inside out.

15. Meditation on *Torah* can be used by the Holy Spirit to bring us to maturity.

What do you think about this?

Torah

Essays on the Fulfilment of Torah
No 3: On Fences and Freedom

A greatly respected tradition from Judaism is to put a fence around the *Torah*, but is this the very thing that leads to bondage?

Among the most respected sections of the Mishnah is 'Aboth', 'The Fathers'. Here we find many wise sayings, even going back to the time of Hillel and Shammai, whose schools of teaching influenced the thinking of Jews even in Jesus' time. Since the Jewish background to the Christian faith has been neglected for many years, the discovery of Aboth by those of us seeking to re-establish our roots can be like a fresh inspiration. Here we find a stimulus to understanding Rabbinic thought which even sheds light on the Lord's teaching. In our zeal to learn about our roots, and through studying what for most of us is a new discovery, we might even begin to sympathise with Jewish traditions and teaching because of what we read. Yet, while sympathising in many ways with our Jewish friends and respecting their great zeal for the truth and their great part in preserving and outworking biblical truth, I suggest that we need to be careful. In the very first paragraph of Aboth is a beguiling idea that we must treat with caution.

Aboth begins with the familiar words: 'Moses received the Law from Sinai and committed it to Joshua, and Joshua to the elders, and the elders to the Prophets; and the Prophets committed it to the men of the Great Synagogue. They said three things: Be deliberate in judgement, raise up many disciples, and make a fence around the Law.'

A fence around the law, on the face of it, is a very wise thing to construct. The principle is that, in order not to break the laws given by God, more stringent requirements should be devised than in the laws themselves. If the more stringent requirements are kept (and even if they are only broken in a minor way) then there will be no danger of breaking the actual commandments of God. How sensible! How holy! Yet surely this is the very route to bondage and self-righteousness.

For example, in the 7th section of the tractate 'Shabbat' in the Mishnah are the thirty-nine classes of work, devised in relation to the command not to work on the Sabbath. They contain issues which the Lord Jesus challenged as He walked through the grainfields (Matthew 12:1-8), concerning reaping, threshing and winnowing. Some of the other issues covered are very detailed such as the sewing of two stitches or the writing of two letters being a breach of the fence around the Law.

If we consider Jesus's challenge to the interpreters of the *Torah* in His day, we have evidence that the very framework he was challenging related to the fence around the law. Heavy burdens were put on ordinary people, which took away their freedom and their delight in the *Torah* of God. Not only that, but Jesus also identified the self-righteousness that resulted from these attempts at piety, as He confronted the religious leaders themselves. Surely, this was also Paul's chief area of concern regarding works rather than faith. It is easy to deceive ourselves that we have come into the safety zone concerning the observance of *Torah* by applying strict rules of interpretation. Yet extreme bondage rather than true freedom is the result.

The key to the exercise of true freedom in relation to *Torah* is faith. It is, dare I say it, not only faith for the forgiveness of sin (which is falling short of the laws of God) through the blood of Jesus, but also faith that the Holy Spirit will enable us to achieve the standards of holiness required by the law, gradually, as we grow in fellowship with Him. This is a sensitive and balanced freedom that can easily turn into licence, but it is the only meaningful route to a truly *Torah* observant lifestyle. A fence around the law is a fleshly device that will lead to bondage and deceive us that we are holy when we are only self-righteous. A fence around the law denies the true freedom we have in Jesus and the faith that is the hallmark of our walk (halachah) with the Holy Spirit.

Paradoxically, as we learn from the Sermon on the Mount, the spiritual fruit that is the consequence of this true life of faith manifests interpretations of *Torah* which, if they were borne by the flesh (if that were possible, which it isn't), would put a fence around even the *Torah* fence of the Rabbis! 'Guard your hearts' is the true fencing process, for from the heart comes forth the fruit of the Spirit, against which there is no law.

Torah

Essays on the Fulfilment of Torah
No 4: A New Beginning

For many of us, the rediscovery of the Jewish Roots of the Christian faith is like a new beginning. This is not just a new beginning for each individual and family, but for the whole Church. It is also the time when the Lord is bringing new beginnings for Israel, both in their Land and, for many, in their spiritual life. Quite suddenly, all of Messianic belief is ready for pruning and correction, even in the words and phrases that are used and have been used for many years. One such phrase, 'born again', is itself associated with the idea of new beginnings.

This phrase is used too lightly by many Christians. It becomes like a badge worn to verify membership of the true Church, while what is seen in the lives of many who wear this badge, far from verifies an understanding of what it means. Indeed, it can be a badge of spiritual pride and shallowness rather than a badge of humility and depth of relationship with God.

Our humbling encounter with the risen Lord should be regarded as no less awesome than that of Nicodemus (John 3). Perhaps we need to consider this carefully, as we seek to re-establish a fulfilled *Torah* perspective in the Church, particularly in these early days of restoration. What should it really mean for either a Jew or a Gentile to claim to be a 'born-again believer'?

First, let me say that we are referring to spiritual birth here, a birth that comes about through the regeneration of the Holy Spirit, a birth that draws us near to our Father in Heaven with the intimacy that gives us the right to call Him Abba. This was surely, what Jesus was leading Nicodemus to desire, in that fascinating interaction between our Jewish Lord and Rabbi and that respected member of the Sanhedrin. Here was an expert in the contemporary understanding of *Torah* in a secret meeting with the One who fulfilled *Torah*. We must remember that this was a meeting on Jewish soil and must look behind what was being said to understand what was intended.

When Nicodemus asked,

How can a man be born when he is old? Surely he cannot enter a second time into his mother's womb to be born! (John 3:4)

he was not showing the ignorance that many have supposed. He was simply trying to get a further response from Jesus by inventing a question that would, hopefully, bring an explanation of how this idea of rebirth was being applied. He would have already understood the concept of being born again. It was a figure of speech applied to a number of circumstances of life. Edersheim, in his 'Life and Times of Jesus the Messiah', mentions a number of circumstances to which this applied. Proselytes to Judaism were considered newly born. So too were the bridegroom in his marriage, the Chief of the Academy on his promotion and the king on his enthronement. It was a term used to describe a new beginning in an important circumstance of life, where the person took a new role as a beginner, like a child, having to start at the bottom and learn a role in life all over again. Nicodemus would already have been 'reborn' a number of times, including when he became a member of the Sanhedrin.

Rebirth into the Kingdom of Heaven was a completely new application to Nicodemus and one which went beyond physical experience. Nevertheless, the Lord Jesus chose to use this familiar metaphor, which would convey an accurate and understandable idea to Nicodemus. What might this have meant for him? It might have led to his spiritual rebirth, so that he could be a fulfilment of Matthew 13:52, a teacher of the law who has been instructed about the kingdom of heaven, and who is like the owner of a house who

brings out of his storeroom new treasures as well as old.

Is a 'night-time' coming upon Israel, in which many like Nicodemus will seek an audience with Yeshua (Jesus)? If so, we can pray for deeper insights into fulfilled *Torah* to become known across the whole world. We are, perhaps, on the verge of something that the world and the Church have never seen, when Messianic Jews and Messianic believers from the nations will discover the true meaning of *Torah* together.

Meanwhile, for those of us who already claim rebirth, there is an important principle to consider from this story. This will prevent us from two errors. One has been prevalent in the Church already. It is as mentioned above, a shallow perception of what this term 'born again' means. The second applies to those who have been reborn by the Spirit of God and are now considering what this means with regard to fulfilled *Torah*. To be born again means that we are like children. Like children, we can be hasty, presumptuous and forceful when we should be teachable, careful, listeners and slow to act hastily. To be born again into the Kingdom of Heaven is a spiritual experience, but it is also understandable in the way that Jesus used the idea with Nicodemus. Let us, in these days of new beginnings, not be too hasty to assume that we have understanding of all that God is doing in the *Jewish Roots* movement, or in the establishment of fulfilled *Torah* lifestyles. Like children, let us learn together and grow to maturity and let Him restore to us all that He intends.

Torah

Essays on the Fulfilment of Torah
No 5: How Much More Jesus

One of the most important aspects of the restoration of our biblical heritage is the correct reading and interpretation of Scripture. The first step is to re-establish the continuity of the whole of Scripture. Even those of us who are totally committed to restoration may need to work on this. We are so accustomed to partitioning Scripture between New and Old Testaments that we have unwittingly classed one (usually the 'Old' Testament) as inferior to the other. For some there has been a sort of fear ingrained into us, that to emphasise the Old Testament is tantamount to legalism or failing to be free to worship Jesus (Yeshua). The opposite, of course, is true. We will know our Saviour better when we see Him emerge from the whole of salvation history. The foundations for understanding who He is and why He came are set in the early books of the Bible. Nowhere else can we find this totally reliable information.

Having established the continuity and importance of all Scripture, we can begin to study it - in a meaningful way. There is much to be discovered in relation to this. I would like to consider just one principle here.

A phrase that occurs more than twenty times in the Bible is, 'How much more.' This phrase illustrates a principle of Bible teaching, in which an idea is first given in a simple form and then developed into a deeper and more important form. Indeed, we see, more generally, that God's teaching is very often through contrasts of one kind or another. Some of the best examples of the principle 'how much

more' come in Jesus' own teaching:

> *If you, then, though you are evil, know how to give good gifts to your children, how much more will your Father in heaven give good gifts to those who ask him! (Matthew 7:11)*

> *If you then, though you are evil, know how to give good gifts to your children, how much more will your Father in heaven give the Holy Spirit to those who ask him! (Luke 11:13)*

> *If that is how God clothes the grass of the field, which is here today, and tomorrow is thrown into the fire, how much more will he clothe you, O you of little faith! (Luke 12:28)*

A use of this phrase in the Epistle to the Hebrews leads to a significant application of the point. Having considered the sacrifices of the Old Covenant the writer speaks of Jesus' more excellent sacrifice:

> *How much more, then, will the blood of Christ, who through the eternal Spirit offered himself unblemished to God, cleanse our consciences from acts that lead to death, so that we may serve the living God! (Hebrews 9:14)*

What began in the Old Covenant had 'much more' meaning in the ministry of Jesus the Messiah. From Jesus' own teaching we learn that He did not come to abolish the *Torah* and the Prophets but to fulfil them. Thus we can read the whole of Scripture (particularly the Old Testament (Tanach)) with the 'how much more' principle in mind. When we do this we somehow ease the burden of interpretation. We can read the whole of Scripture asking what this teaches us about Jesus. This helps us to establish the continuity of Scripture and also saves us from trying to force too much out of a given text. Let us look at one example of this, where there can be a danger of taking the text too literally as speaking about Jesus, while there is also a profound pointer to Jesus.

The Song of Songs is a deeply evocative love story with much human sensuality, so much so that it might even seem out of place to be in Scripture at all. Many people see this as an exact parable to the relationship between Jesus and His bride. Others see it as no more than a love story between human beings, particularly because of the emotive sensuality. First, we must say that God made mankind in His own image, so that we must be free to express the sexuality that he intended between a man and his wife. Secondly, however, in interpreting a love story at the human level into a heavenly picture, we might be perceiving God too much in the image of fallen mankind. Here is the tension in interpreting Song of Songs as pointing to Jesus. However, if we consider this as the most beautiful of love stories that we will ever encounter at the human level, we can then consider whatever pure ideas come from it, and say that if this could be true for human beings then how much more will God's intimate love for us through Jesus be shown. This is subtly different from saying that the lover in the Song of Songs is Jesus.

Now consider all the types and shadows in the same way. Just as the writer to the Hebrews sees Jesus as 'how much more' than the Temple sacrifices, so we can look at every type and shadow and express the 'how much more'. This frees us from the bondage of trying to be too literal over every aspect of an image pointing to Jesus. While there are some exact parallels, such as in the model of the Tabernacle and the Feasts of the Lord, we need not strain for ideas that were not intended. For example, we see Joseph as a 'type of' Jesus, but don't expect Jesus to go step by step through everything that Joseph did. There are many parallels, of course, but we can begin with some straightforward and safe ones before probing more deeply, and we need not be concerned if we can't make some ideas fit.

We might say, for example, 'If Joseph went down to Egypt and was used by God to save the children of Israel from famine, how much more will Jesus feed us spiritually.' Or, 'If Joseph wept over his brothers and forgave them when he revealed himself to them, how much more will Jesus forgive and save His brothers when He finally reveals Himself to Israel in the last days.' With this approach, we can gently dig into the truths that Scripture gives about Jesus without running the risk of distortion, particularly regarding eschatology.

There are many examples that could be taken to further illustrate the point. Some comparisons are more literal than others, but everywhere we see what was achieved prior to Messiah and pointing to Him, even in the lives of human beings. No-one has achieved what Jesus has. He has done more than the best, and always in regard to servanthood. We end with two of the more remote examples. Samson gave one last push in the Temple of Dagon, destroying many of the Philistines as the pillars of the Temple collapsed. How much more did Jesus destroy the works of the evil one as, at the last, He suffered on the cross. The children of Israel served Solomon's son Rehoboam who was made King of the Jews. Rehoboam ruled unwisely, following the advice of false counsellors, who said,

> Tell these people who have said to you, 'Your father put a heavy yoke on us, but make our yoke lighter'-tell them, 'My little finger is thicker than my father's waist.' (1 Kings 12:10)

How much more shall we serve Jesus, King of the Jews, who said,

> Come to me, all you who are weary and burdened, and I will give you rest. Take my yoke upon you and learn from me, for I am gentle and humble in heart, and you will find rest for your souls. For my yoke is easy and my burden is light. (Matthew 11:28-30)

Torah

Essays on the Fulfilment of Torah
No 6: Offerings from the Heart

In Genesis Chapter 4 we read about the offerings of Cain and Abel:

In the course of time Cain brought some of the fruits of the soil as an offering to the LORD. But Abel brought fat portions from some of the firstborn of his flock. The LORD looked with favour on Abel and his offering, but on Cain and his offering he did not look with favour. So Cain was very angry, and his face was downcast.

It is often said that God favoured Abel's offering because it was from among the flocks, a foreshadowing of Yeshua (Jesus), the Lamb who was slain for us. There must be a good deal of truth in this. To study this further, we can move forward in our Bible studies to the time when the Tabernacle was constructed to see the types and shadows of Messiah more fully, in the offerings of animals on the brazen altar. It is hard for us to picture the full force of these day-by-day, week-by-week, year-by-year offerings. Mingled with the stench of blood is the smell of burning flesh - the best of the animals from the flocks of Israel slaughtered before the Lord and burnt as sacrifice before Him. Yet, here is *Torah* at work in its deepest sense. Here is a teaching about the cost of sin and the only way of forgiveness, through the shedding of blood, life for life. Add this to all the other types and shadows of *Torah* and we see an image forming before us of Yeshua (Jesus), the only acceptable sacrifice for our sins. Yes, Abel's sacrifice was a foreshadowing of all this.

That seems to be that, on first reading. But is that really all there is to it? Was Abel's sacrifice only acceptable because it was from among the flocks, while Cain's was unacceptable, being from the produce of the earth and so less costly? Look at Leviticus 2 for the answer:

> When someone brings a grain offering to the LORD, his offering is to be of fine flour. He is to pour oil on it, put incense on it and take it to Aaron's sons the priests. The priest shall take a handful of the fine flour and oil, together with all the incense, and burn this as a memorial portion on the altar, an offering made by fire, an aroma pleasing to the LORD. The rest of the grain offering belongs to Aaron and his sons; it is a most holy part of the offerings made to the LORD by fire.

There is a perfectly acceptable offering to the Lord from the produce of the soil, so it is not the offering alone that counts, there is something more to be seen. I particularly like the picture of the priest taking a handful of the grain offering and burning it before the Lord. Apart from this handful, the grain offering was for the consumption of the priests. Imagine yourself in the position of the priest. Here is your food handed to you. If you put a big handful on the altar fire, then there is less left over to eat. Is it not a waste to burn such good food? Surely the Lord doesn't want wastage. He only wants a small handful as a symbol. Perhaps one grain will do. Surely He wants my hunger to be satisfied. But picture the open-hearted response of taking a large, almost careless handful and throwing it on the fire with abandon, enjoying the moment, risking a small dinner for the joy of giving freely, in the prescribed way, to the Lord. This reminds us of what Paul said:

> Each man should give what he has decided in his heart to give, not reluctantly or under compulsion, for God loves a cheerful giver. (2 Corinthians 9:7)

In both the grain offering of the person coming to the priests at the altar, and the handful offered to the Lord by the priests, God looks for the same principle - an obedient and willing heart. How often do we hear in Scripture that God does not look on the outward appearance, but looks on the heart? This is why the widow's mite that Yeshua saw being put into the Temple collecting box is recorded in the Scripture as an everlasting memorial. A king could give half his kingdom, but it might not be worth as much as the widow's mite in God's eyes. How blessed God was when that mite went into the Temple treasury.

Now go back to Cain's offering. What did God say to Him?

Why are you angry? Why is your face downcast? If you do what is right, will you not be accepted? But if you do not do what is right, sin is crouching at your door; it desires to have you, but you must master it. (Genesis 4:6-7)

God did not mention the fact that this was fruit of the ground rather than an animal from the flock, but showed Cain that his heart condition had been found out through his offering. A sinful heart had been exposed. Indeed, Yeshua fulfilled the Grain Offering as much as He fulfilled the other offerings when He gave Himself for us, and always His heart was right before His Father as the offerings were given, no mean handful, but a whole-hearted and Holy sacrifice of every part of Himself. If He had not done this, He, like Cain, would have sinned, but He did not.

There is an awesome holiness in all the giving and receiving that the Kingdom of God requires. This is *Torah* at its deepest level. The practical manifestations are but an outward symbol of a heart condition. Whether it be in our tithes or in our works of service, whether it is the Grain Offering or the Burnt Offering (as fulfilled in Yeshua) God is looking at our heart beyond anything else. We can deceive ourselves and we can deceive those who see what we give, but we cannot deceive God. We must go beyond the practical to the spiritual in our understanding of *Torah*. *Torah* goes from the practices of life to the heart. Ultimately they lead to Messiah. Perhaps, when we realise just what was going on deep down in the heart of Yeshua as He fulfilled all the sacrifices for us we might just begin to realise the difference between Cain and Abel, and what Paul meant when he said:

Therefore, I urge you, brothers, in view of God's mercy, to offer your bodies as living sacrifices, holy and pleasing to God–this is your spiritual act of worship. (Romans 12:1)

And we might realise what Samuel meant when he rebuked Saul, saying:

Does the LORD delight in burnt offerings and sacrifices as much as in obeying the voice of the LORD? To obey is better than sacrifice, and to heed is better than the fat of rams. (1 Samuel 15:22)

Torah

Essays on the Fulfilment of Torah
No 7: On Oxen and Parapets

In his reference to oxen the Apostle Paul gave new meaning to an old Mitzvah. Have we reached this same maturity of interpretation after 2000 years of Church history?

When we have understood the role and nature of *Torah*, meditations upon its principles will lead to the right kinds of questions. In prayerfully considering these questions and waiting upon the Lord for enlightenment we can see, like the Apostle Paul, general principles at the heart of various commandments and we can learn to apply these general principles in new and relevant ways.

The Bible records two occasions when Paul referred to the commandment of Deuteronomy 25:4 which stated that an ox should not be muzzled as it treads the grain (1 Corinthians 9:9 and 1 Timothy 5:18). On both occasions he used the commandment to show how ministers of the Gospel should receive appropriate payment. Jews might say he was applying midrashic method here, to extract a truth from a particular part of Scripture to apply it to a different circumstance. Christians might say that Paul, having seen the law as now having no continuing meaning since the coming of Yeshua (Jesus), was treating the ideas rather loosely and liberally. I would suggest that Paul had found the keys to the principle of the law (*Torah*) being written on the heart. Indeed, there is a kind of midrashic interpretation of *Torah*, but led by the Spirit of God rather than through a scientific method of biblical interpretation.

It is interesting that there are very few references in the New Testament to the individual Mitzvot such as the one above. Again, after 2000 years of Christendom, the general impression is that this is because they are not important now that Messiah has come. It is rather strange, however, that Paul uses this one rather remote example twice. I would suggest that this should give us a clue to the way that we should read both the 'New' and 'Old' Testaments. Far from Paul dismissing the 'Old', he is applying the teaching in the way that he expects us to apply it. This is simply one example that he uses in passing and which has found its way into the New Testament writings. Indeed, because there is so little interpretation of the Mitzvot, in terms of the New Covenant, we should realise that we are expected to find interpretations for ourselves. If this were not so we might be inclined to treat the New Testament as a new and complete rulebook, assuming that it has a literal completeness, replacing what went before. Indeed, I would suggest that this is just what many Christians have (unwittingly) done. Instead, we have the final steps of revelation that can now be applied alongside the earlier revelations of Scripture bringing all to fullness, by the power of the Holy Spirit and in the Light of Messiah. We should not expect all the answers to be in the pages of the New Testament, but we should find ourselves on a walk of faith with the Holy Spirit filling out the truth of the whole of Scripture for us.

I would also suggest that this is of extreme importance to those of us in the early stages of the restoration of the Jewish roots of the Christian faith. Going back to the Old Testament, for some, can be a return to literal application of what is found there, missing the spirit of the teaching and the wider application. This is what leads to dry ritual observance of the Feasts, to wearing of Tzit-Tzit and, possibly, to putting self-righteously inspired parapets around one's roof.

The heart of all Mitzvot is to love the Lord with all our heart and our neighbour as ourself. This spiritual principle can only be applied to our hearts by the Holy Spirit Himself, but once there, all the Mitzvot can rise to a higher and more general plane, as well as being perfect examples in themselves of how to apply the principles in certain circumstances. Thus Paul was able to see that in practising, year by year, the principle of not muzzling an ox when treading the grain, letting it feed freely and generously as it worked, there is a principle that can be manifest on the heart and which can be applied in a variety of circumstances, including payment of ministers of the Gospel. Paul had learned to read the heart intent of these Mitzvot and expects us to do the same.

Another seemingly remote example (this time, however, not quoted in the New Testament) is Deuteronomy 22:8 - When you build a new house, make a parapet around your roof so that you may not bring the guilt of bloodshed on your house if someone falls from the roof. Is this principle now to be taken literally, to be of no effect, or does it speak of a general principle? This is an excellent example of loving our neighbour and a perfect example for Middle-Eastern houses with flat roofs, so that there are circumstances even today where it is what we should do quite literally. However, through meditating on the principle, it speaks of care for safety in every area of our interaction with our neighbours. It challenges our heart as to whether we care for our neighbour, and hence challenges our maturity in our spiritual rebirth. Parapets speak of fire extinguishers, first aid boxes, guards on our machinery, and careful safety precautions in all that we do. The *Torah* principle is a profound and perfect prompt to a general principle that can be applied in millions of circumstances, prompted from the heart, but impossible to contain, in the entirety of its applications, in the covers of our Bible. Indeed, we can go further, from the practical to the spiritual. For example, we as parents should put scriptural principles into the lives of our children so that they have spiritual guard rails in their lives. This is the principle that Ezekiel was to bring to his nation as a watchman (Ezekiel 33) so that he would be free of bloodguilt. This is also what Paul meant when he declared himself to be free of bloodguilt because he had declared the whole counsel of God to the people (Acts 20:18-26). He set up a spiritual parapet for their protection, just as we should in our families and fellowships.

I would add one more point in light of our search for the Jewish roots of our faith, so that we do not despise too readily what was achieved through the Church. I can take my example from Britain, my own nation, but it applies to other countries where the Gospel message took root in the fabric of the nation, including the USA. For over a thousand years, from the time of King Alfred the Great, the laws of Britain have reflected the heart of *Torah*. Alfred the Great caused the Ten Commandments and other parts of the law of Moses to be written into our law books. This is why, for example, we developed a consciousness for health and safety in our industries. The heart of the teaching about parapets has been applied in our nations albeit that we have forgotten when and how. Now, as we seek to recover and make more explicit what *Torah* is in our Churches, we must not forget our heritage and we can recognise that there has been a *Torah* impact to our nations, and hence a hope for recovery in these days of growing *Torah*lessness. Furthermore, we must be among those who add depth to the lives of believers and not those who lead them to a new form of superficiality.

Torah

Daily Readings from Torah

An introduction to a Bible Reading Scheme

It is possible to utilise a *Torah* based approach to Bible studies in many ways. One way would be to break up the weekly *Torah* portion into sections for study day by day so that a family could achieve in-depth personal study throughout each week. In this section of the book an example of this is offered for consideration, in which the portion 'Bereshit' is divided up for study over a period of one week. We see how some of the issues raised are considered alongside other appropriate Scriptures so that there are topics for meditation three times each day, which could coincide with regular times for study and prayer, say at morning noon and evening. This is presented as an example of what can be done to restore *Torah* foundations to Bible study for the individual and for the family. If this method is adopted it could be the responsibility of the head of a household to plan the way that *Torah* portions are divided and introduced within the family. Year by year it will be found that different issues spring to mind as the same portions are read over again. There is no end to what we can find when we are freed to study in this way.

Introduction to this method of Bible study

When Jesus was handed the book of the prophet Isaiah in the synagogue at Nazareth (Luke 4:16), He was expected to read from the set portion of Scripture for that particular Sabbath. It was the tradition that set portions from the *Torah* and the Prophets were read each week. There were two possible cycles for these readings, extending over either one year or three years. The tradition continues to this day.

The word *Torah* is a Hebrew word with rich meaning. It means teaching, God's teaching and instruction for life. The word Law is not adequate to define what *Torah* is, while it is true that *Torah* contains Law and leads to a well-ordered life. It is recognised that God teaches us through the whole Bible. In the Old Testament (what the Jews would call the Tanakh) is the foundational teaching on all matters of truth. This view was supported by Jesus in His teaching, particularly when He said that He had not come to destroy the Law (*Torah*) and the Prophets, but to fulfil them (Matthew 5:17). If we were restricted to the Old Testament we could still set the foundations of our faith, but we would fall short of the full revelation of Jesus Christ.

When we are grafted into the Olive Tree of the family of faith in Jesus (Romans 11), we become members of the household of God (Ephesians 2:19), and inheritors of the covenants of promise with the Commonwealth of Israel (Ephesians 2:12). Our inheritance begins in the truths set out in the pages of the Old Testament. The foundations of truth that God built up from Genesis onwards are the foundations of our faith. We find, for example, that our model for the life of faith, the man Abraham, is in the book of Genesis. We find the character of God and the nature of man developing from the early books of the Bible. We find pointers towards the coming of Jesus embedded in the pages of all Scripture. If we read the Bible starting from the foundational books we will discover that the fulfilment that is revealed in Jesus' ministry and the teaching of the Apostles, contained in the New Testament, has much deeper impact. If we know our Bible well we will see that threads of truth develop right across Scripture.

The synagogue tradition was to treat the first five books of the Bible as the foundational reference point for all teaching. Thus the word *Torah* is often applied directly to these books. Christian tradition gave these five books the title Pentateuch. There is great benefit in using the teaching of the first five books of the Bible as the foundations upon which our Bible studies are built

If this method of Bible study is adopted it will soon be realised that there is no limit to the way links can be made across Scripture. An idea that begins in the early books of the Bible is developed in many ways throughout the rest of the Bible. This is why this method of reading the Bible is so rich. Year by year, day by day, ideas develop in different ways, often in step with the experiences of life, through which God is teaching us. There is no one Bible commentary. We can each develop our own commentary through our individual walk with Jesus in fellowship with the Holy Spirit. We each have our walk on our 'Emmaus Road' where Jesus reveals Himself to us through the *Torah*, Prophets and Writings of Scripture.

This study utilises a portion (Parashot, in Hebrew) from the book of Genesis which the synagogues use for their one-year cycle. The studies begin with the portion from *Torah* and then develop the themes through the whole of Scripture. A method of Bible study is introduced rather than a definitive commentary, which it cannot be. This method has been used by individuals and by heads of families at family devotions in the morning and evening. The studies are divided up so that a fraction of the weekly Bible portion is studied each day, and so that each portion is taken over the whole week. This allows additional complementary readings to be brought in. It will be seen that the ideas taken up from Genesis develop across the whole of Scripture. Though the studies begin in Genesis they link easily to the fulfilled message of Jesus the Messiah and to the eternal hope expressed by the prophets, pointing to the message of Revelation in particular

The main aim of the study is to explore the process of studying all Scripture from its original foundations. Each person might then continue with this method but in ways which suit themselves. The *Torah* and *Haftarah* Portions have been divided up into suitable sections to give six separate studies. Each day two additional and related studies have been found so that there is a Bible Study for morning, midday and evening on each day. Short notes have been given with each Bible reading to give some food for thought, discussion and prayer. The ideas starting from the *Torah* portion are developed through studying other scriptures, demonstrating how threads of truth weave through the whole Bible, from Genesis to Revelation, from foundation to fulfilment.

The morning and evening studies are suitable for brief times of teaching and devotion for the whole family, when they can gather together led by the head of the home. It is appropriate to read the Bible passages together and then enter into a short discussion, finishing with prayer. The head of the home should have some ideas already prepared to feed into these discussions and to help to draw conclusions.

Longer studies can take place when possible (for instance around the meal table on the Sabbath Day) when ideas can be reviewed for the whole week.

Torah studies help us to understand both God and ourselves. They point specifically to Jesus. In practical terms, they are also relevant to our understanding of situations in the world around us. As a stimulus for prayer, they should encourage us to draw near to God in praise and worship, to pray for our personal and family needs and to pray for the situation in the Church and among the nations.

An Example from *Torah*
Bereshit: In the Beginning: Genesis 1:1-6:8, Isaiah 42:5-43:11

First Day

Morning reading: Genesis 1:1-2:3.
    Comment: Around 6000 years ago God created the universe. This is the first thing that we read in the Bible and this fact is at the foundation of our faith. It is not something that we can prove by science, but all the world displays evidence of Creation and of our Creator. Just as men, in their pride, do not want to believe in God, so they will find every excuse not to believe that the universe was created. See if you can think of one example from the world around that is evidence of our Creator. There are simple examples and more complicated ones, but everywhere we look, we can discover

evidence. Here is one example from the millions that you can find. If you look at an egg, it is shaped in a very special way. Mathematicians can show that the shape of an egg gives it the maximum strength at its ends (the shape is called a catenary in mathematics. Each end of the egg is a catenary, the strongest possible shape). When an egg falls to the ground it will land on one of these strong ends and so be protected from breaking. Yet the middle of the egg, where the two ends meet is weak and so when a chick is ready to hatch it can easily break out of the side. This is a sign of the Creator. It is difficult to imagine an eggshell coming to this design by chance! Now find some more evidence for our Creator and praise God for the wonder of His Creation.

Midday reading: Romans 1:18-21, Psalm 24.

Comment: The evidence for God our Creator is all around us. Paul taught, in the Letter to the Romans, that the evidence in the universe is so clear that there is no excuse for anyone not to recognise this and worship God. Yet men and women from every generation have ignored or distorted this evidence. Psalm 24 leads us to worship God from meditation on the Creation, our recognition of God's greatness and our need for holiness. The Psalm also points to the King of Glory, Jesus the Messiah.

Evening reading: Psalm 19.

Comment: End the day with a further meditation on the wonder of God's Creation. This Psalm reminds us that God speaks to us through His Creation, with a language that everyone can understand. From His Creation, we see His character. All God's works are well-ordered. His *Torah* shows how our lives can be well-ordered, coming from the same mind that created the ordered universe. His laws reveal our faults and His order and steadfastness reveal His character. All this leads us to repentance and worship.

Second Day

Morning reading: Genesis 2:4-25.

Comment: Here is a second account of the Creation. This time we have a picture of Adam living in the Garden of Eden in the perfection that God had created. It is difficult for us to imagine this perfection. Perhaps we have a taste of it on those quiet mornings in the countryside, when dew is rising and the air is still and clear, but perfection is not to be found in today's world as it was then, even though there is still great beauty. Not only was there peace in the environment, but there was also peace between man and God. Also, Adam was also given a helper. This was the beginning of the family of mankind. The Lord God created the woman from the man, demonstrating the unity that He desired for this family. He wants a family on earth. The family's members are to be in unity with one another and with Him.

Midday reading: Isaiah 65:17-25, Ephesians 5:15-33.

Comment: There will come a day when there will be peace and order again. We must wait for the New Creation. In the meantime, it is God's plan that family life and order is maintained in the Body of disciples of Jesus. As well as this being important in its own right, for the ordering of society, Paul shows us that our family structure is a picture and practical teaching point for the order in God's own Family, of which Jesus is the Head. It is no wonder that Satan is setting out to destroy the family structure of mankind. We are somewhere in between the establishment of a family at the Creation of the World and the time of the New Creation, and we are to focus on family life as God's priority, despite all the pressures around us.

Evening reading: Isaiah 42:5-43:11.

Comment: For our evening meditations, and following our theme of family which began this morning, it is appropriate to read this week's Haftarah Portion. The reading from Isaiah shows how, despite all the troubles of this world and despite the sinfulness of mankind, there is a plan for recovery. Here we see God, as the Father, overseeing all history and ensuring that His great promise to Israel will be accomplished. We who come from the Gentile Nations, and have been adopted into this family through the atoning sacrifice of Jesus the Messiah, can also praise Him. What Adam and Eve experienced temporarily in the Garden of Eden has been lost, but we can look forward to a permanent and perfect future prepared by

God our Father, in the World that is to come.

Third Day

Morning reading: Genesis 3:1-24

Comment: When we read this account of how both Adam and Eve were tempted to do what God had told them not to do, we have a glimpse into human nature as it continues today. The first sin is like all the others - disobedience to the commandments of God. We see that God gave mankind choice and made it clear what should and should not be done. We cannot tell if the Fall was inevitable but we know that sin entered the world and caused separation from God at that time and mankind continues to go against the will of God to this day. Whatever rules God sets up, mankind has free will and exercises that will against God's perfect will. This is inevitable since the Fall. The situation before us in today's Bible reading is arguably the saddest day that mankind has experienced in the whole of history, leading to all the wars, all the strife, all the division, all the sickness, all the toil, all the pain, all the fear, all the hunger and all the poverty that the world has seen. Decay came into the Creation. It affected the animal kingdom, the trees and flowers and all living things, as well as mankind. Yet we go on rebelling against God and not learning from this first sin.

Midday reading: 1 Timothy 2.

Comment: Paul, when writing to Timothy, was conscious of the way community life should be ordered. It was clear to him that the temptation of Adam through Eve was something to bear in mind when considering the authority and responsibility structure of community and family life among believers. Perhaps the reason why there is such a disregard for this order of society in today's world is that most people consider the world far older than six thousand years. Adam and Eve either have become myth or seem to exist in a meaningless past. Nothing could be further from the truth. This passage from the Letter to Timothy puts the right priorities before us. The Salvation of all who will believe in Jesus the Messiah is the reason for the continuance of this order of creation, and we are to establish godly order to our lives in our believing communities while the day of opportunity still remains for some to turn, and, in so doing, recover from the consequences of the Fall.

Evening reading: Revelation 7:1-17.

Comment: It is only when we have put the Fall into perspective that we can put the recovery from the Fall into true perspective. The height of our recovery equals the depth of the Fall. Indeed, it has not only been made possible for us to recover what was lost by Adam and Eve, but our recovery is permanent. Our duty to live according to God's standards on this earth and to persevere until the end is to be measured by this wonderful picture from the Book of Revelation, when the recovery is complete and we, who believe, will be gathered into one family forever, worshipping our Saviour. Our worship can begin this evening in some small way, perhaps. Everything has been made possible for us because of Jesus, the second Adam, who came down from Heaven.

Fourth Day

Morning reading: Genesis 4:1-24.

Comment: When Adam and Eve were sent out of the Garden of Eden, God could easily have abandoned them, even have put them to death there and then. Yet He chose to let them live, and, more than that, to have children. We might have expected that this little family would look back with regret on what had happened to Adam and Eve and to do their very best to lead a disciplined life that would please God, but they were not able to do so. Not only do we see sin taking root in mankind but also we see the terrible evil of murder, which was the result of envy and resentment. This is human nature displayed before us at the dawn of the world, at the beginning of time, at the foundations of the family of man. Also hidden in this story of Cain and Abel is the first hint of the sacrifice that would please God, the firstling of the flock. Here is a pointer to the Lamb of God. Did God already have in mind what it would take to recover mankind from the horrors of sin even as He watched Cain murder Abel? He looked ahead to the time when His only Son, Jesus would be the acceptable sacrifice for our sins. In this chapter of Genesis we have both the depth of the sin nature of mankind and the pointer to the means of atonement. God's choice was not to destroy all mankind on account of Adam and Eve, but to patiently accept that sin would rise, counting the cost of His own Son's life as an atonement. Here, already, the second Adam, Jesus, was a substitute for the first Adam (and his children, including us), because Adam was allowed to live, despite his sin and the sin of his son Cain. God had already made the decision.

Midday reading: Galatians 5:16-26.

Comment: The murder of Abel by Cain is not an exception. It is in the flesh nature of every human being to commit the most terrible sins. Paul sets out clear examples of what the flesh will achieve, in this portion from the Letter to the Galatians, but there is a remedy. God has sent His Holy Spirit to empower all who have been redeemed through the shed blood of Jesus the Messiah. The life of the Holy Spirit in us gives us the ability to produce pure fruit in our lives. There is no other way than to learn to live like this. Otherwise we are no better than Cain, however much we try to subdue our natural fleshly lusts.

Evening reading: Isaiah 53.

Comment: We should end our day not gloating over Cain, but humbled by the thought that we could naturally go the same way ourselves. Isaiah 53 reminds us of the price of our recovery. God's ways are not according to man's logic, but no man could find a more logical solution to the recovery of the fallen human race than the substitute. The cost of life is life. We can receive new life because a Lamb, our substitute, was slain for us. That Lamb was Jesus the Messiah, the Son of God. Cain and Abel reveal our fallen nature, but Jesus can transform that nature, though first we must accept the truth which Isaiah prophesied, and which came to pass when Jesus went to the Cross for us at Calvary – but we must accept the substitute for ourselves.

Fifth Day

Morning reading: Genesis 4:25-5:24.

Comment: Here we have the family line from Adam. A new

beginning was made through Seth. Here we also see pointers to Jesus. Cain is left to roam the world, banished, suffering a life of torment, living in fear but not finding death. Cain reminds us of those cast out of God's presence, while Seth reminds us of Jesus, through whom will come salvation. The line of Seth goes directly to Enoch, the man who walked with God, and to Noah, the one to bring rest, another reminder of Jesus. These are types rather than the final manifestation, of course. If the names of Adam and his offspring are written down side by side in the Hebrew and translated into our language, we find a statement of the plan of Salvation: 'Man (Adam) (is)appointed (Seth) (a)mortal (Enosh) possession (Cainan) (to the) praise of God (Mahalaleel) (there will) descend (Jared) (a) dedicated (Enoch)man of increase (Methuselah) (a)strong man (Lamech) (who will bring) rest (Noah)'. As we see the families of the earth expanding, so we also realise that God has in mind a sure plan of Salvation. By the way, every one of the men on this list is in the physical family line of every person on earth, including you and me.

Midday reading: Psalm 2.

Comment: All around us, in the whole world, we see evidence that Psalm 2 is true. The Nations are still raging and people everywhere will do their utmost to avoid bowing the knee to Jesus. Yet God will redeem a people and they will serve Jesus, His Son, whom He has appointed to rule from His holy hill. One day those who worship the Son will live in the peace (Shalom) that is promised, while the raging of the nations will be brought to nothing.

Evening reading: Hebrews 10:35-11:7.

Comment: The writer to the Hebrews speaks of the life of faith. He begins with the fact that it is faith alone that pleases God. Indeed this faith is a gift from God and we please Him when we allow Him to build our faith. Later in our *Torah* studies, we will come to Abraham, our 'father' of faith, but in the opening chapters of Genesis we have already met models for our faith. We join these men in the Body of believers through faith in Jesus. Notice that the first item on the list is faith that God created the world. Perhaps Abel, Enoch and Noah being closer to the Creation had fewer problems with this than our present generation. Yet, they only saw Jesus through types and shadows. We know the reality. Surely then we can walk with God like Enoch, even as the nations rage and make their stand against God and His anointed Son.

Sixth Day

Morning reading: Genesis: 5:25-6:8.

Comment: God, through His grace, preserved mankind, yet all the abominations possible rose among us. Verses 5 and 6 of Chapter 6 must be one of the saddest statements of the whole Bible. The rise of wickedness was so great that God regretted creating mankind. We must face this truth with realism. The nature of man has not changed from that day, except through the transformation that comes through the New Birth brought about by the Holy Spirit to those who believe in Jesus. Although God has done so much, we continue to live in a fallen world with the same manifestations of wickedness as at the time of Noah. Yet, God was able to find one man who found grace in His eyes. Through that man, Noah, salvation was to come for one family while the rest of mankind was destroyed. This points to Jesus and to the end of the world, as we know it. Noah is simply a signpost to the greater fulfilment through Jesus. If we check the records from chapter five we can discover that Methuselah lived to the year of the Flood. He saw the increase of wickedness on the earth and surely must have been sad and possibly, he was partly instrumental in tutoring Noah whom God chose out of this world. This makes us think about our standing in this world and our influence on others.

Midday reading: Ezekiel 22:23-31.

Comment: The story of the Fall and the growth of wickedness in the world was not contained by the Flood. In this portion from Ezekiel we see that men are still in rebellion, but God is constantly looking for those whose hearts are turned towards Him. The sadness of Ezekiel's day is shown in verse 30 of this section. God was looking for a man to intercede for the people and found none. At the time of Noah God found such a man. What about today? Where are those whom the Lord God seeks whose hearts are turned to Him and who are grieved by the wickedness of the nations?

Evening reading: Philippians 2.

Comment: We have seen how God looked for a man through whom He could show His grace at the time of Noah and found one, but we know that the world continued to decline even after the Flood. We have considered how God is still looking for those He can save in every generation, and this challenges us to consider our own standing before Him. Our response is that our righteousness is because of Jesus, and for this reason alone, we are counted among those whom the Lord favours. He is the only Man through whom the final and perfect plan of Salvation can be accomplished, our only perfect model, who in all humility went to the Cross for us. In Paul's letter to the Philippians we read about the character of our Saviour, to whom Noah pointed. Into this world full of sins and wickedness came our Saviour, to whom point all the verses of Scripture and the travails of history.

The Sabbath Day (Shabbat)

Morning reading: John 1:1-18.

Comment: We have reviewed the account of the Creation of the World and its Fall. This has led us to consider our life of faith and to consider the family of God. We have seen that, even as mankind was increasing in those early days, God had a plan of recovery in mind. Our meditations should help us to appreciate what Jesus has done for us, and so it is fitting to contrast John 1 with our readings from Genesis. We see that Jesus (The Word) was with God in the beginning and before Creation, because everything was made for Him and through Him. He decided to save a family for Himself even as He watched sin rise and even while realising that He would pay the price one day. That was done for all who will believe. As John says, He gave us the right to become children of God. Let us praise Him on this Sabbath Day.

Midday reading: Romans 8.

Comment: We have considered the Creation of the World this

week and, though the Fall has spoilt its original perfection, there is still a great remnant of beauty. It is good to celebrate the beauty of God's Creation this Sabbath Day, perhaps finding some activity or study which focuses our attention on what God has done. Then we can go on and read how all of Creation is groaning, waiting for the fulfilment of the purpose for which it was allowed to continue. This purpose is the revealing of those who are adopted into God's family through faith in Jesus the Messiah. We have the standing of sons of God. This is the highest reason for God's creation, to call people like us into His family! Praise the Lord!

Evening reading: Revelation 21:1-8.

Comment: We have considered the Creation of the World and stood in awe at its magnificence, and yet more in awe at the plan that God has had for us, despite the terrible sin of mankind. Now, we look into the future. When all has been accomplished, we will be in a new Heaven and on a new Earth. What has faded through the Fall will be recovered, and those who believe in Jesus, those who make up the family of God, will be in this Paradise forever.

Additional Reading for the Sabbath Day: Read right through the Letter to the Hebrews.

Steps Leading to Zion Gate.

Section 3

Halakhah

God's plan for all His people is that they walk by faith as one worldwide community. Far from interpreting Torah as legalism and rules to learn by rote, the ultimate aim of God's programme of teaching is that we exercise our freedom to live by the power of the Holy Spirit in step with Him and in harmony with His plans for us.

Halakhah

Part 1: A Walk with God

Halakhah for the Local Community

The responsibility of Elders

Most of us will probably remember the scene from Fiddler on the Roof where men from the Jewish Community gathered around the Rabbi to ask, 'Is there a blessing for the Tzar?' After some reflection, came the two edged humorous reply, 'May the Lord bless him and keep him.....far from us'. Albeit that this is an amusing incident, it reminds us of an important principle - the need that people have in a local community to have questions answered. This also reminds us of the Jewish tradition of Halakhah and the need for communities to have an authoritative person or persons to help with decisions relating to the life of the community. Jewish tradition of having a local Rabbi or a Bet Din or even a Sanhedrin comes from the time of Moses, when it was necessary to bring community judgements on practical day to day issues. Moses was advised by Jethro, his father in law, to appoint deputies to settle the easier matters of Halakhah :

'Moses said unto his father in law ... the people come unto me to inquire of God: when they have a matter, they come unto me; and I judge between one and another, and I do make them know the statutes of God, and his laws. And Moses' father in law said unto him, The thing that thou doest is not good. Thou wilt surely wear away, both thou, and this people that is with thee: for this thing is too heavy for thee; thou art not able to perform it thyself alone. Hearken now unto my voice, I will give thee counsel, and God

shall be with thee: Be thou for the people to God-ward, that thou mayest bring the causes unto God: and thou shalt teach them ordinances and laws, and shalt show them the way wherein they must walk, and the work that they must do. Moreover thou shalt provide out of all the people able men, such as fear God, men of truth, hating covetousness; and place such over them, to be rulers of thousands, and rulers of hundreds, rulers of fifties, and rulers of tens: and let them judge the people at all seasons: and it shall be, that every great matter they shall bring unto thee, but every small matter they shall judge: so shall it be easier for thyself, and they shall bear the burden with thee.' (Exodus 18:15-22)

The Sanhedrin, at the time of Jesus, was the central body for issues of Halakhah to be resolved, and the members had the right to 'Sit in Moses' seat' (Matthew 23), but it is clear that they were not what they ought to have been. Generally, the teaching of the Torah had become a set of rules made by men that were burdensome to the Israelites. Indeed, Jesus told His followers that none should be called Rabbi (Matthew 23:8), since there was only one Master (the Lord Himself).

Though the incident of the Rabbi in Fiddler on the Roof is amusing, there is also a serious side to the situation that is caricatured in the musical. Just as the teachers in Jesus' day interpreted Torah inaccurately, so a teacher of Torah today, if he does not have the wisdom of God, can make pronouncements out of his own head, and the same can happen through any local individual or group that has authority in local congregations of believers.

In the coming days Halakhah is going to be an important issue for the worldwide Messianic movement. Since Moses' day there has been a need to interpret Torah into everyday life of the covenant community. It is still the Lord's way. In Jewish tradition, Halakhah is a set of rulings for the living out of Torah, but should this be the way for the Messianic community? The potential pitfall of adopting a centralised rabbinical background to Halakhah, as in the Sanhedrin of Jesus' day, is that rulings for the worldwide community will become burdensome and lifeless. Indeed, the Church among the nations did not avoid this pitfall when it centralised authority in Rome with the Popes. It is very easy to give authority into the hands of a central organisation and thereby deprive the believing community of its source of life. Indeed, this can happen in the local community as much as at international level, when the responsibility of the head of the home is taken into the hands of the local pastorate (or Rabbi). Dr Karl Coke is right in calling the Church back to recognise the authority and responsibility to be restored to the home within the believing community.

The issue of Halakhah must be considered very carefully in the coming days and the implications for the worldwide Messianic movement are profound. There will be a need for some reference points no doubt, but authority must chiefly be recognised as within the sensitive balance of home life and local eldership. It is the local elders who sit in Moses' seat on behalf of the heads of homes, more than any central body, whether based in Jerusalem or elsewhere. There must be no Pope of the Messianic movement. The Holy Spirit has promised to be among two or three who gather in the Name of the Lord. The Lord does not require a minyan of ten members, but He will work among small groups who truly meet in His Name, and for His purposes, particularly with local groups of elders.

We can learn much from the Acts 15 Council of Jerusalem, which could be seen as a Messianic Bet Din (House of ruling). The issue of the Law of Moses first arose there in response to questions of Halakhah for the communities among the Gentile nations. In brief, the four injunctions that were sent out in a letter to the congregations could be associated with those things that would lead believers into spiritual idolatry. If this is so, then an interpretation of the letter to the Churches was that they should flee idolatry and serve the One True God. No other burden was placed upon them, with the supposition that control of the developing body of believers was not to be centralised, but authority was to be kept in the hands of local congregations. This did not mean that other issues of Torah did not matter, but that the Holy Spirit will work through local elders to bring understanding to the essential aspects of Torah for that community. For this, local elders are to be open to learning their pastoral role through the interpretation of Torah into life-giving Halakhah, for families and individuals in the local setting. Halakhah itself is then a walk with the Living God and not obedience of dry and lifeless rules. In this way, we should realise that local eldership has a strategic role to play in the developing Messianic movement and the time is here to learn how to listen together to the Holy Spirit for the interpretation of Torah into living Halakhah, in service of the local communities of believers, and to put aside any temptation to form a central authoritative body that replaces local eldership. Indeed, the local eldership must be mature, not imposing burdens, but serving the needs of the community.

For Study and Meditation:
Study the word 'walk' in the Bible and consider how this refers to the way that we should apply the teaching of Scripture in our practical and spiritual lives. Read Exodus 18:15-22, Titus 1:5-9 and Acts 15, and consider the responsibility of Elders in the local community of believers to interpret the Scriptures as they protect, teach and pastor disciples of Yeshua to walk in His ways.

Halakhah

Halakhah

The word *Halakhah* comes from the Hebrew root *Halakh*, 'to walk', 'to go' or 'to go forth'. In Jewish tradition, *Halakhah* is the way a person should 'walk' or 'go' through life. It is the legal side of Judaism covering the code of conduct in all affairs of life. The principles of *Halakhah* are believed to go back to the teaching of Moses that was given at Sinai. It is considered that there is a written tradition of Scripture (founded on the first five books of the Bible - the *Torah*) and also an oral tradition (passed on by word of mouth until codified in the *Mishnah* by about 200 AD). Throughout the ages, there have been authoritative bodies in Jewish communities that interpreted the teaching of the Scriptures and the oral traditions to determine how a person should live. This has produced many volumes of rabbinical writings over the centuries, and such has been the effort to interpret Scripture into a conduct of life that there have been times when the *Bet Dins* (legal courts) have had the right to inflict punishments, within Jewish communities, for transgressions of Halakhic rulings.

While there is a Halakhah that is burdensome, walking out our response to Scripture is what God expects of us. The Bible itself confirms this. For example, we can consider Scriptures like:

And thou shalt teach them ordinances and laws, and shalt show them the way wherein they must walk, and the work that they must do. (Exodus 18:20)

Train up a child in the way he should go: and when he is old, he will not depart from it. (Proverbs 22:6)

And thou shalt teach them diligently unto thy children, and shalt talk of them when thou sittest in thine house, and when thou walkest by the way, and when thou liest down, and when thou risest up. (Deuteronomy 6:7)

Blessed is the man that walketh not in the counsel of the ungodly, nor standeth in the way of sinners, nor sitteth in the seat of the scornful. But his delight is in the law of the LORD; and in his law doth he meditate day and night. And he shall be like a tree planted by the rivers of water, that bringeth forth his fruit in his season; his leaf also shall not wither; and whatsoever he doeth shall prosper. (Psalm 1:1-3)

Thus saith the LORD, Stand ye in the ways, and see, and ask for the old paths, where is the good way, and walk therein, and ye shall find rest for your souls. (Jeremiah 6:16)

There is an appeal to all people to meditate upon the teaching of God and to apply it to the way they live their life. This Halakhah, which all should seek, represents the good life, in every way. The teaching of God is to be applied and is not meant to be theory alone. Nevertheless, the mistake is to see all that God has taught as simply legalistic - as a set of rules alone. Such rules, ultimately, can become lifeless. This was the reason for Yeshua (Jesus) strongly criticising the interpreters of the Torah of His day:

But woe unto you, Pharisees! for ye tithe mint and rue and all manner of herbs, and pass over judgment and the love of God: these ought ye to have done, and not to leave the other undone. (Luke 11:42)

Woe unto you also, ye lawyers! for ye lade men with burdens grievous to be borne, and ye yourselves touch not the burdens with one of your fingers. (Luke 11:46)

The Apostles of Yeshua HaMashiach (Jesus the Messiah) were conscious of the way He brought fulfilment to, and gave the true interpretation of, all Scripture. They witnessed the perfection of what Halakhah should be as they observed the life of the Lord, every word, every step, every gesture, every obedience of the Father's will, every act of loving-kindness being a perfect representation of God's teaching. Here, at last, was an embodiment of the true Halakhah to envision those who sought to walk in the ways of God. As the Apostles proclaimed the Gospel message of salvation, they also called believers to a way of life that faithfully interpreted God's teaching, in word and deed:

> But be ye doers of the word, and not hearers only, deceiving your own selves. (James 1:22)

> For the grace of God that bringeth salvation hath appeared to all men, teaching us that, denying ungodliness and worldly lusts, we should live soberly, righteously, and godly, in this present world. (Titus 2:11-12)

Acts 15 records the coming together of leaders of the body of disciples of the risen Lord Jesus Christ to discuss the application of the Bible teaching (the Law/Torah of Moses) to Gentiles who were being saved. This can be seen as a Bet Din, where Halakhic ruling was sought in the manner of Jewish custom. This indicates the care that was being taken to abide by a correct interpretation of Scripture into the lifestyle of believers, and the continuity of the idea of Halakhah, even as the Gospel message was going forth.

By making reference to 2 Timothy 3:16, which in turn would have referred to the existing Scriptures of Paul's day (the Tanakh or Old Testament):

> All scripture is given by inspiration of God, and is profitable for doctrine, for reproof, for correction, for instruction in righteousness: that the man of God may be perfect, thoroughly furnished unto all good works.

we can deduce that believers in the Lord Jesus Christ need to be as concerned for Halakhah as the Jews have been over all the centuries, seeking to live out the true interpretation of all Scripture,

but bearing in mind the lifeless legalism that the Lord condemned, despite the determined efforts of the Jewish leaders. We must be careful not to misinterpret the idea of what Halakhah should be. It is possible to interpret both the New Testament and the Old Testament into a lifeless legalism, living scripturally, but independent of God's fellowship, forgetting that the promise of Yeshua was: **I am come that they might have life, and that they might have it more abundantly.** (John 10:10). Particularly in this day when many Jews are turning to faith in Yeshua, questions of Halakhah are arising as at the time of Acts 15. What is the true Halakhah that will unite believers in the faith, free of bondage and full of living witness?

True Halakhah neither denies the commandments of God nor the freedom given to us through the Gospel message. Secure in our relationship with the Father through faith in Yeshua, His Son, we are called to a walk with God in fellowship with the Holy Spirit. Scripture is brought to life through this walk and is no longer flat and theoretical. This true Halakhah depends on the life of the Holy Spirit being in us as we seek to interpret Scripture. The living God, by His Holy Spirit leads us to live by the principles of Scripture step by step. When we learn to walk with Him we become conscious of His willingness to walk with us and teach us along the way. We are called to be friends of God, growing into a mature application of Scripture in an individual walk with God. Herein lies our security against both lawlessness or dry legality. This is our inheritance in Yeshua, recovering the fellowship with the Father that was lost through Adam and Eve. This was Paul's central theme of teaching. Far from leading us away from obedience to God's 'law' he showed us that the true walk of faith, was to be through our relationship with the Father and Son through His Spirit. Halakhah fails when it becomes a set of rules for the interpretation of Scripture, whether out of Judaism or Christianity. Halakhah means 'walk' and we walk out our faith in fellowship with the Living God. This is an experience founded on Scripture as fulfilled in Yeshua. This is the only true Halakhah for all who are saved through faith in Yeshua, whether from among the Jews or from the Gentile nations.

For as many as are led by the Spirit of God, they are the sons of

God. For ye have not received the spirit of bondage again to fear; but ye have received the Spirit of adoption, whereby we cry, Abba, Father. (Romans 8:14-15)

For study and meditation:
Consider the walk with God that Enoch had (Genesis 5:22-24).
Consider the walk with God that the Hebrews had in the wilderness (Exodus).
Consider the walk with Yeshua on the road to Emmaus (Luke 24).
Read Romans 8.

Halakhah

The Walk of Faith

If our life of faith is likened to a walk then we are right to consider where we are going, and what God expects of us on the journey. The Bible contains a number of examples for us to consider.

One of the most important examples is the journey of the Children of Israel through the wilderness. They left Egypt and began a physical journey to the Promised Land. On this journey they were to learn all of God's requirements for their lives. They learned the practical aspects of Torah for living their lives as a holy community of God's people. However, this journey was also to be a spiritual journey, in which they were intended to learn to walk by faith. It is made clear in the book of Hebrews (Chapters 3 and 4), that their journey should have resulted in faith in God. It is also clear that this was the most important part of their walk with God and one in which a whole generation failed:

> *Who were they who heard and rebelled? Were they not all those Moses led out of Egypt? And with whom was he angry for forty years? Was it not with those who sinned, whose bodies fell in the desert? And to whom did God swear that they would never enter his rest if not to those who disobeyed ? So we see that they were not able to enter, because of their unbelief. (Hebrews 3:16-19)*

Their journey was to the Promised Land and we are intended to learn from their example. This fact is mentioned by Paul in the First Epistle to the Corinthians:

> *Now all these things happened unto them for ensamples: and they are written for our admonition, upon whom the ends of the*

world are come. *(1 Corinthians 10:11)*

If we study the Epistle to the Hebrews carefully, we see that just as Moses led the Children of Israel to the Promised Land, so Yeshua (Jesus) leads us to our promised rest, which is the fulfilment of the Sabbath rest. He leads us to our final resting place. We are on a journey in which our physical life has to be lived, but in which we are to look forward to the final objective of our heavenly home. Just as through our physical journey, like the Children of Israel, we are to apply God's teaching (His Torah) to become holy people, the main objective is to grow in faith for our final resting place in our heavenly home. We are warned that we must not fail in this important issue:

Therefore, since the promise of entering his rest still stands, let us be careful that none of you be found to have fallen short of it. For we also have had the gospel preached to us, just as they did; but the message they heard was of no value to them, because those who heard did not combine it with faith. (Hebrews 4:1-2)

This gives us a very important principal for the way we understand Halakhah. When we study the foundational books of Torah (the first five books of the Bible) we find many rules that are associated with holy living. Indeed, we are people living in this world and we need to know how to live to please God. We must consider this aspect of Halakhah in some detail, but we must realise that there is also a higher goal for our life of obedience and faith. We must not let this higher goal be a licence for sin in this world, but we must have this higher goal in mind. If we do not lay this foundation for our Halakhah (walk of faith) then we might be tempted to form some sort of Messianic Halakhah which is based on works alone and even be diverted into the sort of short-sightedness and self-righteousness that typified the teachers of Torah at the time of Yeshua (Jesus). In humility, therefore, we should establish this foundational principle of our walk of faith.

The writer to the Hebrews goes on to consider the importance of this faith, particularly in Chapters 10 and 11 of the Epistle:

Now faith is being sure of what we hope for and certain of what we do not see. This is what the ancients were commended for. (Hebrews 11:1-2)

Among the ancients who were commended by God we find Enoch. Very little is written about him, but the major thing is recorded in Genesis 5:24:

Enoch walked with God; then he was no more, because God took him away.

Before Moses and even before Abraham we have a testimony of a man who pleased God, walking with him by faith so well that God simply took him away. Surely this gives an important clue to the goal of this faith, of which Habakkuk wrote and which was later quoted by the writer to the Hebrews:

The righteous will live by his faith (Habakkuk 2:4, Hebrews 10:38)

Much is said of the life of faith among believers today. It is an error to consider this faith as relevant only to our life on earth, as some seem to do. Of course, just as the Children of Israel learned to depend on God for their daily provision in the wilderness, so it is a part of our walk of faith to depend on God for our daily needs. While this is important, the higher object for our faith is the goal of our salvation in Yeshua, the promised rest after all the troubles and trials of this life. This is the life that the righteous will live that Habakkuk foresaw and which the writer to the Hebrews emphasised.

Abraham is our 'father' regarding this faith (Romans 4:11-16). He gives us the supreme model and the Book of Genesis contains all the relevant details. From his first steps of faith coming out of Ur of the Chaldees, to the supreme test on Mount Moriah we follow his progress and growth in faith. In Isaac, his son, the focus of his faith is to be fulfilled, that he will have multitudes of descendants from all nations. We learn later in the Bible that this promise referred to those who would inherit salvation faith:

Nor because they are his descendants are they all Abraham's children. On the contrary, 'It is through Isaac that your offspring will be reckoned.' In other words, it is not the natural children who are God's children, but it is the children of the promise who are regarded as Abraham's offspring. (Romans 9:7-8)

The promise is given in Genesis 17:

As for me, this is my covenant with you: You will be the father of many nations. No longer will you be called Abram ; your name will be Abraham, for I have made you a father of many nations. (Genesis 17:4-5)

It is fulfilled in Revelation 7:

After this I looked and there before me was a great multitude that no one could count, from every nation, tribe, people and language, standing before the throne and in front of the Lamb. They were wearing white robes and were holding palm branches in their hands. And they cried out in a loud voice: 'Salvation belongs to our God, who sits on the throne, and to the Lamb. (Revelation 7:9-10)

The covenant promise given to Abraham is the foundational issue of all Scripture. It was fulfilled through the sacrificial death of Yeshua. Our inclusion in the covenant promise is the goal and hope of our lives. We please God if we have faith which is the substance of this hope (Hebrews 11: 1,6). This faith can only be acquired as a gift of God, however (Ephesians 2:8).

What then, is this walk of faith, our Halakhah? We must not be short sighted. Our Halakhah, like Abraham's, has in view a city without foundations whose architect and builder is God (Hebrews 11:10). There are many practical aspects of our everyday life to consider as we walk according to this faith while on this earth. This too is Halakhah. However, the supreme goal is to live in humble and thankful submission to God so that through our daily experiences we will grow in salvation faith. If we do not establish this fact then we might fall short of the mark and consider Halakhah as only relating to our interpretation of Torah in practical ways for this life, as many are prone to do.

For study and meditation:
Read the Epistle to the Hebrews.
Read Genesis 12 to 25.
Read Romans 3 to 5.

Halakhah

Seek Those Things Which Are Above (Colossians 3:1)

Halakhah is important to every disciple of the Lord Jesus Christ (Yeshua HaMashiach). The primary goal is the life of faith and the primary objective is the final abiding place in the heavenly kingdom. We must never lose this vision. However, once we have established this ultimate goal, we must recognise that we also have a practical life to live on this earth, and we must all decide how to order our lives on account of our faith. We cannot simply think about what the Bible teaches and not do it. We are not philosophers alone. We must be practitioners. We must find the principles of our life of faith and then do them. This applies to every aspect of our life, but while this is a high priority, most of us fail in one way or another in understanding or applying this teaching. Even at the time when Yeshua walked on this earth, and even though the interpreters of the law of Moses were in error, the Lord emphasised the importance of Halakhah:

> The scribes and the Pharisees sit in Moses' seat: all therefore what-soever they bid you observe, that observe and do. (Matthew 23:2-3)

Torah (the teaching of God) is what we must study, and Halakhah (the way that we walk) is how we apply this teaching. Throughout our life-time we must both learn and apply all that God will teach us by His Spirit and through the written Word, the Bible. This walk of faith requires us to be good students. It is not easy to balance faith for our final resting place with practical steps for each day. One extreme of our interpretation of Torah can bring negligence of the practical things of a holy life. The other extreme can bring short-sighted legalism.

It was short-sighted legalism that Yeshua condemned in the teachers of Torah of His day, which had led to them having self-righteous attitudes. Indeed, they had so misinterpreted Torah that they failed to recognise Yeshua Himself, the fulfilment of Torah. His penetrating words condemned them:

> Woe unto you, scribes and Pharisees, hypocrites! for ye pay tithe of mint and anise and cummin, and have omitted the weightier matters of the law, judgment, mercy, and faith: these ought ye to have done, and not to leave the other undone. Ye blind guides, which strain at a gnat, and swallow a camel. (Matthew 23:23-24)

It may even be fear of this extreme that throws some of us to the other extreme. In trying to learn from the mistakes of the Jews of Yeshua's day or of the Children of Israel in the wilderness, it is possible that we neglect the Law of Moses completely, thinking that it does not apply to us now. Rather than seeking a balanced view and a balanced lifestyle, it is possible, as many have done, to neglect practical aspects of Torah, thinking that the teaching of Moses has been replaced by the teaching of Yeshua.

A key to understanding comes in Paul's letter to the Corinthians:

> Moreover, brethren, I would not that ye should be ignorant, how that all our fathers were under the cloud, and all passed through the sea; and were all baptized unto Moses in the cloud and in the sea; and did all eat the same spiritual meat; and did all drink the same spiritual drink: for they drank of that spiritual Rock that followed them: and that Rock was Christ. But with many of them God was not well pleased: for they were overthrown in the wilderness. Now these things were our examples, to the intent we should not lust after evil things, as they also lusted. (1 Corinthians 10:1-6)

At first sight we might be tempted to read this as implying that those who came out of Egypt were baptized into Moses while we are baptized into Yeshua. We might take the walk through the wilderness as only symbolic. Yet, closer reading of the whole of the letter shows us that Paul is using this teaching to show the Corinthians that they must not make the same mistakes as the Children of Israel did. Elsewhere (in the Epistle to the Hebrews, for example) we are shown that there is indeed a symbolic meaning to the wilderness walk of the Children of Israel, but we must also realise that there is a practical teaching that we should learn as well. Indeed, Paul specifically warned the Corinthians that they should not fall into the sins of the flesh that beset the Children of Israel - a very practical reminder of the Law of Moses!

We need to consider what this means for us, because Israel's experience was intended as an example to us. First, let us consider Israel. Their wilderness experience seems at first sight to be simply connected with practical lifestyle, practical application of Torah. One might imagine that they were given a practical experience that would lead us to a spiritual experience. However, Paul, in his letter to the Corinthians, shows that behind the practical walk was also the experience of Christ. Through all the symbolism within their practical experience was the pointer to the life of faith in Him. This is why the covenant with Abraham was given before the Law of Moses. The two were to be lived in harmony. Faith was the higher call, but it was to be within the reality of practical applications of Torah for the covenant community. The criticism of Israel was that they did not combine their response to the message given to them with faith (Hebrews 4:2). In the end they turned their Halakhah into dead works that missed the goal of their faith, namely, Yeshua (Romans 10:4).

The message of Paul to the Corinthians is that it is the same for us as it was for them. Of course, we have the benefit of knowing more fully the revelation of Yeshua and we have been given the Holy Spirit to write the Law on our hearts. While taking this into account, we must recognise that Paul warned the Corinthians about sins of the flesh in particular, showing that the practical aspects of Torah are relevant to us as they were to the Children of Israel and that, despite all, it is possible to miss the mark. The issue is not about the relevance of Torah, including the Law of Moses, but how we should understand and obey it.

Before us is a walk of faith. If we lower our sights we will see Torah as simply a set of rules for life and our Halakhah could become a bondage or a route to self-righteousness. If we see that the goal of Torah is the life of faith, we are ready to interpret Torah in all its fullness, correctly interpreting the practical requirements in the light of Messiah. This is what the Children of Israel failed to do and this is what the Corinthians (like us) might also have failed to do. It is not easy. True Halakhah is the goal of our lives. We are to discover how to walk with God by faith, with our mind on things above, in fellowship with the Holy Spirit, who will enable us to interpret all of God's Torah, including the teaching given through Moses, into a practical lifestyle. Our Halakhah is to be both spiritual and practical.

For Study and Meditation:
Read 1Corinthians 9 and 10.
Read Romans 10.
Read James 1.
Read Matthew 5-7.

Halakhah

Baptism to Yeshua

To fulfil the Lord's call to walk (Halakh) with Him, we must respond to His invitation to be united with Him by the power of His Spirit. This is brought about by a spiritual baptism associated with repentance and faith. Our walk of faith and baptism to Yeshua and His covenant community is within the Covenant that God made with Abraham:

As for me, behold, my covenant is with thee, and thou shalt be a father of many nations. Neither shall thy name any more be called Abram, but thy name shall be Abraham; for a father of many nations have I made thee. And I will make thee exceeding fruitful, and I will make nations of thee, and kings shall come out of thee. And I will establish my covenant between me and thee and thy seed after thee in their generations for an everlasting covenant, to be a God unto thee, and to thy seed after thee. (Genesis 17:4-7)

Within the framework of this Covenant made with Abraham, based on faith, the Lord made another Covenant through Moses, pointing to repentance. The Children of Israel came before the Lord at Mount Sinai to receive the Covenant by which they would be required to order their lives as a holy nation. They were given God's requirements through Moses. Within this Covenant was given a means for the forgiveness of sins through the sacrifice of animals. Through the failure of the Children of Israel, we learn that repentance is necessary, but it is not sufficient, even with the sacrificial system of the Tabernacle and Temple, to attain the righteousness required by God. A new Covenant in the blood of Yeshua HaMashiach (Jesus the Messiah) is the only means of obtaining this righteousness:

Behold, the days come, saith the LORD, that I will make a new covenant with the house of Israel, and with the house of Judah: not according to the covenant that I made with their fathers in the day that I took them by the hand to bring them out of the land of Egypt; which my covenant they brake, although I was an husband unto them, saith the LORD: but this shall be the covenant that I will make with the house of Israel; After those days, saith the LORD, I will put my law in their inward parts, and write it in their hearts; and will be their God, and they shall be my people. (Jeremiah 31:31-33)

Salvation is by repentance and through faith in Yeshua. While the Torah given through Moses is holy, it is only through the righteousness imputed to us through Yeshua that we can be saved, becoming members of the covenant community promised to Abraham. Saved by grace and not through works, we embark on our walk as disciples of Yeshua.

There is no escaping the reality that a spiritual transformation is required in us if we are to become members of the covenant community. This transformation is the work of God by His Holy Spirit. We require a baptism of the Holy Spirit for the cleansing of our hearts so that we can be born anew into the kingdom of heaven. No external works or physical exercise will bring this about and it is entirely a work of God to the willing and repentant sinner. There is a spiritual immersion required at a meeting place with God for all who are called into the covenant community. It is more than indoctrination, more than philosophy, it is a spiritual transformation and an immersion into God's Holy Spirit beginning with repentance and faith in Yeshua. This same Holy Spirit is the enabler of our ability to grow in faith and grow in holiness as disciples of Yeshua. If we are to truly walk with God, that is live out our Halakhah experience, we must live in the experience of this spiritual transformation. We cannot side-step it if we are to live fulfilled Halakhah.

While this is a totally spiritual experience, and can be given by God independent of any physical practice, God has chosen to offer us a meeting place with Him through water baptism. Here, a spiritual truth can be paralleled by the physical symbol. As we begin on our road of discipleship, our walk with God, our Halakhah, we would be wise to relate it to the unity with Yeshua that water baptism symbolises and which is brought about through a spiritual baptism of our hearts. This spiritual transformation is the only means of discovering true Halakhah.

Ritual immersion in water was practised among ancient nations, even before Israel was a nation. The qualities of water symbolised spiritual power. Sometimes magic was associated with ritual immersion, wherein it was thought that the water itself contained the power of gods or demons. Immersion in water for ritual washing became a practice among the Jews. It was associated with purification for Temple service and it was sometimes connected with conversion from other faiths. It was realised that immersion in water could not itself wash away sins of the heart, while being a practical means of demonstrating the desire for that inner truth. As with many aspects of the Torah of God, a practical exercise was an aid to and a link with a deeper spiritual reality. The echo of truth relating to the crossing of the Red Sea by the Israelites was contained in the ritual washings relating to purification from sin. The passing through the Red Sea was likened to a baptism involving death, burial and resurrection. God has taken the ancient practice of ritual immersion, cleansed of any ideas of magical powers, and offers it to repentant sinners as a meeting place for their initiation into discipleship, immersed in His Spirit and into Yeshua.

At the time of Yeshua, there was a growing movement around the Jordan River calling for repentant sinners to be baptised. At the baptism, witnesses (particularly the baptiser) would stand and verify the self-baptism of repentant sinners who totally immersed themselves in water, face downwards. John the baptiser had the special call from God to fulfil the commission of Isaiah 40:3. Repentant sinners from all Israel came to him at the Jordan for baptism. These repentant sinners were obeying the call of God, and expressed their desire for inner purification through their act of ritual immersion, because of which God sealed them for the coming

Kingdom. Into the midst of these repentant sinners, who had no means of saving themselves, came the sinless Yeshua. In fulfilment of righteousness, he was baptised before John and in the presence of the company of repentant sinners. In submitting Himself to baptism, He became completely identified with helpless sinners, whose hearts are moved to repentance. He knew that their salvation would only be complete through Him. Just as Moses led the Children of Israel to the Promised Land, so Yeshua, in complete solidarity with repentant sinners, committed Himself to leading them to the 'Promised Land' of the Kingdom of Heaven. The extent of Yeshua's commitment to all repentant sinners, whether at the Jordan that day or in future years, was that the symbols of death, burial and resurrection of His baptism pointed forward to His death on the Cross, His burial in the tomb and His resurrection on the third day. The commitment was made that day at the Jordan River and the Holy Spirit came upon Yeshua empowering Him for His ministry.

Among Yeshua's last words (Matthew 28:19), was the command for His future disciples to be baptised. Having heard the preaching of the Gospel those who respond will come to repentance and faith. They are called upon to take the step of baptism as they begin the walk of discipleship, going on to learn all that Yeshua would expect of His disciples (their Halakhah). The empowering given by the Holy Spirit, as at the Day of Pentecost (Acts 2), is the essential means by which the inner transformation takes place and whereby the disciple is empowered for service. Water baptism is offered to future disciples as the practical means of bringing them to a meeting place with God. Just as Yeshua declared His solidarity with repentant sinners through water baptism, so repentant sinners are given the opportunity of declaring their solidarity with Him through their water baptism. Before witnesses they declare their faith and commitment. As they go through the waters of baptism they should expect to experience death in Yeshua's death, death to the carnal and sinful nature, burial of the old man under the atoning blood of Yeshua, and resurrection in the power of Yeshua's resurrection, into Kingdom life. This is more than the baptism of John, because it goes beyond repentance – into new life. A believer's baptism affords an appropriate time for asking the Holy Spirit to bring the spiritual manifestations of the new birth and the equipping for discipleship and works of service. The newly baptised believer rises from the water expecting to now live in union with Yeshua, committed to a holy life and sealed with faith, the substance of the hope for eternal life.

Water baptism is offered to believers as a practical step in relation to a deep commitment to Yeshua, and as a profound commitment to discipleship. It should be a natural step for those who are called to partake of eternal life. Because Yeshua Himself offered this meeting place, instructing His disciples to undergo baptism, it is to be considered as an important step which God will honour by the power of His Spirit. Since Yeshua demonstrated solidarity with repentant sinners even to commitment to death on the Cross, it is appropriate that we, in humility, make our step of commitment to Him. Whether we take the opportunity of water baptism or not, the spiritual change and commitment of the believer that baptism represents cannot be ignored if we are to fulfil our Halakhah, our walk with God, as disciples of Yeshua.

For Study and Meditation:
John 1.
Matthew 3.
Romans 6-8.
Matthew 26-28.

Halakhah

Friends of God

The plan of salvation is a story that is more intimate than any love story on earth. The closest that the Bible comes to revealing the intimacy of this love story, in terms of human relationships, is the Song of Solomon. Here is a pure account of loving relationships at human level, which maintains its purity within the context of sensuality. As we read the account, we might just dare to believe that this story could be a parable of the love between the Lord and His Bride, the Covenant Community of all of His disciples.

This idea is amplified through the most profound Torah principle of all: the unity in marriage between a man and his wife. Much, if not all, of Torah has practical activities or principles that teach us about higher things. So it is with marriage. Paul makes this plain as he merges the principles of marriage with the principles of relationship between Yeshua (Jesus) and the Church, in Ephesians 5:

> So ought men to love their wives as their own bodies. He that loveth his wife loveth himself. For no man ever yet hated his own flesh; but nourisheth and cherisheth it, even as the Lord the church: for we are members of his body, of his flesh, and of his bones. For this cause shall a man leave his father and mother, and shall be joined unto his wife, and they two shall be one flesh. This is a great mystery: but I speak concerning Christ and the church. Nevertheless let every one of you in particular so love his wife even as himself; and the wife see that she reverence her husband. (Ephesians 5:28-33)

Indeed, this is a principle of Halakhah, Torah in action. We cannot sit at home simply thinking about principles of marriage, they are to be lived, and in living them we are also walking with God. Marriage is where the second Great Commandment concerning love at the human level (loving our neighbour as ourself) is worked out most intimately, and where we have the deepest meditation from a human standpoint regarding the higher truth of the first Great Commandment:

> Thou shalt love the LORD thy God with all thine heart, and with all thy soul, and with all thy might.

It is a lifelong challenge to learn what this means, but neither the first nor second commandment is empty and harsh, requiring religious response that is bereft of relationship. Indeed, in the purest sense, these commandments are invitations to loving relationship. Through practice of loving relationship at the human level, the most intimate expression being between husband and wife, we are to begin to learn about the love of God.

Another way of understanding this is through the principle of knowing. The concept of 'knowing' is related to intimacy or familiarity. At the lowest level this applies to practical things of life. If we have knowledge of a fact or idea, we have familiarity with it. The more we know, the more this fact or idea is part of us so that we can use it quite freely and naturally. In relationships too, knowledge of a person is related to intimacy that goes far deeper than formal relationships. There is a sympathy and an empathy in knowledge of a person - a relationship with the person. At the deepest level, knowledge is spiritual and is the result of mature and loving relationships that draw people together. Through the best of human relationships (all of which are unfortunately tarnished by sin) we can just begin to understand the relationship that the Lord God has prepared for us through Yeshua. The relationship of men and women with God was spoiled in the Garden of Eden. Salvation through Yeshua is to reconcile men and women with God, restoring what was lost. This is why Yeshua prayed for this before He went to the Cross:

> Father, the hour is come; glorify thy Son, that thy Son also may

glorify thee: as thou hast given him power over all flesh, that he should give eternal life to as many as thou hast given him. And this is life eternal, that they might know thee the only true God, and Jesus Christ, whom thou hast sent. (John 17:1-3)

His purpose was not that we might know about the Father and His Son Yeshua but that we might know the Father and the Son. We are to experience this knowledge and not simply think about it. This is why Torah is a set of static, potentially lifeless, principles until it becomes Halakhah. We are reborn into our salvation in order that we walk out and experience our life of faith in living relationship and unity with the Lord God, in the purest and most intimate relationship.

Abraham is our father regarding the walk of faith, and the most important thing that was said of him was that he was the friend of God:

And the scripture was fulfilled which saith, Abraham believed God, and it was imputed unto him for righteousness: and he was called the Friend of God. (James 2:23)

But thou, Israel, art my servant, Jacob whom I have chosen, the seed of Abraham my friend. (Isaiah 41:8)

The sons of Abraham are intended to be like him. It is our inheritance to be called friends of God. How many friends does God really have in this fallen world? He is not looking for self-righteous legalists, but softhearted friends, who desire to live in purity but realise their need of a Saviour. Abraham achieved the great commendation of being a friend of God because he found the path of faith in his walk of obedience. He, like us, was imperfect, but he was willing to let God walk with Him, teach him and strengthen him through faith. He was a friend of God because he knew how to walk with God.

There is a senior partner in this walk. It is the Lord Himself to which we are yoked, but He has promised to make our walk easy if we will go His way:

Come unto me, all ye that labour and are heavy laden, and I will give you rest. Take my yoke upon you, and learn of me; for I am meek and lowly in heart: and ye shall find rest unto your souls. (Matthew 11:28-29)

Abraham was God's friend because he was willing to be taught how to walk with Him according to God's principles and requirements. It must be the same for us. As the Scripture says:

Can two walk together, except they be agreed? (Amos 3:3)

We have then, an invitation to walk with God through all of our life. This is to be a walk in loving friendship, intimate fellowship, growing deeper as the days go by. Such friendship is personal and experiential, where we talk as we walk, where we listen and learn and grow in faith that pleases our Lord with whom we are walking more closely than with any earthly friend, part of Him, bound to Him in covenant relationship. Will it be said of us as we learn Halakhah, that we are a friend of God? Moreover, as all of God's friends learn how to walk with Him, they are together being prepared as a bride for a husband. Our Halakhah starts with the relationship of friendship and ends with a marriage supper.

For Study and Meditation:
Song of Songs.
John 17.
Ephesians 5.
James 2:14-26.
Revelation 19:5-9.

Halakhah

Flee from Idolatry

Torah combines both positive and negative principles to help us to stay on the narrow road that leads to life (Matthew 7:14). The most important positive command is that we must love the Lord our God with all our heart, soul, mind and strength. This lies behind all of God's teaching. The first Commandment is the negative counterpart of this:

> I am the LORD thy God, which have brought thee out of the land of Egypt, out of the house of bondage. Thou shalt have no other gods before me. Thou shalt not make unto thee any graven image, or any likeness of any thing that is in heaven above, or that is in the earth beneath, or that is in the water under the earth: Thou shalt not bow down thyself to them, nor serve them: for I the LORD thy God am a jealous God, visiting the iniquity of the fathers upon the children unto the third and fourth generation of them that hate me; and showing mercy unto thousands of them that love me, and keep my commandments. (Exodus 20:2-6)

Idolatry is the major sin to be avoided. Because it is of the utmost importance, we can be sure that there will be temptations along the path of life related to this. There are many ways we can be seduced gradually away from that one main objective of loving our Lord God in an undivided way. When we realise this, we will discover that the warning to flee idolatry is behind much of Torah, giving us an important principle to remember along the path of life.

The Book of Proverbs shows how wisdom is the spiritual gift that enables us to walk the path of life that is pleasing to God. If we are walking according to the wisdom of God we are walking in fellowship with God, in the life of His Spirit. The temptations that divert us from the true path of life are likened, by contrast, to a seductive woman:

> My son, keep thy father's commandment, and forsake not the law of thy mother: bind them continually upon thine heart, and tie them about thy neck. When thou goest, it shall lead thee; when thou sleepest, it shall keep thee; and when thou awakest, it shall talk with thee. For the commandment is a lamp; and the law is light; and reproofs of instruction are the way of life: to keep thee from the evil woman, from the flattery of the tongue of a strange woman. Lust not after her beauty in thine heart; neither let her take thee with her eyelids. For by means of a whorish woman a man is brought to a piece of bread: and the adulteress will hunt for the precious life. (Proverbs 4:20-26)

Just as a pure marriage is a profound parable for the relationship between the Lord and His Church, so harlotry is a parable of being seduced to follow foreign gods.

The most serious sin of the Children of Israel was following false gods. Even when Moses was on the mountain receiving the Ten Commandments the Children of Israel were building a golden calf like the gods of Egypt (Exodus 32). Despite all that they were taught, they continued to fall into this sin, as the prophets declared so often:

> Hast thou seen that which backsliding Israel hath done? she is gone up upon every high mountain and under every green tree, and there hath played the harlot. And I said after she had done all these things, Turn thou unto me. But she returned not. And her treacherous sister Judah saw it. And I saw, when for all the causes whereby backsliding Israel committed adultery I had put her away, and given her a bill of divorce; yet her treacherous sister Judah feared not, but went and played the harlot also. And it came to pass through the lightness of her whoredom, that she defiled the land, and committed adultery with stones and with stocks. (Jeremiah 3:6-9)

There are many ways of making and worshipping idols. They are not necessarily the sticks and stones that typified ancient cultures. Anything that takes priority in the heart over our love for God can become an idol and the spiritual powers that would try to seduce us have ways of taking us gradually off into spiritual adultery. As we walk forward as disciples of Yeshua we must be aware of this.

Torah is intended to teach us discernment, the difference between right and wrong. The Lord teaches us through contrasts. It is even said that Yeshua would learn discernment in this way, typified by the sweet and sour contrast of curds and honey:

> *Therefore the Lord himself shall give you a sign; Behold, a virgin shall conceive, and bear a son, and shall call his name Immanuel. Curds and honey shall he eat, that he may know to refuse the evil, and choose the good. (Isaiah 7:14-15)*

Discernment as the goal of the mature is emphasised in the Epistle to the Hebrews:

> *But strong meat belongeth to them that are of full age, even those who by reason of use have their senses exercised to discern both good and evil. (Hebrews 5:14)*

The most important evil to discern is that which seduces a person to idolatry. How sad it is when a person is so seduced that he or she serves the powers of Satan thinking that he or she is serving the One True God.

The importance of this is emphasised through the teaching of the Council of Jerusalem (Acts 15). When Gentiles were beginning to be saved, a problem arose as to how the Law of Moses might apply to them. A council was called in Jerusalem, which followed the model of a Bet Din (House of Judgement). In accordance with Jewish tradition, whenever an issue of Halakhah arose a ruling of the eldership was sought. Thus, the Council of Jerusalem was the place where an issue of Halakhah relating to those saved from the Gentile nations was discussed. Paul gave evidence as to how the

Holy Spirit was at work among the Gentiles, and there was vigorous discussion as to how converts should be expected to follow the Law of Moses. James summed up the halakhik ruling:

> *Wherefore my sentence is, that we trouble not them, which from among the Gentiles are turned to God: but that we write unto them, that they abstain from pollutions of idols, and from fornication, and from things strangled, and from blood. (Acts 15:19-20)*

There is explicit reference to idols. Indeed, it can be argued that all of these four injunctions have some link with spiritual adultery. These injunctions seems to be a reference to what are called the noahide laws (principles given directly to Noah), which are also emphasised in the teaching of Moses (Leviticus 17). The eating of meat sacrificed to idols can be linked to spiritual adultery, and the cleansing of meat from its blood (which is not possible with strangled animals) is associated with keeping separate from impure life sources. Sexual adultery has clear relationship with making intimate partnerships with adulterous spiritual powers. It can be argued that these injunctions, from the Council of Jerusalem, pointed towards the care with which disciples of the Lord Yeshua should keep away from things that were associated with idolatry and spiritual adultery - teaching that has been passed on from the time of Noah. Out of the whole scope of Torah, at this important council came a specific warning to be guarded against idolatry and spiritual adultery, the very sins that Israel as a nation committed over and over again.

We recall that it was sins equivalent to those major sins that brought down King Saul. As Samuel pointed out, when Saul had failed God:

> *For rebellion is as the sin of witchcraft, and stubbornness is as iniquity and idolatry. Because thou hast rejected the word of the LORD, he hath also rejected thee from being king. (1 Samuel 15:23)*

Paul, in the context of his teaching on communion, also warned

of these things:

> *Wherefore, my dearly beloved, flee from idolatry. (1 Corinthians 10:14)*

As we set out on our walk of faith, we are to seek to be united with the Lord alone. He will teach us His ways. He will teach us how to interpret Torah into Halakhah, but at the very start, it is wise to take heed of the warning that our chief battles are against the seductions that seek to rob us of this relationship.

Having said this, we are not to live a life of uncertainty. Providing we look for purity in our walk, our Jewish heritage assures us that we are to enjoy a full life on this earth. If we are free of idolatry and guarded against spiritual seduction, our life can be full to the brim of all the good things that the Lord would give us. While guarding our hearts against the evil one, we are to live in the joy and provision of the Lord, as we walk with Him.

For Study and Meditation:
Read Proverbs 1 to 9.
Read Acts 15.

Halakhah

The Blessing of Discipleship

Disciples of the Lord Jesus Christ (Yeshua HaMashiach) must have a balanced approach to all of Scripture. They need to be confident to use both the Old and the New Testament, including the Law of Moses, as a basis for study and practice. True Halakhah is not ritualistic, but neither is it a licence to sin. James had this truth in mind when he wrote:

But whoso looketh into the perfect law of liberty, and continueth therein, he being not a forgetful hearer, but a doer of the work, this man shall be blessed in his deed. (James 1:25)

This statement shows us the perfect balance of studying Torah (the whole of God's teaching programme of the Old and New Testaments), applying it, living in freedom and being blessed by God.

One of the reasons why some people find it difficult to study and apply the teaching of the Old Testament, which is in fact foundational for our Halakhah, is that there is confusion regarding the blessings and curses.

There is no doubt that Israel lived in the context of both blessing and curse. It is written:

Behold, I set before you this day a blessing and a curse; a blessing, if ye obey the commandments of the LORD your God, which I command you this day: and a curse, if ye will not obey the com- mandments of the LORD your God, but turn aside out of the way which I command you this day, to go after other gods, which ye have not known. (Deuteronomy 11:26-28)

These words were not said lightly and God fulfilled them to the letter. For example, we read about the time when a curse was over Israel at the time of David:

There was a famine for three successive years; so David sought the face of the LORD. The LORD said, 'It is on account of Saul and his blood-stained house; it is because he put the Gibeonites to death.' (2 Samuel 21:1)

Furthermore, when Israel continued to sin they were eventually exiled, according to what God had said to Solomon:

'But if you turn away and forsake the decrees and commands I have given you and go off to serve other gods and worship them, then I will uproot Israel from my land, which I have given them, and will reject this temple I have consecrated for my Name. I will make it a byword and an object of ridicule among all peoples. And though this temple is now so imposing, all who pass by will be appalled and say, 'Why has the LORD done such a thing to this land and to this temple?' People will answer, 'Because they have forsaken the LORD, the God of their fathers, who brought them out of Egypt, and have embraced other gods, worshiping and serving them--that is why he brought all this disaster on them.'' (2 Chronicles 7:19-22)

Israel came under the curse of the Law, quite literally, and the consequences of this are set before us as we seek to study Torah for ourselves. Hence, we must be very clear on how this applies to true disciples of the Lord Yeshua, who also said:

So in everything, do to others what you would have them do to you, for this sums up the Law and the Prophets. 'Enter through the narrow gate. For wide is the gate and broad is the road that leads to destruction, and many enter through it. But small is the gate and narrow the road that leads to life, and only a few find it. (Matthew 7:12-14)

The key to understanding begins with the sacrificial system, which was also within the framework of Torah. There was a means of reconciliation with God if there was true repentance from the people of Israel. The sacrificial system of the Temple was established to give a means by which true repentance could be expressed. A telling example of repentance is found in Psalm 51. King David should have lost his life for his adultery with Bathsheba, but he was spared through true repentance. This was always possible within the framework of the Old Covenant, but there was not a permanent remedy. It was unrepentant Israel who came under the curse of Torah, and it was inevitable that this would happen.

The main lesson that we learn from Israel is that no person can achieve righteousness through works of the Law of Moses. If we try to obtain righteousness through obeying this Law in the manner it was first given to Israel, eventually we will fail. The Law is so high and holy that those with an unregenerate heart will fail. This is why Paul teaches us that the prime purpose of the Law of Moses is to reveal sin and point to the need of our Saviour, rather than bring us to salvation independent of our Him (Romans 7:7).

Yeshua came to free us from the bondage of this curse. If it were not for His permanent sacrifice for us then we would all come under the curse of the Law today. It is this curse that Yeshua has removed, not the Law itself, whose requirements still stand, albeit that we will fail to achieve them perfectly:

> *Christ redeemed us from the curse of the law by becoming a curse for us, for it is written: 'Cursed is everyone who is hung on a tree.' He redeemed us in order that the blessing given to Abraham might come to the Gentiles through Christ Jesus, so that by faith we might receive the promise of the Spirit. (Galatians 3:13-14)*

The curse of the Law is not the Law itself, but the curse for transgression of the Law. This curse still stands for all outside the Covenant Community of Yeshua, a darkness which is over the face of all the nations of the earth:

Whoever believes in him is not condemned, but whoever does not believe stands condemned already because he has not believed in the name of God's one and only Son. (John 3:18)

All of the teaching of God found in the Bible is relevant to disciples of Yeshua. Disciples of Yeshua are those people who through faith and repentance are bound into Him through the baptism of the Holy Spirit, empowered by His Spirit to manifest the fruit of Torah. Through faith, they are free of the curse that was always before Israel. This gives us the freedom to explore all of the teaching of God and to learn, by the power of the Holy Spirit, to apply it. Halakhah is a joyous walk in freedom of the curse providing we are bound close to our Saviour. This is the blessing of our salvation, that we can please God within the framework of humility and repentance that draws us close to Yeshua. The curse of the Law - the punishment for our transgressions - was laid on Him. This is the basis of our freedom, the cause for our joy and the reason why we, as devoted disciples, should now live to please Him, studying the Torah from the whole of the written Word and letting the Holy Spirit make it manifest on our heart with an overflow of fruitfulness and righteousness. This is blessing indeed.

For Study and Meditation:
Read Deuteronomy 4-11.
Read Romans 1-8.
Read Psalm 51.
Read Lamentations 1-5.
Read Matthew 26-27.

Halakhah

Characteristics of our Halakhah

It is important to establish the fact that Halakhah, for disciples of the Lord Jesus Christ (Yeshua HaMashiach), is not to be totally in the sort of legalistic framework that characterised Jewish Halakhah at the time of Yeshua, and characterises much of Judaism today, based only on formal rulings that appear in the Mishnah and Talmud. It is important to remember this fact in the day of re-establishment of Israel as a nation, a day of great expectancy for a mighty move of the Holy Spirit in bringing many of the nation to salvation in Yeshua. We must, as disciples of Yeshua, be those who live by the power and indwelling of His Spirit to interpret Torah correctly. With the faith of Abraham we must live out the fulfilment of the Law of Moses. This is indeed a walk of faith, a walk that has distinct fruit, distinct characteristics. It is a disciplined walk but not one that brings bondage. The writers of Scripture were familiar with the concept of Halakhah (walking with God) and always saw discipleship in these terms. Thus it was natural for them to consider the way that the truths of Scripture should be living within us and characterising our life. It is a very useful exercise, therefore, to do a word study based on the concept of walking out our faith, to see what the characteristics of our Halakhah should be. We will quote some examples as a beginning to such a study, which can then be completed with the assistance of a Bible Concordance.

For Study and Meditation:

When Abram was ninety-nine years old, the LORD appeared to him and said, 'I am God Almighty ; walk before me and be blameless. (Genesis 17:1)

I will walk among you and be your God, and you will be my people. I am the LORD your God, who brought you out of Egypt so that you would no longer be slaves to the Egyptians; I broke the bars of your yoke and enabled you to walk with heads held high. (Leviticus 26:12-13)

Walk in all the way that the LORD your God has commanded you, so that you may live and prosper and prolong your days in the land that you will possess. (Deuteronomy 5:33)

And now, O Israel, what does the LORD your God ask of you but to fear the LORD your God, to walk in all his ways, to love him, to serve the LORD your God with all your heart and with all your soul, and to observe the Lord's commands and decrees that I am giving you today for your own good? (Deuteronomy 10:12-13)

When the time drew near for David to die, he gave a charge to Solomon his son. 'I am about to go the way of all the earth,' he said. 'So be strong, show yourself a man, and observe what the LORD your God requires: Walk in his ways, and keep his decrees and commands, his laws and requirements, as written in the Law of Moses, so that you may prosper in all you do and wherever you go, and that the LORD may keep his promise to me: 'If your descendants watch how they live, and if they walk faithfully before me with all their heart and soul, you will never fail to have a man on the throne of Israel.' (1 Kings 2:1-4)

Blessed is the man who does not walk in the counsel of the wicked or stand in the way of sinners or sit in the seat of mockers. (Psalm 1:1)

Even though I walk through the valley of the shadow of death, I will fear no evil, for you are with me; your rod and your staff, they comfort me. (Psalm 23:4)

Blessed are they whose ways are blameless, who walk according to the law of the LORD. (Psalm 119:1)

He whose walk is upright fears the LORD, but he whose ways are devious despises him. (Proverbs 14:2)

In the last days the mountain of the Lord's temple will be established as chief among the mountains; it will be raised above the hills, and all nations will stream to it. Many peoples will come and say, 'Come, let us go up to the mountain of the LORD, to the house of the God of Jacob. He will teach us his ways, so that we may walk in his paths.' The law will go out from Zion, the word of the LORD from Jerusalem. (Isaiah 2:2-3)

When Jesus spoke again to the people, he said, 'I am the light of the world. Whoever follows me will never walk in darkness, but will have the light of life.' (John 8:12)

He is also the father of the circumcised who not only are circumcised but who also walk in the footsteps of the faith that our father Abraham had before he was circumcised. (Romans 4:12)

What agreement is there between the temple of God and idols? For we are the temple of the living God. As God has said: 'I will live with them and walk among them, and I will be their God, and they will be my people. Therefore come out from them and be separate, says the Lord. Touch no unclean thing, and I will receive you. I will be a Father to you, and you will be my sons and daughters, says the Lord Almighty.' Since we have these promises, dear friends, let us purify ourselves from everything that contaminates body and spirit, perfecting holiness out of reverence for God. (2 Corinthians 6:16-7:1)

But the fruit of the Spirit is love, joy, peace, patience, kindness, goodness, faithfulness, gentleness and self-control. Against such things there is no law. Those who belong to Christ Jesus have crucified the sinful nature with its passions and desires. Since we live by the Spirit, let us keep in step with the Spirit. (Galatians 5:22-25)

You used to walk in these ways, in the life you once lived. But now you must rid yourselves of all such things as these: anger, rage, malice, slander, and filthy language from your lips. (Colossians 3:7-8)

If we claim to have fellowship with him yet walk in the darkness, we lie and do not live by the truth. But if we walk in the light, as he is in the light, we have fellowship with one another, and the blood of Jesus, his Son, purifies us from all sin. (1 John 1:6-7)

Whoever claims to live in him must walk as Jesus did. (1 John 2:6)

And this is love: that we walk in obedience to his commands. As you have heard from the beginning, his command is that you walk in love. (2 John 1:6)

It gave me great joy to have some brothers come and tell about your faithfulness to the truth and how you continue to walk in the truth. (3 John 1:3)

Yet you have a few people in Sardis who have not soiled their clothes. They will walk with me, dressed in white, for they are worthy. (Revelation 3:4)

The city does not need the sun or the moon to shine on it, for the glory of God gives it light, and the Lamb is its lamp. The nations will walk by its light, and the kings of the earth will bring their splendor into it. (Revelation 23:23-24)

He has showed you, O man, what is good, and what does the LORD require of you? To act justly and to love mercy and to walk humbly with your God. (Micah 6:8)

Halakhah

Community

Each individual is responsible for his or her walk of faith, but the application of Halakhah is mainly related to community. It was a *nation* that came out of Egypt, not a set of individuals. Abraham is to be the father of nations - one family. At the end of time there will be one body of believers collectively known as the Bride of Messiah. Paul taught us that:

We were all baptized by one Spirit into one body–whether Jews or Greeks, slave or free–and we were all given the one Spirit to drink. (1 Corinthians 12:13)

and that:

Now in Christ Jesus you who once were far away have been brought near through the blood of Christ. For he himself is our peace, who has made the two one and has destroyed the barrier, the dividing wall of hostility, by abolishing in his flesh the law with its commandments and regulations. His purpose was to create in himself one new man out of the two, thus making peace, and in this one body to reconcile both of them to God through the cross, by which he put to death their hostility. (Ephesians 2:13-16)

We are a community built out of families and the outworking of our Halakhah is in terms of the relationships that develop among us. How can parents teach their children, if they do not have relationships with them? Why should it be important for husbands to love their wives if family is not the priority of Torah? Why are justice, mercy and care for the lonely, the widows and the orphans a priority if community is not the context of Halakhah?

The Reformation of the Sixteenth Century taught strongly about salvation by faith, but the Church has focussed more on individual salvation than on community life. Therefore, at the heart of our present day restoration of the Church to her true biblical roots, there must be the strengthening of family and community. Thus the principles of Halakhah, a central component of this restoration, must be in relation to family and community life above all else.

Israel came out of Egypt as one nation and stood before Mount Sinai together to receive Torah. Torah is a complete teaching programme for a nation, involving instructions for the family, instructions for the nation coming before God at the times of the Feasts, instructions for commerce and for all manner of social interaction. If our application of Torah fails it is because community life has broken down. This happens when the principle of loving ones neighbours as oneself has not been fulfilled. Hear the words of the prophets who revealed the sins of Israel and Judah:

> You trample on the poor and force him to give you grain.
> Therefore, though you have built stone mansions, you will not live
> in them; though you have planted lush vineyards, you will not
> drink their wine. For I know how many are your offenses and how
> great your sins. You oppress the righteous and take bribes and you
> deprive the poor of justice in the courts. (Amos 5:11-12)

> Is this the kind of fast I have chosen, only a day for a man to
> humble himself? Is it only for bowing one's head like a reed and
> for lying on sackcloth and ashes? Is that what you call a fast, a day
> acceptable to the LORD? Is not this the kind of fasting I have cho-
> sen: to loose the chains of injustice and untie the cords of the
> yoke, to set the oppressed free and break every yoke? Is it not to
> share your food with the hungry and to provide the poor wander-
> er with shelter-- when you see the naked, to clothe him, and not
> to turn away from your own flesh and blood? (Isaiah 58:5-7)

The Ten Commandments are all manifestations of the two great commandments to love the Lord God with all our heart, soul and strength and our neighbours as ourselves. Starting with these commandments and working through all of Torah, we discover that the application of Torah is always through relationships. Israel sinned as a nation and was exiled as a nation. Though each person is responsible before God for his or her sins, the Lord is always building a community to which each individual has responsibility.

As well as praying that each of us, as individuals, should know God (John 17:3), the Lord also prayed that we would be one:

I pray for them: I pray not for the world, but for them which thou hast given me; for they are thine. And all mine are thine, and thine are mine; and I am glorified in them. And now I am no more in the world, but these are in the world, and I come to thee. Holy Father, keep through thine own name those whom thou hast given me, that they may be one, as we are. (John 17:9-11)

The purpose for Israel as they came out of Egypt was that they should be a community that, through their combined Halakhah, would become a light to the world. The building of this community is still the Lord's priority and He, by His grace, has added many that are saved from among the Gentile nations to the covenant community. The priority of family based community still stands, as Paul implied in his teaching (Ephesians 4-6):

And he gave some, apostles; and some, prophets; and some, evangelists; and some, pastors and teachers; for the perfecting of the saints, for the work of the ministry, for the edifying of the body of Christ: till we all come in the unity of the faith, and of the knowledge of the Son of God, unto a perfect man, unto the measure of the stature of the fulness of Christ.........

And walk in love, as Christ also hath loved us, and hath given himself for us an offering and a sacrifice to God for a sweet-smelling savour........

Submitting yourselves one to another in the fear of God. Wives, submit yourselves unto your own husbands, as unto the Lord........

*Honour thy father and mother; which is the first command-
ment.....*

Thus, when we learn Halakhah we should realise that the
application is to be within our relationships in the home and
believing community. Issues relating to our life of faith, while learned
by individuals are also to be learned together. The principle of the
Lord being with us when two or three are gathered in His Name
(Matthew 18:20) implies that He will teach as we meet together. As
we sit around the family table, we can expect the Lord, by His Spirit,
to help us understand matters relating to family life. As the elders of
a congregation meet together, perhaps in the manner of a Yeshiva
(open discussion/ debate), they can expect the Lord, by His Spirit,
to bring understanding to the issues of Halakhah for the community
as a whole, brought to the meeting and discussed prayerfully, in His
presence. Though this seems to be a basic issue, we must
recognise that alternatives can be either to learn Halakhah privately,
as individuals, or to have Halakhah rulings made in a more general
and legalistic framework from some central organisation. Neither of
these alternatives lead to a community full of the Lord's life. The
Lord is building us through families and communities and it is within
this framework that He will teach us together, the way to walk with
Him.

For Study and Meditation:
Read Ephesians.
Read 1 Corinthians 12-14.

Halakhah

Guidance

Even inanimate objects need to be guided. How will a lawnmower cut the grass successfully if it is not guided as it moves forward? How much more do living disciples of the Lord Jesus also need guidance from the Master? However much we have studied the general principles of Scripture, however firmly they are written on our hearts and however much we have learned from others, we still need guidance for the day to day walk with the Lord. Our walk is one of fellowship, one of particular application of the general principles of Scripture. If we do not expect such guidance, we can only expect a walk based on dry principles, a legal framework to our Halakhah. This is not the inheritance of the children of the Living God, who called us into intimate fellowship. Thus as we learn to walk with Him, we must learn how to receive guidance.

There is no formula for this; the Lord communicates in different ways appropriate to each of us, but we can be sure that God, who is the same yesterday, today and forever, can and will communicate to His people as He always has done. We must not be presumptuous, but we must seek Him for guidance. There are still angels. There is still prophecy. There are still visions and dreams and many other ways that God leads.

We must not think that the Lord is a chatterbox. He does not waste His words. If our head is full of ideas then it is probably not the Lord who is speaking, just our fertile mind in action. The Lord does speak, but His guidance is clear and direct. He can say in two words what may take us a lifetime to understand. He was not constantly chattering even to the major biblical prophets - what is recorded in the Scriptures was communicated over many centuries.

Some of the prophets have very small writings, to represent their lifetime's calling. Sometimes the Lord is very quiet and is, in a paradoxical sense, able to say more through silence than through many words.

If we are living in fellowship with Him, we will always have questions and we will be listening for answers, reading the signs in our life, waiting for the clear guidance that will come, but only at the right time and in the Lord's way. When He speaks, He does it in a way that increases fellowship rather than releasing us to independence. One question will lead to another as we seek and receive guidance, as we live in fellowship with the Lord on our walk of faith. The Lord's guidance is always in accord with His character, which has been revealed through Scripture and totally revealed in Yeshua. Thus, we can be sure that any guidance will not be against the pattern of Scripture. Here is the first way that we should test our guidance - and test it we must, for we can be very prone to vain imagination and to seductive influences.

We must also be careful to distinguish guidance from prophecy. We are all called to be prophetic people, but we are not all prophets. There is a prophetic ministry within the Church, but not everyone will be called to this:

And God hath set some in the church, first apostles, secondarily prophets, thirdly teachers, after that miracles, then gifts of heal-ings, helps, governments, diversities of tongue. Are all apostles? are all prophets? are all teachers? are all workers of miracles? (1 Corinthians 12:28-29)

When Moses said:

Would God that all the LORD'S people were prophets, and that the LORD would put his spirit upon them! (Numbers 11:29)

he was looking forward to the day when the prophecy of Joel would be fulfilled, as it began to be dramatically fulfilled on the Day of Pentecost:

And it shall come to pass in the last days, saith God, I will pour out of my Spirit upon all flesh: and your sons and your daughters shall prophesy, and your young men shall see visions, and your old men shall dream dreams: and on my servants and on my handmaidens I will pour out in those days of my Spirit; and they shall prophesy. (Acts 2:17-18)

Guidance is connected with prophecy but it does not make us all prophets. God, through His Spirit, comes alongside us on our walk of faith to guide us according to His will and purpose. When we are submitted to Him, He will take the initiative to guide us. He is looking for willingness to be led according to His purposes and expecting us to pray for guidance, patiently waiting for that guidance to come and patiently learning how to recognise His voice. It was said of Yeshua:

This is my beloved Son, in whom I am well pleased; hear ye him. (Matthew 17:5)

and:

He calleth his own sheep by name, and leadeth them out. And when he putteth forth his own sheep, he goeth before them, and the sheep follow him: for they know his voice. (John 10:3-4)

Some, who are called by God, will hear the voice of the Holy Spirit on behalf of their communities, but all of us should expect to be guided by the Lord as His disciples. This can be in any way that God communicates, as He has always done. The Lord will guide each person, each family and each community.

We must be students of the Scriptures and know the general principles by which we are to live. We must seek to allow the Holy Spirit to impart these principles to our hearts. Then we must walk a prayerful path before our God. He will sometimes mould the circumstances of our lives to guide us, by simply and imperceptibly orientating our lives in accord with His will, so that, in a gentle way by which the circumstances themselves speak to us, we move forward feeling secure in His hands. This does not require a dramatic word. At other times, though He is silent, we continue to move forward on the path before us. Sometimes a Scripture is made alive in our minds to confirm a general principle of guidance. Sometimes He wakes us up with thoughts that He has placed into us. Sometimes He will use visions and dreams, (which, however, should not be interpreted too hastily). In all these ways, guidance can come.

We must all expect to be guided by the Living God. Halakhah is dry and formal without this personal guidance. We are called into fellowship with the Living God, and this fellowship is real. As we grow more in fellowship with the Lord, guidance will become as natural as walking. We will be conscious of the Lord's fellowship in all that we do. The Lord is gentle and patient. His guidance is clear and is not harsh to those listening to Him from moment to moment. In guiding His people as a whole, He will use the ministries of the Church, causing us to be dependent on each other as well as directly dependent on Him. He will give guidance to heads of homes so that they can guide their families. He will shepherd the community through pastors. He will teach through teachers. He will use all the ministries for the edification and guidance of the body as well as walking with us as individuals. We must learn to trust Him for guidance as He builds us up to be His own people.

For Study and Meditation:
Read Psalm 63.
Read John 10.
Read John 14.
Read Hebrews 4:16, 12:25.
Read 1 John 1:1-7.

Halakhah

A Matter of the Heart

Torah is the teaching of God. Halakhah is the 'doing' of Torah. Halakhah depends on our receiving the wisdom of God, which is the spiritual gift that directs us along the path of life, mobilising the principles of Torah into practical action. When wisdom is interpreted into the logic of our minds, we might call it guidance. With heart and mind conscious of the principles of Torah we are to take prayerful steps in our life in fellowship with the Lord Himself. Halakhah is a sensitively balanced matter of heart response within the practical things of life.

When Israel, through Moses, was given the principles of holy living, the way had not been generally opened for Halakhah to proceed from the prompting of the heart. If it had been so there would have been no need for Jeremiah to prophesy:

Behold, the days come, saith the LORD, that I will make a new covenant with the house of Israel, and with the house of Judah: not according to the covenant that I made with their fathers in the day that I took them by the hand to bring them out of the land of Egypt; which my covenant they brake, although I was an husband unto them, saith the LORD: but this shall be the covenant that I will make with the house of Israel; After those days, saith the LORD, I will put my law in their inward parts, and write it in their hearts; and will be their God, and they shall be my people. (Jeremiah 31:31-33)

We must understand our situation in relation to that of Israel, regarding Torah, the Law of Moses and Halakhah. Torah, the whole teaching of God, always required us to live the life of faith (like our father Abraham). The Law of Moses made it explicitly clear what is required of a holy people. These principles stand. When we read them, they seem to be attainable, but we forget the sinful nature that wars against the holy principles of God. Thus, the moment we know about these holy principles and try to put them into practice, sin comes in to prevent us. The result is that the knowledge of principles of holiness simply reveals our inability to live them in all holiness. If faith had been mixed with heart intent to obey the code of holiness, Israel would have been in the same position as we are. They failed, however, and this was to teach us our need of our Yeshua as our permanent sacrifice for sin and the enabling of the Holy Spirit to live by faith. Grafted into the covenant community by faith we are now enabled to walk with God as was intended. This is a matter of the heart, because the principles of Torah are now imparted to our heart. Our call to holiness is the same as that of Israel, but the context has changed to enable us to please God. As James taught, faith should now result in works. The manifestations of Torah should be evident in our Halakhah, as we walk according to the prompting of the Holy Spirit. Our call is the same as for the Children of Israel, but now we can succeed, through Yeshua's sacrifice and through the gift of the Holy Spirit.

The teaching of the New Testament is to be put alongside the teaching of the Tanakh (Old Testament). It is a mistake to see the Scriptures of the New Testament as replacing those of the Old Testament. Torah still contains the revelation of God the Creator, shown in the first book of the Bible. Torah still contains the life of faith typified in the life of Abraham, as taught in the first book of the Bible. The pictures of Messiah which He later fulfilled are still there in all of the Torah, the Prophets and the Writings as He taught the disciples on the Road to Emmaus (Luke 24). The Law of Moses still shows the principles of life for the covenant community. The book of Proverbs still gives us the best teaching on wisdom in the whole Bible. The Book of Psalms still reflects the pattern of worship emerging from every aspect of life, like no other book. The prophets still warn us of the awesome consequences of failure not to live as a faith community pursuing our walk of faith. The usefulness of Scripture that Paul taught Timothy still stands, and he was referring to the Tanakh when he wrote:

All scripture is given by inspiration of God, and is profitable for doctrine, for reproof, for correction, for instruction in righteousness: that the man of God may be perfect, thoroughly furnished unto all good works. (2 Timothy 3:16-17)

The New Testament is not a replacement for the Old Testament. The Sermon on the Mount did not replace the Law of Moses. Instead, Jesus gave us an understanding of the heart intent of the Law of Moses. The Law said that the heart should not be so sinful as to lead to murder, but it is the same sinful heart that is angry. The Law said that a person should not commit adultery, but it is the same sinful heart that causes a person to look lustfully at another. The Law of Moses should have been the result of heart responses to God's law, in relation to anger as well as murder. Perhaps, as is often the case with the Lord's teaching, He was expecting us to consider carefully what He said in the Sermon on the Mount, discussing it, and drawing our conclusions. Surely, the correct conclusion was that He was talking heart to heart with His disciples. He was showing them that sin is a thing of the heart and that there was no escaping the fact that self-righteously obeying the strong commands, such as adultery and murder, could mask the fact that the heart was still sinful, being prone to lust and anger. He was pointing out the need of all people for a Saviour, above all else that was being taught that day on the Mount.

Having said this, we can go on further. People could not obey the Law of Moses without an inner transformation, but the Law of Moses did succeed in revealing the need of our Saviour Yeshua. The Law of Moses pointed to Him. This was the goal of the Law. This is the Gospel message. This is the primary message of the New Testament. None of the New Testament writers set out to write a complete commentary on the Old Testament. Why should they, when the Gospel message was also about a living relationship with God? It was about regeneration by the power of the Holy Spirit, who lives in us and manifests the Law of Moses at heart level. The Gospel message is about a living relationship with God because of the atoning blood of Yeshua, by the power of the Holy Spirit. A theoretical and philosophical set of writings about the Law of Moses cannot replace this. There is no need to write a full commentary on the Tanakh, because we have the Tanakh itself and the Holy Spirit is given to us so that we might study all the Scriptures in fellowship with Him and with one another. This should transform our view of the New Testament and release us to a walk with God within a balanced view of all Scripture.

Torah is now a matter of the heart. We have the truths of it available in a way that the Children of Israel did not, at heart level. The manifestations of Torah that are contained in the Tanakh concern some of the fruit of heart principles. When we read about them, the Holy Spirit can and will use them to stimulate the deeper truths that are to be embedded on our hearts, just as Yeshua was doing in the Sermon on the Mount. It is up to us to study the full range of these things.

Halakhah begins with the written code that Moses recorded for us and moves into the deeper spiritual truths that come from our life bound up in the life of the Holy Spirit. Perhaps this is why some of the teaching of the New Testament seems to be new teaching, rather than showing the heart manifestations of Torah principles already established. This is because the deeper spiritual manifestations of Torah overflow, where once they were only typified by Commandments written on stone:

> But the fruit of the Spirit is love, joy, peace, longsuffering, gentleness, goodness, faith, meekness, temperance: against such there is no law. (Galatians 5:22-23)

For Study and Meditation:
Read Matthew 5-7.
Read Romans 1-8.
Read Exodus 20.
Read Deuteronomy 15.
Read Galatians 5.

Halakhah

Practical Examples

The New Testament gives us a beginning to Halakhah, but leaves us to discover, in fellowship with one another and with the Holy Spirit, the full scope of what this should be. To this end, it is useful to approach our study of Halakhah through the device of open debate and discussion that is typified in a Yeshiva. This is where ideas are explored openly and where everyone can participate in the discussion. If this is done in good order and with prayer, led by mature Bible teachers, to keep discussions on track, we can expect the Holy Spirit to bring revelation and answers to our questions, as we meet and discuss them:

For where two or three come together in my name, there am I with them." *(Matthew 18:20)*

Indeed, it is essential that we tackle some of the important issues of Halakhah in our communities in this way. There are many practical issues of our life of faith to consider.

The first criterion is that we become very well acquainted with all that Scripture contains, so that relevant principles can be brought to our mind as we consider our questions together. Scripture does not contain ideas that are logically set out one after the other like a rulebook. The ideas develop here and there and are to be searched out. Thus, our method of Bible study should follow, in general terms, the idea of Jewish Midrash - searching the Scriptures for truth. This should not be a mechanical or scientific system, however, but with the aid of the Holy Spirit, as we link the threads of ideas together, we can discover truth.

We should be disciples who have many questions. Sometimes questions are as powerful as answers. It was Jesus' questions that astonished the teachers of the Law when He was only twelve:

They found him in the temple courts, sitting among the teachers, listening to them and asking them questions. Everyone who heard him was amazed at his understanding and his answers. (Luke 2:46-47)

If we have questions then we have a starting point to our prayerful investigations of Scripture. The key is to then find the heart principles to which Scripture points. It is these heart principles that are to be mobilised into our Halakhah. We should learn to 'yeshiva' in the home and have a central place for this in our community gatherings.

There are fewer examples in the New Testament than we might think, of the practical outworking of heart principles according to what is written in the Law of Moses. There is one clear example, however. If we were to ask the question about paying ministers of the Gospel, then we would find the Halakhah principle on this point. Paul gives us the teaching as if it is quite natural for him to interpret Torah in this way. This can help us to model his method. In Deuteronomy 25:4, it says:

Thou shalt not muzzle the ox when he treadeth out the corn.

Paul had clearly understood the heart principle of this. He had realised that as the Children of Israel had done this very practical thing in their agricultural community, it should have been a prompt to deeper heart truths. This is so with much of the Law of Moses. Practical things are given for a person to do, which are profound examples of heart principals. They are good things to do of themselves, but are also intended to be points of meditation leading, by the power of the Holy Spirit, to deeper general principles that can then be manifested in a multitude of other ways. In two places (1 Corinthians 9 and 1 Timothy 5) Paul showed that the heart principle behind this Mitzvot (commandment) would lead to paying ministers of the Gospel:

For it is written in the law of Moses, Thou shalt not muzzle the mouth of the ox that treadeth out the corn. Doth God take care for oxen? Or saith he it altogether for our sakes? For our sakes, no doubt, this is written: that he that ploweth should plow in hope; and that he that thresheth in hope should be partaker of his hope. If we have sown unto you spiritual things, is it a great thing if we shall reap your carnal things? If others be partakers of this power over you, are not we rather? Nevertheless we have not used this power; but suffer all things, lest we should hinder the gospel of Christ. Do ye not know that they which minister about holy things live of the things of the temple? and they which wait at the altar are partakers with the altar? Even so hath the Lord ordained that they which preach the gospel should live of the gospel. (1 Corinthians 9:9-14)

However, we will not get answers to all our practical questions direct from Paul and we must do some prayerful searching for ourselves on the questions that are important to us.

Take another example. In Deuteronomy 22:8 the Children of Israel were told to build a wall (otherwise called a parapet or battlement) around the roof of their house:

When thou buildest a new house, then thou shalt make a battle-ment for thy roof, that thou bring not blood upon thine house, if any man fall from thence.

If a person walked on a flat roof, it would be very easy to slip and fall off. A wall would save him and hence save his life. When we meditate upon this principle, we might see how wonderful this caring attitude is. We might see how this is a wonderful manifestation of the principle that we must love our neighbour as ourselves. It is not difficult to see how this principal can be extended. It is about love in a practical and caring way regarding the safety of our neighbours, ensuring that there are safety standards in every avenue of life. The heart principle is clear and then the manifestation should be in a million different ways in the health and safety precautions of our homes and work-places. Parapets on roofs are the prime example of fire-extinguishers, safety rails, protective helmets, properly laid carpets and a host of other things that just flow out of our heart when we know the principle. Furthermore, in the spirit of Ezekiel 33 and Acts 20:18–26 we go from the practical to the spiritual, recognising the need to put 'parapets around our hearts' through the protection imparted in response to the preaching and teaching of the whole Torah of God.

Another example comes from Leviticus 19:32:

Thou shalt rise up before the hoary head, and honour the face of the old man, and fear thy God: I am the LORD.

What a wonderful principle! When an elderly person comes into the room, the younger ones should stand. What a wonderful principle, perfect in itself and one that we should study just for the beauty of what it means when an older person is honoured in this way. We could write a book on this one principal of Halakhah and not come to the end of the beauty of it. Yet, it is again simply a wonderful example of God's teaching us a heart principal. God is so wonderfully practical with His teaching! By practising this one thing, our heart will be stirred to respect the elderly in every way. Beginning with standing in their presence, we will honour them in every part of community life. We will love our parents as we ought. We will care for them and all of the elderly, taking practical steps to exalt them and this will have innumerable profound effects on all of our community life.

This is the way to approach Halakhah. Let us study it and practice it with all our heart.

For Study and Meditation:
Read Psalm 119.

Halakhah

Part 2: One Covenant Community

The Living Covenant:
Israel's next step, and the consequences
for all of the Covenant community

When we read the Bible, the whole of Covenant history is laid before us. However, we must not think the Covenant that God made with Israel is all in the past. It is a living Covenant and applies to all those who are called to walk with God today, as much as it applied to those who were called in the past. Indeed, we are at a very special time, because the nation of Israel is also coming into the foreground of Covenant history, after many generations of exile. As surely as God brought Israel back from exile at the time of Ezra and Nehemiah, He is bringing the nation back today. Israel is going through a time of preparation so that, in the coming days, they will learn to walk with the Lord as never before, even since the time of Jacob. This has consequences for all who are called according to the Covenant promises. The Covenant is real and relevant to us all. Its history is still being unfolded and we have a part in it. Halakhah, as it applies to communities, will undoubtedly come alive as this present phase of history unfolds. Halakhah is related directly to the Covenant that God cut with Abraham.

Israel's walk with God as a nation began with their deliverance from Egypt. In a way, this was also the beginning of Halakhah for all of us who believe in the One True God. All who come into Covenant relationship with YHWH look back to Abraham our 'father' of faith, and to Moses through whom the Law came, and try to live a balanced life, learning to walk with God by faith. Our teaching programme begins with all that happened to the Children of Israel. Then, having learned from Abraham and Moses, we realise more and more our need of Yeshua (Jesus) and we look to Him, the author and finisher of our faith (Hebrews 12:2). Our understanding of how to walk with God develops from these interacting principles.

The Lord God chose Israel, and has put the nation into the centre of His teaching programme for us all. We understand the Covenant promises through them. We learn of mankind's inability to obey all that Moses taught and of the need for a Saviour by studying the history of Israel. We learn of the love of God through His love for Israel. We learn of the righteousness of God through the history of Israel, both in the Land of Israel and in exile. Through Israel, contrasts are also drawn with other nations, so that we can understand how all of mankind needs a Saviour, and that there will be no compromise in the judgement of God on all those who are not redeemed through the shed blood of Yeshua HaMashiach (Jesus the Messiah).

All these things and more, we learn by studying our Bibles, through the inspiration of the Holy Spirit. The Covenant with God is real. It was given to Abraham, passed down through Isaac and Jacob, and through successive generations of the Children of Israel. It is a Covenant made with living people, and the record of it is within the lives of these people throughout the centuries. When we read of the time when the Covenant was cut with Abraham, there is life and inspiration from the scriptural account. We know that Abraham was a real man and this really happened. This inspires us to believe in the ongoing truth and validity of the Covenant and its fulfilment through Yeshua (Jesus). If it were possible to go back and witness the cutting of the Covenant with Abraham, we would expect to find a real man and a real episode of history. Indeed, it would be an awe-inspiring situation and a great privilege to witness the moment when history was made. It would be similarly satisfying to witness any of the great steps of salvation history as they happened - the Exodus, the giving of the Ten Commandments, the setting up of the Tabernacle, the building of the Temple, the times of the Judges and Kings of Israel, the ministry of Yeshua, the coming of the Holy Spirit and many other things that are vivid in the Bible accounts and which actually took place. All this is our history. Yet, is the Covenant embedded in history alone? Is our walk of faith less for us than for those who went before us?

We probably have a tendency to look back at the history of Salvation - the progressive steps of God's Covenant plan - and consider that it has more to do with history than present reality. Yet, if we begin to meditate upon this, we should realise that Covenant history goes on in our day as vividly as in any generation. The Covenant lives with each succeeding generation. We are no lesser heirs to the Covenant promises than Abraham or Moses or the Children of Israel. Indeed, their walk of faith is completed on this earth and we are the people who are involved with God's continuing plans in our day. Some of us need to wake up to the reality of this.

One particular thing that still stands is God's Covenant promises to Israel. It is as alive today as it ever was. We may not know exactly how the last steps of Israel's Covenant walk (Halakhah) will work out, but we know that in general terms God will never completely cast off the Children of Israel. There are many Bible passages to verify this, for example:

Sing O heavens; and be joyful, O earth; and break forth into singing, O mountains: for the LORD hath comforted his people, and will have mercy upon his afflicted. But Zion said, The LORD hath forsaken me, and my Lord hath forgotten me. Can a woman forget her sucking child, that she should not have compassion on the son of her womb? Yea, they may forget, yet will I not forget thee. (Isaiah 49:13-15)

Hear the word of the LORD, O ye nations, and declare it in the isles afar off, and say, He that scattered Israel will gather him, and keep him, as a shepherd doth his flock. For the LORD hath redeemed Jacob, and ransomed him from the hand of him that was stronger than he. (Jeremiah 31:10-11)

All of the Covenant promises are fulfilled in Yeshua HaMashiach.

While Israel has been scattered among the Gentile nations, many from these nations have found an equal place with believers from the Children of Israel, now that the mysteries of the Covenant have been revealed in Yeshua. Yet there are still the final steps of the Covenant which include the physical descendants of Israel who are alive in our day, and we are witnessing these steps just as certainly as any other part of Covenant history has taken place.

What is happening in the land of Israel today is a preparation for the fulfilment of the Covenant promises through Yeshua of the remnant of the nation. Covenant history is not ancient history but living history. As surely as Abraham stood before God and received the Covenant promises, so we witness the outworking of the Covenant today. All of the things that we learn from the Scriptures regarding our Halakhah are related to this. In particular, we know that when the nation of Israel is, at any time, given possession of the Land of Israel they must study the terms of the Covenant and live according to all that the Lord expects of His Covenant people. On two occasions in history their failure to mix faith with their obedience to the Law of Moses (see Hebrews 4:2) has led to a painful exile. The first exile ended when the nation was led back from captivity at the time of Ezra and Nehemiah. Now the second exile is coming to an end as Israel gathers in the Land once more.

What then are the last steps in this Halakhah, which began in Egypt thousands of years ago? The conditions are the same as in all other generations. The Torah of God still stands. It was not understood by previous generations, but it still stands for the Covenant nation. Even when the law of Moses was read again at the time of Ezra, the whole understanding of Torah was not imparted. Torah is fulfilled in Yeshua; the Covenant is fulfilled in Yeshua; true Halakhah is a walk to Yeshua and a walk of faith in and with Yeshua, but even when Yeshua walked on this earth, the majority of Israel failed to see Him as the fulfilment of Torah, and so they were scattered among the nations. The law of Moses (properly understood) is still in force, but Torah and Halakhah cannot be fulfilled unless there is faith in Yeshua. These issues face us today as they did when Israel was last in the Land, and these days are even more significant than in the time of Ezra. Present-day Israel, however, is as yet far from seeking to live according to the Covenant and, as a nation, is far from faith in Yeshua. With Israel back in the Land we must see the understanding of these truths gradually (or suddenly) come, as God Himself sheds His light on the fullest meaning of the Covenant for all of us. This last step of the Covenant promises is still to take place.

Far from Covenant history being ancient history contained in the Bible alone, it is living history and we who are accepted in the Commonwealth of Israel from among the nations (Ephesians 2:12-13) are involved with all of God's plans in this day. We will be witnesses of the ancient promises of God being worked out among both Jews and Gentiles, and the time will come when Israel itself will bear testimony to the faithfulness of God in these last steps of human history. These are days which Abraham would have longed to see. We are in one of the most exciting days of Covenant history, days when all of God's Covenant people are being called to walk with Him as has never before been witnessed on this earth. It is time to wake up to this and for all of us to learn to walk accordingly. Can't you feel a stirring within, compelling us to walk together with God forward into the last phase of Covenant history?

For Study and Meditation: Look up some of the Covenant promises given to Moses and the Prophets. Consider how we are a part of the outworking of the Covenant in our day, at least as much as others were in the generations that have gone before.

Halakhah

Arise, shine; for Thy Light is come

Halakhah should not be a private walk of faith where Scripture is used selfishly and shallowly. It should be a walk of faith within the whole community purposes of God. We were drawn into fellowship with Him in the context of the plan of salvation for Israel, extending to the whole world. Once we understand the full context of our walk of faith (Halakhah), we can also study the Scriptures deeply, accurately and meaningfully. For too long, it has been a practice of the Church to dip into Scriptures, and accept only part of the truth that they convey. Particularly in these days, our Halakhah must be considered within the fullness of what is written and in the context of what is happening in the world today, as the Lord continues to fulfil His covenant promises. In particular, we are waking up to the fact that the Lord has not forgotten Israel, and believers saved from the Gentile nations have not replaced Israel. Instead, according to Romans 11 and Ephesians 2, they have joined the covenant community. The Lord's plan is as wide and deep as His love, and He has not forgotten that Israel is to be included in the last phase of salvation history, as well as believers from the Gentile nations. This is born out by Scripture when we read it correctly.

The quotation from Isaiah 60:1 illustrates the point very well: 'Arise, Shine; for Thy Light is Come.' The poetry in this sentence is beautiful - compelling. When we come upon the sentence, we want it to apply to ourselves. There is healing in it. Perhaps we might consider that the Lord Himself has led us to the passage to bless us personally. There is a focus on light, which can be contrasted with darkness. There is a command to get up. There is the indication of a change of circumstances. There is perhaps the expectation that by the power of the Holy Spirit, the Lord will send deliverance from some pressure situation that a believer has come into. This idea might be strengthened if one considered the Hebrew of the text, which transliterated is: 'Kumi auri ki ba aurekh'. It is discovered that the sentence is in the singular as if directed to one single person. If a single believer, desiring a blessing from God, comes across this passage, it can appear to be a personal message from God to encourage him or her to put problems aside and get moving again in faith. Who would not want such encouragement?

While all of this can be so, the passage contains far more than this. Taken in context, it comes from a section of Isaiah that includes the following:

> *We grope for the wall like the blind, and we grope as if we had no eyes: we stumble at noon day as in the night; we are in desolate places as dead men. We roar all like bears, and mourn sore like doves: we look for judgment, but there is none; for salvation, but it is far off from us. For our transgressions are multiplied before thee, and our sins testify against us: for our transgressions are with us; and as for our iniquities, we know them; in transgressing and lying against the LORD, and departing away from our God, speaking oppression and revolt, conceiving and uttering from the heart words of falsehood. And judgment is turned away backward, and justice standeth afar off: for truth is fallen in the street, and equity cannot enter. Yea, truth faileth; and he that departeth from evil maketh himself a prey: and the LORD saw it, and it displeased him that there was no judgment. And he saw that there was no man, and wondered that there was no intercessor: therefore his arm brought salvation unto him; and his righteousness, it sustained him. For he put on righteousness as a breastplate, and an helmet of salvation upon his head; and he put on the garments of vengeance for clothing, and was clad with zeal as a cloak. According to their deeds, accordingly he will repay, fury to his adversaries, recompense to his enemies; to the islands he will repay recompense. So shall they fear the name of the LORD from the west, and his glory from the rising of the sun. When the enemy shall come in like a flood, the Spirit of the LORD shall lift up a standard against him. And the Redeemer shall come to Zion,*

and unto them that turn from transgression in Jacob, saith the LORD. As for me, this is my covenant with them, saith the LORD; My spirit that is upon thee, and my words which I have put in thy mouth, shall not depart out of thy mouth, nor out of the mouth of thy seed, nor out of the mouth of thy seed's seed, saith the LORD, from henceforth and for ever. Arise, shine; for thy light is come, and the glory of the LORD is risen upon thee. For, behold, the darkness shall cover the earth, and gross darkness the people: but the LORD shall arise upon thee, and his glory shall be seen upon thee. And the Gentiles shall come to thy light, and kings to the brightness of thy rising. (Isaiah 59:10-60:3)

We see here something far more encompassing than a message to one believer. It is a message to a nation. The message is in the singular, because the Lord sees His covenant people together as one family. It is not only a personal message; it is a corporate message. It is not a promise of healing a small ailment. It is the message of hope for all people, centred on a promise of restoration to Judah. It is a message that has its deepest relevance in times such as the Holocaust of the Second World War. At a time of deep despair and darkness, deliverance will come. The picture language is intense, because of course darkness applies to the sinful state as well as a state of physical hardship.

Isaiah, like other Prophets, brought a message of coming judgement to Judah, but woven into the message was a promise of hope and a promise of redemption. This passage speaks of the time when there will be no other help for fallen Judah and of the time when the Lord Himself will save the nation. It is a messianic passage, pointing to the time when Yeshua would come to announce salvation to His people. He is the light of the world that would come. The message is directly to the Jews, that one day, they would, at a time of utter helplessness, as it were, hear the compelling message of restoration, healing and salvation through Yeshua, 'Arise, shine; for Thy Light is come.'

The passage is echoed in the Gospels: 'The people which sat in darkness saw great light; and to them which sat in the region and shadow of death light is sprung up.' (Matthew 4:16), which is taken directly from another passage in Isaiah 9:1-2.

In Isaiah 60:3, we read that, 'Gentiles shall come to thy light'. Salvation through the Messiah of Israel will also be offered to the Gentiles.

In these days where the prophecies of Isaiah are deeply relevant regarding the salvation of the Jews, we must read the Scriptures in context and take in the full scope of their meaning. Our Halakhah is not to remain at the shallow level of dipping into the Scriptures for a personal blessing, but we must realise that the promises of Scripture are deep and meaningful, pointing to the climax of all salvation history. Will God cease to bless us individually through these Scriptures? I don't think so, but we must see personal blessings in the context of the full measure of meaning that they carry. The Light of God has come to all that will believe. The blessings that this brings to each of us are a small (though significant) part of the fullness of blessing that is to be brought to all of His Covenant people. The Light that came to Israel has spread to all nations and into every part of our lives, if we believe in the One who is the Light.

For Study and Meditation: Find some other passages of Scripture that carry deep messages concerning the Lord's promises to His covenant people. Consider prayerfully the full meaning of these passages, and how personal blessings are but a part of the fuller promise.

Halakhah

Pray for the Peace of Jerusalem

It is a part of our Halakhah to be conscious of the Lord's present work in Israel and to have Israel constantly in our prayers. The prophet Isaiah shows us this principle:

For Zion's sake will I not hold my peace, and for Jerusalem's sake I will not rest, until the righteousness thereof go forth as brightness, and the salvation thereof as a lamp that burneth. And the Gentiles shall see thy righteousness, and all kings thy glory: and thou shalt be called by a new name, which the mouth of the LORD shall name. Thou shalt also be a crown of glory in the hand of the LORD, and a royal diadem in the hand of thy God. Thou shalt no more be termed Forsaken; neither shall thy land any more be termed Desolate: but thou shalt be called Hephzibah, and thy land Beulah: for the LORD delighteth in thee, and thy land shall be married. For as a young man marrieth a virgin, so shall thy sons marry thee: and as the bridegroom rejoiceth over the bride, so shall thy God rejoice over thee. I have set watchmen upon thy walls, O Jerusalem, which shall never hold their peace day nor night: ye that make mention of the LORD, keep not silence. And give him no rest, till he establish, and till he make Jerusalem a praise in the earth. (Isaiah 62:1-7)

If we are walking with God then we will share His concerns. Isaiah reflected the heart of the Lord when he prophesied in this way. Neither Isaiah nor the Lord will recognise a final rest until all is accomplished for Jerusalem and the Jewish nation. The earth will continue in its fallen and painful condition until this is brought about. There will be no true Sabbath rest for God's people until this is accomplished. We will not rest until all is accomplished and we should not cease to pray for this, as Psalm 122 also implies:

> *I was glad when they said unto me, Let us go into the house of*
> *the LORD.*
> *Our feet shall stand within thy gates, O Jerusalem.*
> *Jerusalem is builded as a city that is compact together:*
> *Whither the tribes go up, the tribes of the LORD, unto the testi-*
> *mony of Israel, to give thanks unto the name of the LORD.*
> *For there are set thrones of judgment, the thrones of the house of*
> *David.*
> *Pray for the peace of Jerusalem: they shall prosper that love thee.*
> *Peace be within thy walls, and prosperity within thy palaces.*
> *For my brethren and companions' sakes, I will now say, Peace be*
> *within thee.*
> *Because of the house of the LORD our God I will seek thy good.*

As well as containing echoes from Israel's past, there is also a pointer in this Psalm towards the future restoration of Israel and to Jerusalem becoming a praise in the earth. When we are caught up in this vision, we will realise that as the Lord works His purposes out for Israel in these days, He will also be working out His purposes for the Covenant community of the whole earth. In praying for the restoration of Israel, we are praying for the restoration of the whole community of believers and the return of Messiah. This is not to set Israel above those saved from the nations, but simply to emphasise the way the plan of salvation in its last phase is being outworked.

However, we must consider the reality of the situation if we are to pray meaningfully. Though there is a growing number of Jewish people who have faith that Yeshua is the Son of God and though the Messianic community is growing in numbers, the greater part of the plan of salvation has yet to be accomplished. At this time, the majority of Jewish people in the world, including the majority who live in the Land of Israel, are blind to the knowledge of their Messiah. We know from Romans 11 that this partial blindness was for the sake of salvation coming to the Gentiles, and that there was always promised a time when the blindness would be removed:

For I would not, brethren, that ye should be ignorant of this mystery, lest ye should be wise in your own conceits; that blindness in part is happened to Israel, until the fulness of the Gentiles be come in. And so all Israel shall be saved: as it is written, There shall come out of Sion the Deliverer, and shall turn away ungodliness from Jacob: for this is my covenant unto them, when I shall take away their sins. (Romans11:25-27)

There are many passages that speak of the time when the Jews return to the Land of Israel and there are some that imply that there will be a return to the Land prior to the completion of the plan of salvation. One such example is in Chapter 31 of Jeremiah. This is the chapter which contains the revelation of the final goal of the Covenant promise that was given to Abraham:

Behold, the days come, saith the LORD, that I will make a new covenant with the house of Israel, and with the house of Judah: not according to the covenant that I made with their fathers in the day that I took them by the hand to bring them out of the land of Egypt; which my covenant they brake, although I was an husband unto them, saith the LORD: but this shall be the covenant that I will make with the house of Israel; After those days, saith the LORD, I will put my law in their inward parts, and write it in their hearts; and will be their God, and they shall be my people. (Jeremiah 31:31-33)

In earlier verses of this chapter, prior to this promise we read that the Lord will gather Israel and then bring them to the joy of their salvation:

Hear the word of the LORD, O ye nations, and declare it in the isles afar off, and say, He that scattered Israel will gather him, and keep him, as a shepherd doth his flock. For the LORD hath redeemed Jacob, and ransomed him from the hand of him that was stronger than he. Therefore they shall come and sing in the height of Zion, and shall flow together to the goodness of the LORD, for wheat, and for wine, and for oil, and for the young of the flock and of the herd: and their soul shall be as a watered gar-

den; and they shall not sorrow any more at all. Then shall the virgin rejoice in the dance, both young men and old together: for I will turn their mourning into joy, and will comfort them, and make them rejoice from their sorrow. (Jeremiah 31:10-13)

Thus, as we consider the condition of Israel today, we must understand that what we see is in the context of these great promises given to the Prophets of old. We know that it has been a painful exile for the Children of Israel (as painful as the persecution that they have experienced among the nations and as painful as the Holocaust which took six million lives of Jews of all ages in the Nazi concentration camps). The pain is not over and we are witnessing the pressures surrounding the nation of Israel in our day.

Scripture is clear that the exile was on account of not fulfilling Torah. For example, this was what God said to Solomon at the time of the dedication of the Temple in Jerusalem:

But if ye turn away, and forsake my statutes and my commandments, which I have set before you, and shall go and serve other gods, and worship them; then will I pluck them up by the roots out of my land which I have given them; and this house, which I have sanctified for my name, will I cast out of my sight, and will make it to be a proverb and a byword among all nations. And this house, which is high, shall be an astonishment to every one that passeth by it; so that he shall say, Why hath the LORD done thus unto this land, and unto this house? And it shall be answered, Because they forsook the LORD God of their fathers, which brought them forth out of the land of Egypt, and laid hold on other gods, and worshipped them, and served them: therefore hath he brought all this evil upon them. (2 Chronicles 7:19-22)

The first exile to Babylon can be understood through the failure to fulfil Torah in the way that it was understood at the time. The second exile to all the nations of the world can be understood through the failure to recognise the fulfilment of Torah when Yeshua came to save His people for their sins.

We have no right to gloat over this, because we now realise that the blindness (and hence the suffering) has continued to this day so that there would be a phase of history for the Gentiles to hear and respond to the Gospel message.

Now that Israel is returning from exile, the nation should first be considering it in comparison with the days of Ezra, when the law of Moses was read and the people made a fresh commitment. It is time for Israel to ask questions about how they should become a Torah community walking with God, at least as much as this was considered at the time of Ezra. However, because there has been a second exile following the ministry of Yeshua, they should also be asking questions that go beyond the understanding of Torah in Ezra's day. When they ask their deeper questions, we can be sure that the Lord will eventually show them that the answer lies in the fulfilment of Torah that Yeshua brings, a deeper understanding of its principles and the way of salvation through Him.

Israel today is not a community fulfilling its Covenant commitments, but the time is approaching for them to become this in the fullest sense that the Prophets foresaw. God is behind the scenes of all that is happening and through the circumstances that will arise in and around Israel, we can assume the nation as a whole (the 'all Israel' of Romans 11) will seek God.

Since these things are before us and since we, who have inherited the Covenant promises along with Israel, can understand these things, a prominent part of our Halakhah in the coming days is a prayerful walk with God, where the gathering of Israel unto salvation is a central theme. If we walk closely with God we will find that we will share the concerns of His heart, and we will find that there are plans in His heart for Israel today, along with the rest of His plans for the whole of the Covenant community.

For Study and Meditation: Search the Scriptures and become thoroughly acquainted with God's plan for Israel, so that your commitment to prayer for Israel will be a central part of your Halakhah in the coming days, as the plan unfolds before our eyes.

Halakhah

Other Sheep

Our Halakhah (walk with God) is at many levels. These levels include the way we live our personal lives, involving the lifestyles of our families and communities, and they also include the wider missionary work of the Church. The closer our walk with God becomes, the more we will understand and be involved in all aspects of His life and ministry. He is working out His Covenant purposes among all of mankind, looking always to the gathering of the redeemed community from every nation. If we walk closely with God, we will share in the wider plans as well as the local ones. We will have an international view of the Covenant as well as a local one. Our Halakhah must have this in mind; our concerns should extend into the harvest fields of the earth, even when our attention is also given to things close to hand or close to home.

We live in the day of the regathering of Israel unto salvation. These are days that the Prophets foresaw. Our concerns for the Covenant plans of God take in the nation of Israel in a renewed and very special way. For centuries, the Church has been deprived of its Hebraic heritage and of fellowship with Jewish believers. Because of this, we are only gradually waking up to what this means. When we do wake up to what God is doing in Israel, then we find many points to consider within the overall framework of Halakhah. The Church's mission takes on a renewed emphasis in the light of Israel today. Yet, this is not all! We must not pay so much attention to even this profound move of God that we neglect other aspects of the Lord's continuing mission in this world.

If we go back to the Covenant with Abraham, we recall the balance of the Lord's promise:

And when Abram was ninety years old and nine, the LORD appeared to Abram, and said unto him, I am the Almighty God; walk before me, and be thou perfect. And I will make my covenant between me and thee, and will multiply thee exceedingly. And Abram fell on his face: and God talked with him, saying, as for me, behold, my covenant is with thee, and thou shalt be a father of many nations. Neither shall thy name any more be called Abram, but thy name shall be Abraham; for a father of many nations have I made thee. (Genesis 17:1-5)

The Covenant began with Abraham, was passed on to Isaac and Jacob and was established through the Children of Israel, but the intention was always that Abraham would be the father of many nations. There is a wonderful method in this, that through one nation many would learn God's ways and be saved. There is wonderful balance in this, that God has compassion on all nations, the Gospel being for all men and women. We must find this balance too, as we consider the missionary call of the Church. In our day, as never before, we can have Israel back at the heart of our understanding of the Covenant and of our meditations on Halakhah, and we can and should be zealous for the lost sheep of the tribes of Israel. However, alongside this we must also have continuing zeal for the salvation of many from all nations.

This is the attitude of Yeshua (Jesus). He came first to Israel, He was and is King of the Jews, but He had His heart and mind also set on gathering people from all nations. Recorded in John 10:16 are these words:

And other sheep I have, which are not of this fold: them also I must bring, and they shall hear my voice; and there shall be one fold, and one shepherd.

In John 17:20-23 we hear Yeshua's prayer for all who will believe:

Neither pray I for these alone, but for them also which shall believe on me through their word; that they all may be one; as thou, Father, art in me, and I in thee, that they also may be one in us: that the world may believe that thou hast sent me. And the glory which thou gavest me I have given them; that they may be one, even as we are one: I in them, and thou in me, that they may be made perfect in one; and that the world may know that thou hast sent me, and hast loved them, as thou hast loved me.

While He gathers Israel unto salvation, Yeshua also continues to gather His sheep from many nations. This was also the commission of His disciples:

All power is given unto me in heaven and in earth. Go ye there-fore, and teach all nations, baptizing them in the name of the Father, and of the Son, and of the Holy Ghost: teaching them to observe all things whatsoever I have commanded you: and, lo, I am with you alway, even unto the end of the world. (Matthew 28:18-20)

Disciples of the Lord Jesus Christ (Yeshua HaMashiach) are still called to walk with Him into the harvest fields of the whole earth. Indeed, we live in a day of immense opportunity when the harvest fields are opened as never before. There will be an immense harvest from among the one billion Muslims of the world. There will be many saved from Hinduism, Buddhism, Taoism, Confucianism, Humanism, New Age and all the other traps that Satan has laid before mankind. Many from China, Africa, India, South America, Europe, North America, Australia, Japan, Tibet, Nepal, Iraq, Iran, Saudi Arabia, and all countries to the ends of the earth. Not only for the sake of Israel, but also for the sake of the whole world, Abraham would have longed to see this day. This is the day of fulfilment and opportunity that the writer to the Hebrews foresaw when he wrote of the joy that Jesus would inherit through the gathering of His one flock:

Looking unto Jesus the author and finisher of our faith; who for the joy that was set before him endured the cross, despising the shame, and is set down at the right hand of the throne of God. (Hebrews 12:2)

Halakhah for today's disciple is in the context of both everyday life at a local level and the Great Commission on a worldwide level. We are involved in possibly the last great harvest of the earth from among all nations, and our attitude must be one of balance and zeal, encompassing all that the Lord is doing, in our prayers and through our commitment. Regarding our commitment to Israel, our own nation and other nations, there is a careful balance to be struck and we must avoid unholy bias. A clear example is that, as far as the Gospel is concerned, we must not be pro-Israel and anti-Arab or pro-Arab and anti-Israel, but this is only one example. We must not be pro-British and anti-American, or pro-white and anti-black, or pro-African and anti-Indian, for example. We must stand on holy ground with regard to all of the Lord's work in this world and be involved with particular zeal where He causes us to walk. We must have the attitude of Joshua who, on entry into the Promised Land, asked the captain of the host of the Lord, "Art thou for us, or for our adversaries?", after which we read:

> And he said, Nay; but as captain of the host of the LORD am I now come. And Joshua fell on his face to the earth, and did worship, and said unto him, What saith my lord unto his servant? And the captain of the LORD'S host said unto Joshua, Loose thy shoe from off thy foot; for the place whereon thou standest is holy. And Joshua did so. (Joshua 5:14-15)

God's Covenant plans transcend our expectations and are without the favouritism that besets short-sighted human viewpoints. We walk with holiness and obedience into the harvest fields of the earth, as the Lord fulfils His Covenant promises in our day.

For Study and Meditation: Consider the passages of the Bible concerning the Covenant promises applying to all nations. Prayerfully consider your own involvement in this.

Halakhah

Israel and the Church

Our Halakhah requires us to have a balanced perspective of the whole covenant plans of God, which include Israel and all nations. Another issue that we need to consider is what the Church is, in relation to Israel. Has the Church replaced Israel? Is Israel the Church? Does the Church contain Israel or does Israel contain the Church? These and other questions trouble disciples of the Lord Jesus in our day and it is important for us to have a rightly-balanced view.

'Israel and the Church' is one of those phrases that we use so often that we think we know what we mean. In particular, those of us who have set our faces to study the biblical foundations of our faith in the light of the role of Israel have been careful not to confuse the two terms 'Israel' and 'Church'. Yet, subconsciously, there may be distinct misunderstandings that need correction even among ourselves. If we consider Israel and the Church as one, we deny the need for salvation through the atoning blood of Yeshua. If we see no overlap, however, between Israel and the Church, we might hold the view that the Church is a body of those saved from among the Gentile nations alone, as distinct from those saved out of the nation of Israel.

One question to stimulate discussion is, 'When did the Church begin?' Many would say, 'At Pentecost', in answer to this question, meaning when the Holy Spirit came as recorded in Acts 2. They would see the outpouring of the Holy Spirit as the 'birthday of the Church'. This answer is, however, flawed. Certainly, the giving of the Holy Spirit was the beginning of a new phase for disciples of Yeshua and a fulfilment of the promise that they would be empowered to witness for Him among all nations, and at that point the community of believers in Yeshua grew and eventually spread among all nations. Yet, the Holy Spirit came to those who were already disciples. The believing community, which we call the Church, already existed. There are other names for this community from the Hebrew or Greek, including *qahal* and *ekklesia*, but our basic point can be made without reference to these terms (though we will return to this point, below). We are concerned with the one universal body of believers who are included in the Lord's community called the Church. This body existed before the coming of the Holy Spirit at Pentecost recorded in Acts 2.

Another question concerns the nationality of the Church. The Holy Spirit came to the disciples of Yeshua who were all Jews, and to those who were converted on that special day of Pentecost and who had come to the Temple for the annual Feast of Shavuot (to which the term Pentecost is related). This was predominantly a gathering of Jews from around the nations. Thus, the Church at this time was a Jewish entity. This fact warns us away from considering the Church today as being a body composed of disciples of Yeshua (Jesus) from among the nations *alone*, as distinct from its Jewish members.

The above two points should lead us to consider the phrase 'Israel and the Church' with care. There is an overlap between Israel and the Church. The Church consists of one body of believers in Yeshua, from among all nations, whether Jews or Gentiles. There are cultural differences and even different applications of some elements of Torah, but there is one body.

When did the Church begin? The reference point for all who believe in Yeshua as Messiah is Abraham, the 'father of the faithful'. Chapter 11 of the Book of Hebrews lists many of those who died in faith and who must be considered as founder members of the Church. This body goes back beyond even Abraham and includes Abel, Enoch and Noah. These are men and women who believed in the One True God, who progressively revealed Himself through history and who will, at the end of time, gather all who died in faith, as His community of believers. They looked forward in a mystical way to Yeshua, while we look back with fuller understanding. Israel played a key role in this plan of salvation and have a key place in the body, though not all Israel are the Israel of God (having faith in Yeshua). The Covenant with Abraham in some ways is more profound than the Covenant with Israel through Moses, though these are deep and sensitive matters that require careful attention. The point, however, is that the Church is a historic community to which all who have faith in Yeshua belong. Indeed we could argue that the Church of the Living God began before Creation, since its founder member already existed – the Son of God, not yet incarnate but through whom and for whom all things were made. Since Yeshua came in the flesh, membership of the Church includes those who are His disciples, drawn from all nations, clearly identifying their leader who came down from Heaven to reveal Himself and to pay the price for our salvation. Many from Israel will become Yeshua's disciples in the last days. Many from the Gentile nations have become His disciples over the last 2000 years and there will be more. Those saved from among the tribes of Israel and from among the nations join the one body of believers that we call the Church.

Those saved from among the nations do not become members of the nation of Israel after the flesh. There is no biblical term 'spiritual Israel', so we must also be careful not to spiritualise the concept of Israel. There is, however, 'the Israel of God' (Galatians 6:16) whom we can say are those of physical Israel and also those gathered from the nations, who have faith in Yeshua. The Israel of God refers first to those of physical Israel who are also disciples of Yeshua, but this is not the complete Church, but the part of the Church from the tribes of Israel, to whom believers from the Gentile nations are joined to complete the Church through grafting into the Israel of God.

If we consider these things, then we see that we must be careful of the phrase 'the Church and Israel'. Because of anti-Semitism in some branches of the Church, there are Jewish believers who consider themselves part of a different body and allow the Church to be a Gentile body. Because believers from the nations have been the majority in the Church for many hundreds of years, there has come another false distinction between them and believing Jews, as if Israel was an entity separate from them which itself contained some believers distinct from the Church. This concept has affected some ideas of the Lord's return, particularly the idea of 'the rapture' when the 'Church' is falsely expected to be taken out, leaving Israel to tribulation, in the eyes of some believers.

It is time for us to realise that there is one worldwide community of believers from all nations who belong to one ancient body spanning history, and for us to work to a unity of the faith - our common heritage. This is an important part of our Halakhah relating to the fulfilment of the Covenant promises. This body is the Lord's special possession and consists of members from Israel and from the other nations. There are also special plans in the heart of God for the remnant of Israel as it is being gathered, and other plans for the nations, including the Arabs, and all tribes of the earth. From all nations, in distinct ways, many will continue to be saved into the one body of believers. Because of ambiguity, by agreement, we may choose to rename what has been called 'the Church', but it must be seen as the one body of disciples of Yeshua. Perhaps it is not necessary to use the phrase 'Israel and the Church' so much as we do, because it may have promoted unconscious divisions that have elements of error. At least let us use the phrase carefully and with understanding.

For Study and Meditation: Read Romans 9-11 and carefully consider how we should view the one body of believers from all nations as the Church of the Lord Jesus Christ (Yeshua HaMashiach). Consider whether it is correct to use the term 'Israel of God' for the Church.

Halakhah

Mount Moriah

Judaism teaches that Halakhah begins at Mount Sinai with the giving of the Law of Moses. Each person should receive Torah as if they themselves were with Moses at the foot of the mountain. However, this approach could incline us to legalism. Halakhah should begin instead at Mount Moriah.

Mount Moriah represents faith while Mount Sinai can represent works, if we do not start at the right mountain. In the Covenant promises of God, faith is the foundation and works the fruit. Overarching all of history is the Covenant that God made with Abraham. This is the Covenant that points to salvation through faith in Yeshua. This arch of history links the obedience of Abraham, in laying Isaac on the altar, to the Father bringing His Son Yeshua to the altar, which was a cross, as our sacrifice. Both the step of faith of Abraham (and Isaac) and of Yeshua took place on Mount Moriah. Mount Moriah reminds us of salvation through faith, the pivotal issue of the Covenant.

We can consider both the accounts of Abraham and of Yeshua as ancient history, even though we know it is relevant. Yet, the relevance of what happened on this mountain range should be living with us constantly. Through Abraham came the Covenant as we read in Genesis 17:4-7:

As for me, behold, my covenant is with thee, and thou shalt be a father of many nations. Neither shall thy name any more be called Abram, but thy name shall be Abraham; for a father of many nations have I made thee. And I will make thee exceeding fruitful, and I will make nations of thee, and kings shall come out of thee.

*And I will establish my covenant between me and thee and thy
seed after thee in their generations for an everlasting covenant, to
be a God unto thee, and to thy seed after thee.*

Yet the Covenant did not remain with Abraham. He was to die
and the custodian of the Covenant for the next generation was to be
Isaac:

*And God said, Sarah thy wife shall bear thee a son indeed; and
thou shalt call his name Isaac: and I will establish my covenant
with him for an everlasting covenant, and with his seed after him.
(Genesis 17:19)*

Then, after Isaac, Jacob was the custodian of the Covenant:

*And Isaac called Jacob, and blessed him ... God Almighty bless
thee, and make thee fruitful, and multiply thee, that thou mayest
be a multitude of people; and give thee the blessing of Abraham,
to thee, and to thy seed with thee; that thou mayest inherit the
land wherein thou art a stranger, which God gave unto Abraham.
Genesis 28:1-4)*

The Covenant with Abraham, Isaac and Jacob was then made
with the Children of Israel and eventually fulfilled in and through
Yeshua. The Covenant is alive in every generation, passed on, as it
were, with its blessings and responsibilities. It lives with each
succeeding generation. It was brought to its fullest meaning in
Yeshua and passed on to His disciples in the Great Commission.
These disciples were empowered through the gift and blessing of
the Holy Spirit on the day of Pentecost (Shavuot):

*Go ye therefore, and teach all nations, baptizing them in the
name of the Father, and of the Son, and of the Holy Ghost: teaching them to observe all things whatsoever I have commanded
you: and, lo, I am with you alway, even unto the end of the
world. (Matthew 28:19-20)*

Responsibility on this earth for the Covenant began with

Abraham and was passed on, like the baton in a relay race, to each succeeding generation. It is a living covenant, alive in those who carry the responsibilities for its proclamation and for holding it in faith, in each successive generation. It is now fulfilled as the Covenant on the heart of Yeshua's disciples. Who then are the custodians of the Covenant in our day? Surely it is the generation of Yeshua's disciples who are now alive, commissioned in various ways to serve His purposes. In this way, the Covenant is no less alive than in the days of Abraham, but instead of one man called to faith, it is one body of believers throughout the whole world.

Halakhah begins at Mount Moriah in the sense that each of us has the commission to live by faith as Abraham did and to uphold the Covenant as the most important part of our walk with God. Like Abraham, we are called to make ourselves available to be tutored in order that we might grow in faith. Our Halakhah is for the prime purpose of enabling us to grow in faith. Like Abraham, we will make mistakes, but it is a part of our walk of faith that we are able, in faith, to put our mistakes behind us and press on to the goal. This is what the writer to the Hebrews meant when he reminded us of the great heroes of faith in Hebrews 11, going on to say:

Wherefore seeing we also are compassed about with so great a cloud of witnesses, let us lay aside every weight, and the sin which doth so easily beset us, and let us run with patience the race that is set before us, looking unto Jesus the author and finisher of our faith; who for the joy that was set before him endured the cross, despising the shame, and is set down at the right hand of the throne of God. (Hebrews 12:1-2)

Our Halakhah (walk with God) is to make a priority of our share in the Covenant that God made with Abraham and fulfilled in Yeshua, to grow in faith through our obedience to God, and to fulfil our call to serve as disciples, in whatever area the Lord chooses.

A paradox occurred on Mount Moriah, a paradox that we should also discover. The Covenant of faith requires us to receive our share in the Great Commission, hold it as the most precious thing, yet lay it before the Lord on the altar. It is to be alive in us and at the same time we are to be dead to it, in human terms. We believe both that what God has for us to do will be completed through us, and we treat it as the most treasured possession, yet we allow it to be on the altar of our hearts so that we are dead to it in the world's sense while alive to it in faith. The paradox is understood through Abraham's sacrifice of Isaac. In preparing to take Isaac up Mount Moriah for sacrifice, he in whom the Covenant promise was to be fulfilled, said to his servants:

Abide ye here with the ass; and I and the lad will go yonder and worship, and come again to you. (Genesis 22:5)

Abraham took Isaac to be sacrificed and also said that they would both return. Abraham had reached the peak of Covenant faith. He lived with the paradox that Isaac would both live and be sacrificed. He trusted God, as he had never before done and could not previously have done, that the most precious thing to him - the Covenant, now embodied in Isaac - was dead to him yet alive through faith.

The supreme goal of our Halakhah, above all else, is our role in the Covenant promises of God (our role in the Great Commission). We must walk, as it were, up Mount Moriah, holding on to this precious promise of service and yet releasing it in faith on the altar. Here we will not only find a walk with Abraham our father of faith, in a metaphorical sense, but a sharing in the death of Yeshua (Jesus) with whom we are to be united in faith for this great work that He has for us all to share. This is the goal of faith and our true Halakhah.

For Study and Meditation: Consider Abraham's walk of faith (particularly Genesis 22) and seek to assess your own role as a custodian of the Covenant promises in our day.

Halakhah

Provoking to Jealousy

Previous generations of the Church among the nations did not have to fully consider the reality of Romans 11. It was possible to read about the one body of believers represented by the Olive Tree and see it as more relevant to a future generation. We are that generation! Believers from the physical descendants of Israel are being grafted back into the Olive Tree, of which they are the natural members. It is time to think very clearly about what this means. Paul warned that there could be those saved from the Gentile nations (the unnatural branches) who might become proud of their position and so be cut off from the tree. We are among those who do not want this to happen to us! Indeed, we are among those who are seeking to deepen our membership of the Olive Tree, which represents the historical body of all believers in Yeshua HaMashiach. It is faith in Him that ensures a firm grafting into the tree.

In our search for our true identity in the Olive Tree, we realise that this identity has its origins in the Jewish people, emerging from ancient Israeli culture and has Hebraic linguistic and philosophical roots. We can begin to look at the practices of the Jews that have been passed on from generation to generation in order to find clues to our 'family identity'. Some of the practices we see in Jewish communities today reflect ancient traditions, and so we are taking a growing interest in these things, to see how they might apply to us. While some of these traditions are biblical, some are cultural developments with no particular biblical link, and we must be careful to consider what is appropriate and what is not.

We are in a privileged position. We are seeking the biblical aspects of our Hebraic/Jewish roots at the very time when many Jews are being drawn to salvation through the shed blood of Yeshua. These things are happening together in this world. As Israel is being drawn back to her Land and prepared for salvation, all believers are being drawn back to their true origins of the faith. Whilst there has been a small number of Jewish believers over all centuries, there is a move of the Holy Spirit in our day that is far more widespread and that reminds us of the time of the early disciples. There is a meeting point within the body of believers that will develop over the coming days, where those saved from the Jewish nation will come into unity and fellowship with those saved from the Gentile world, as never before. Some are coming out of a Jewish background to salvation. Others are seeking a true biblical character based on the true foundations of the faith, realising there is something to rediscover that has been neglected in the Church, relating to the Jewish and Hebraic background.

These things relate to the one Covenant for all believers. They are also profoundly related to Halakhah - how we live our lives on account of these things.

There are warnings in Romans 11 written by Paul with our day in mind, preparing us for this day when many Jewish believers would come to faith and when there would be a refocusing of the Church to its true origins. As we seek to discover how to live in the light of this, we should consider a major theme of Romans 11. In verse 11 we read:

> I say then, have they stumbled that they should fall? God forbid: but rather through their fall salvation is come unto the Gentiles, for to provoke them to jealousy.

There has been a phase of history when a partial blindness has remained on the majority of the Children of Israel, giving many Gentiles the opportunity to come to salvation. Always, God has had in mind that there would be a time of gathering of the Jewish remnant. The branches of the Church in the Gentile nations were meant to have this in mind as well. Even though there have been many centuries of waiting, the day that we are living in was eventually to come round. Believers, who were called into the Covenant first offered to Israel, were meant to live lives that might provoke the Jews to jealousy. Now we are in the day when this is vitally important.

There are many sorts of responses in the Church to our search for our Hebraic/Jewish/biblical heritage. Some are shallow responses, where Jewish dress and traditions take high priority over the fruits of the Holy Spirit. Indeed, some things that we might do are more likely to provoke anger than jealousy, particularly when we simply mimic the superficial aspects of Jewish lifestyle. Instead, Jews should be able to recognise that our walk with God was intended as their inheritance in Messiah. Judaism is dry and legalistic without the life of the Holy Spirit, and we should not be so fascinated by Judaism that it appears that we would prefer Jewish tradition to biblical faith. There is so much in Jewish communities that has been retained over the years of exile that it makes us full of praise that Israel is still a nation. However, this was not so that we might become Jews, but that they might retain their identity and also be saved.

It is necessary for us to rediscover our Jewish roots, but in a biblically sound way and in a way that fulfils Paul's teaching that we should provoke the Jews to jealousy. This is far from easy. When we consider, in the coming days, our ideas of Halakhah, which will include considerations of Shabbat, the Feasts, the use of the Hebrew language, interest in the Land of Israel, application of Bible teaching to our family and community life, and much more, and as we consider these things in relation to the Jewish people, we must have in mind Paul's teaching. We must consider if our Halakhah has the characteristics that would provoke Jewish unbelievers to the sort of jealousy that would make them want to be a part of our community, retaining their own Jewishness so far as it is biblical and does not conflict with biblical teaching. They must see our lifestyles, particularly our family lives, as bearing witness to true fulfilment of Messianic promise and hope and not something that is alien - a different religion, perhaps, as some branches of Christianity seem to be. They must see us as walking with God - their God - and overflowing with the fruits of the Holy Spirit. In the coming days, there will be one body of believers that is represented by the Olive Tree in full fruit, and we must have this in mind in all that we do.

For Study and Meditation: Consider Romans 11. Begin to ask questions about the lifestyle of the believer who would be seen as properly rooted in the ancient heritage of the Church, provoking unbelieving Jews to jealousy (and not anger).

Halakhah

The Reading of Scripture

If we read all Scripture with a balanced and mature view of the outworking of God's Covenant promises, we will understand our place and the place of all believers in these plans throughout history. If we do not read Scripture with a balanced view of the Covenant, we may misinterpret some passages and other passages will not convey any meaning at all.

We all filter what we read, see or hear through our own way of thinking, which has been cultivated through our experiences and our education. If we have our minds renewed (Romans 12:2) to conform to the full and balanced perspective of Scripture, then we will read, understand and act upon all that we read in an appropriate way. If our way of thinking is not properly founded or has some misconceptions, then we will have biased and erroneous views of what Scripture says.

Anti-Semitism and misunderstanding of God's Covenant with Israel has given many believers the view that Israel was completely rejected as a nation after the time of Yeshua (Jesus) and was replaced by a new body called the Church. True, there was a cutting out of Jewish branches through unbelief (Romans 11:20), but not forever (Romans 11:23-27). Those who are saved through faith in Yeshua are grafted into an ancient body that goes back to Yeshua through Abraham. Yeshua was there (though not manifest in the flesh) before creation, and the roots of the Church go back even before Abraham, and before the dawn of time. Thus, we must never read Scripture with an idea of replacement in mind, but of joining. One thing that this means is that we should not read the Scriptures of the Tanakh (Old Testament) as if their meaning is now to be fully interpreted in the light of a Church that has replaced Israel. Indeed, the Scriptures cannot all be read in this way. When we read Isaiah or Ezekiel, for example, their messages were directly to the nations of Israel and Judah of their day, and must be read in that way today. There are things for us to learn of a contemporary nature, reflected in the writings to Israel and Judah, but this must be held in balance with their original intent.

Another error is to treat the New Testament Scriptures as for the Church and the Old Testament Scriptures as ancient history and of little relevance. Again, we must understand that it was through the Children of Israel, and all God's dealings with them, that our own teaching begins. The Covenant is put into perspective, as is Yeshua's fulfilment of the Covenant promises, through this foundational teaching. Here are elements of the roots of our faith and all Scripture is made meaningful through correct and balanced study of the whole of Scripture.

All of us, whether disciples of Yeshua from a Jewish or from a Gentile background, are called into the same covenant relationship with God. Granted there may be some differences of cultural identity and some differences of interpretation of some aspects of Torah within our communities that have to be considered, but our family history is the same. We trace our spiritual ancestry and the practical history of the covenant people through the same line. We all have Abraham as our 'father ' in relation to faith, and what God taught us through his physical descendants is relevant to us all. There is only one path to salvation and this is through faith in Yeshua through His sacrifice for us:

> There is one body, and one Spirit, even as ye are called in one hope of your calling; one Lord, one faith, one baptism, one God and Father of all, who is above all, and through all, and in you all. (Ephesians 4:4-6)

For all of us, Torah (the teaching of God) begins in the first five books of the Bible. We should read these books regularly and methodically and establish a mind-set that responds to these books as the foundation of all Scripture. This does not replace Yeshua (Jesus) as the head of the Church, but gives us a scriptural foundation from which our understanding of Him and the life of faith in Him emerge. When we have established this foundation, we will discover that the message of the Prophets is dependent on these Torah foundations. Israel and Judah were addressed directly by the Prophets so that we all might learn. The call of the Prophets is for God's people to live by faith and to return to the Torah foundations of the Covenant. We 'hear' God speaking to His people and so find a reflection of this to apply to our own lives, but without replacing Israel in our concepts. We let God teach us through them. The call to return to Torah becomes a call to find saving faith in Yeshua. We do not read the Prophets as if the United Kingdom or India or the USA or Africa replaced Israel, but we meditate upon what God said to His covenant nation and seek the Lord for ourselves. The writings of the Tanakh are also found to rely on the Torah foundations of Scripture. They are Torah (teaching) of themselves, amplifying, like the Prophets, what has been previously been taught, but resting on the foundations set in the first five books of the Bible. Through Messiah, God created the universe from nothing. Mankind fell and God established a Covenant that would bring about redemption through this same Messiah. With a balanced view of Israel and the inclusion of all that believe in Yeshua, we must constantly go back to the Tanakh to discover the context and relevance of the Covenant to us. We learn directly from the Scriptures about a Covenant lifestyle, and indirectly through the history of God's dealings with Israel how we should seek to balance faith with covenant lifestyle.

Through mature consideration of the Tanakh (Old Testament) we have a framework for a deeper understanding of Yeshua's fulfilment of all Torah and for a deeper appreciation of the rest of the teaching of the New Testament.

Beyond this, we have a clearer view of the end times. The book of Revelation is mysterious and speaks of things that have happened and things that are still to come. This is a book that can only be understood if we have a sense of the continuity of covenant history and have established a foundational understanding of the symbolism and contrasts that have already been set in place. The clearest example is perhaps the imagery relating to Babylon, which we can understand most fully when we have studied the relationship between Jerusalem and Babylon in the Tanakh and the sorrow of the exile to Babylon for God's people. We must imbibe these principles through our constant prayerful reading of all Scripture, starting with a relevant and balanced view of the Covenant and the consequent balanced reading of the Tanakh. Babylon is a clear example, but there are many other images in the book of Revelation, relating to the continuing history of the plan of salvation to the end of time, that can only be understood when we have a mature grasp of all Scripture.

Surely, all of us who are redeemed according to the Covenant promise first given to Abraham and fulfilled completely in Yeshua, are being called to a lifestyle that reflects a complete and balanced view of this. We are also being called to study Scripture in the same balanced and mature way, considering our heritage, our present life and our future, within the one body with many parts, and being prepared for the coming of the Lord.

For Study and Meditation: Select one of the Prophetic Books of the Tanakh and read it carefully, checking how well-balanced your view of its message is, in light of the Covenant promises of God to Israel and to the nations.

Halakhah

A Holy Walk

The principle of holiness is central to the teaching of Scripture. Yet, we all know that our Saviour came and paid the price for our inability to achieve holiness through our own efforts. Indeed, this is what we learn from the history of the Children of Israel. Despite being shown God's holy requirements in the Law of Moses, they failed, giving us the following teaching:

Moreover the law entered, that the offence might abound. But where sin abounded, grace did much more abound. (Romans 5:20)

For Christ is the end of the law for righteousness to every one that believeth. (Romans 10:4)

We learn that Jesus is the objective of the teaching of the law and the law's primary purpose is to lead us to faith because it reveals sin. Of course, we remember that Paul gave us a balanced teaching, even though he was strong on this issue of grace. In the context of one of his fullest references to baptism (death to sin and alive in Messiah through the power of the Holy Spirit), he wrote:

What shall we say then? Shall we continue in sin, that grace may abound? God forbid. How shall we, that are dead to sin, live any longer therein? (Romans 6:1-2)

We also read:

Follow peace with all men, and holiness, without which no man shall see the Lord. (Hebrews 12:14)

Holiness is as much a part of the Covenant as it always was. Israel failed not on account of the Law of Moses, but because they did not live in faith, while seeking to follow the precepts of the Law of Moses:

> For unto us was the gospel preached, as well as unto them: but the word preached did not profit them, not being mixed with faith in them that heard it. (Hebrews 4:2)

We have the advantage over the Children of Israel in two respects, at least. First, we have been shown the fullness of teaching, whereby we see Yeshua (Jesus) as the goal of Torah, the fulfilment of sacrifice, the one who died that we might live. Secondly, the gift of the Holy Spirit has been given to Yeshua's disciples to edify them and to empower them for service. We are enabled to walk in faith in a way that Abraham foresaw, but which his physical descendants, on the whole, did not achieve. If we consider these things, we must realise that our call to holiness is no less than their call to holiness.

What is holiness? It is being set apart from things that are unclean and potentially idolatrous. Many things of the world are of this nature. A central part of Torah was to teach the people the difference between holiness and profanity. This was the reason for physical reminders, such as in clean and unclean meats. It was the role of the priests to teach about these things:

> And the LORD spake unto Aaron, saying, do not drink wine nor strong drink, thou, nor thy sons with thee, when ye go into the tabernacle of the congregation, lest ye die: it shall be a statute for ever throughout your generations: and that ye may put difference between holy and unholy, and between unclean and clean; and that ye may teach the children of Israel all the statutes which the LORD hath spoken unto them by the hand of Moses. (Leviticus 10:8-11)

It is the role of the Royal Priesthood today:

But ye are a chosen generation, a royal priesthood, an holy nation, a peculiar people; that ye should show forth the praises of him who hath called you out of darkness into his marvellous light: which in time past were not a people, but are now the people of God: which had not obtained mercy, but now have obtained mercy. Dearly beloved, I beseech you as strangers and pilgrims, abstain from fleshly lusts, which war against the soul; having your conversation honest among the Gentiles: that, whereas they speak against you as evildoers, they may by your good works, which they shall behold, glorify God in the day of visitation. (1 Peter 2:9-12)

To be able to distinguish the holy from the profane is a sign of maturity:

....strong meat belongeth to them that are of full age, even those who by reason of use have their senses exercised to discern both good and evil. (Hebrews 5:14)

After the altar of sacrifice of the Temple came the Laver, where the Priests washed. This symbolises the fact that after receiving salvation through the atoning blood of Yeshua, we should go on to sanctification (inner cleansing). This is a thing of the heart. Actually, it always was a thing of the heart even though there was physical washing to act as an outward symbol. Ezekiel carried a powerful condemnation to those in exile who were unclean in their heart:

Therefore speak unto them, and say unto them, Thus saith the Lord GOD; Every man of the house of Israel that setteth up his idols in his heart, and putteth the stumblingblock of his iniquity before his face, and cometh to the prophet; I the LORD will answer him that cometh according to the multitude of his idols; that I may take the house of Israel in their own heart, because they are all estranged from me through their idols. (Ezekiel 14:4-5)

Uncleanness of heart separates a person from God. How then can we walk with God? How does this principle affect our Halakhah? First remember that above all, our Halakhah is a walk of faith, within which is a desire to be in fellowship with the Living God

rather than to serve idols. It is this desire, mixed with faith that pleases God. Nevertheless, we must realise that idolatry will be a snare to this walk, and idolatry is anything in our heart that we love that is not acceptable to our Lord. We cannot walk with Him and carry such uncleanness, knowingly and deliberately.

However, there is another principle of life and this comes from our Jewish roots. We are to live life to the full, enjoying all that is good. In the past, members of the Church have had a sort of fear of offending God that has deprived them of living a full life. Christianity at times has seemed austere and lifeless to those who have observed the Christian community - even self-righteous and legalistic. Holiness does not mean lifelessness, self-righteousness or bondage. Some will be called to a greater sacrificial lifestyle than others, and we must not deny this, but on the whole our walk of holiness can still be a walk in the fullness of life. This is a profound challenge to the Halakhah of those who are seeking to walk within their Jewish roots tradition of fullness of life while remaining holy to the Lord. There was a great failure in ancient Judaism to do this. If we can achieve it - and achieve it we must - this will be the means of provoking the Jews to jealousy, as then we will have inherited what was offered to them. It is not easy and we need to let the Lord teach us. We cannot walk close to Him with unholy compromises in our lives, yet strong faith frees us to walk with Him and enjoy life in all its fullness. We must find the things that please Him and with which He will share fellowship in our family and community lives. Actually, there is no shortage of good things in this life. As we walk with Him, He will be with us confirming and approving that which is pure in His sight, as we learn to live life to the full in fellowship with Him.

For Study and Meditation: Consider how Yeshua (Jesus) shared in the ordinary things of family and community life. Is it possible to live a holy life and walk in holiness and fellowship with the Lord, while still having a full, free and joyous life in our families and communities?

Halakhah

Some from Every Tribe

There is a glorious picture in Chapter 7 of the Book of Revelation, where we look ahead to the gathering of people from all tribes and tongues of the earth, redeemed by the Lamb of God and worshipping round the throne. In the first nine verses of this chapter, there is an interesting and important balance to the picture. We see that Israel is identified through its tribes separately from the tribes of the earth. A distinction remains concerning the physical offspring of Israel, from which we can assume a distinction remains concerning the rest of the tribes of the earth. Thus, while we are all one in Yeshua (Jesus) there is something of distinction that remains. Even as we seek to come into the unity of the faith therefore, it is good to consider what characteristics of our own country, clan or family may remain with us as pleasing to the Lord.

There are two extremes, which we should avoid. We must neither be wrongly rooted in our own background nor over-absorbed in all that is Israel.

On the one hand, we must remember that there was a period of history, following the scattering at Babel, when the Gentile nations went their own way, 'separate from Christ, excluded from citizenship in Israel and foreigners to the covenants of the promise, without hope and without God in the world.' (Ephesians 2:12) This means that we are drawn into fellowship with God through Yeshua in the context of the revelation given through Israel. There is a distinct character to the people of faith which determines the point of unity of the body, and which makes us, 'fellow citizens with God's people and members of God's household, built on the foundation of the apostles and prophets, with Christ Jesus himself as the chief cornerstone.' (Ephesians 2:19-20) This causes us to focus our attention on all the history of salvation worked out through the tribes of Israel and coming to fulfilment in Yeshua. This is the reason why we need to find the valid separation points from the world and its systems, and the points of unity with Israel. The empires of Babylon, Greece and Rome grew and infiltrated all the Gentile nations with philosophies and religions that characterise those outside the commonwealth of Israel. Perhaps some things can honour God among the tribes of the world. Perhaps there is a seedbed where the Word of God can flourish in the hearts of some from those tribes, where, even there, there was a preparation for the Gospel message. Something of this character can be retained. However, we must not go so far as to consider that there can be salvation through the man-made or demonic philosophies and religions that these tribes and empires developed. There must be a renewing of the mind (Romans 12:1-3), a spiritual rebirth (John 3) and a grafting into the true Israel of God (Romans 11). There is a distinctiveness that we can retain, but there must be a change of character as well.

On the other hand, we must realise that 'not all who are descended from Israel are Israel.' (Romans 9:6) The picture of the 144,000 from Israel who are sealed suggests that there are some from physical Israel who are not and will not be saved. This further indicates that there are some characteristics to be found in Israel itself that are not pleasing to God. Indeed, Yeshua's ministry demonstrated, through the confrontations with the religious leaders, that there was much that had been misunderstood relating to God's purposes even in the chosen Nation. Thus, we must avoid the extreme of fascination with all that comes from Israel.

This should lead us to value some things of our own family and, perhaps, national heritage, while we also adopt a new character relevant to our grafting into the Commonwealth of Israel. We need not strive to become what we were not meant to be concerning, say, dress or lifestyle. We can remain to some extent what we were when we were called. Nevertheless, it is interesting to see that, in the picture in Revelation, the tribes of the world are waving palm branches before the throne, reminding us of the biblical feasts of the

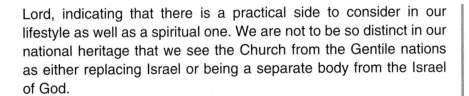

Lord, indicating that there is a practical side to consider in our lifestyle as well as a spiritual one. We are not to be so distinct in our national heritage that we see the Church from the Gentile nations as either replacing Israel or being a separate body from the Israel of God.

While the totality of the redeemed people of God are recognisable as distinct tribes from Israel and distinct tribes from among the nations, there are principles of unity in our faith which the Lord will use to draw us together into one body, particularly as the day of His return draws near. It is our privilege to discover what this unity in diversity is meant to be, and to live content and at peace as we discover it together. There is undoubtedly a work of restoration to bring the worldwide community of believers back into the right balance, but we must not go out of balance as we do so.

For Study and Meditation: Consider which of your national characteristics are pleasing to God.

Halakhah

Root and Fruit

Yeshua (Jesus) gave us a very clear test as to the acceptability of our work. He used the word 'fruit' on many occasions. There are several uses of this metaphor which should cause us to *fear the Lord* in the correct sense of the phrase. For example, in Matthew 7 we read,

By their fruit you will recognise them. (verse 20).

We also read,

….every good tree bears good fruit, but a bad tree bears bad fruit. A good tree cannot bear bad fruit, and a bad tree cannot bear good fruit.' (verse 18)

and

Not everyone who says to me, 'Lord, Lord,' will enter the kingdom of heaven, but only he who does the will of my Father who is in heaven.

Fruitful lives are a consequence of being true believers and hence of doing the will of God. Furthermore, there will be some who *thought* they were doing the will of God, but who were never known by Yeshua. There is no other way to bear good fruit than to be grafted into the Vine, which is Yeshua. John 15 makes this plain, with several references to fruitfulness, including,

Remain in me, and I will remain in you. No branch can bear fruit by itself; it must remain in the vine. Neither can you bear fruit

unless you remain in me.

One of the most awesome references comes from the cursing of the Fig Tree (Matthew 21), and also from the parable of the Fig Tree (Luke 13). In both these cases we can infer that Yeshua is making reference to the fruitlessness of the teachers of the Torah in His day. This can be a warning to those of us who are looking for fruitfulness in the outworking of what we have called the Jewish Roots Movement. We have been inspired to restore what we believe to have been neglected in the Church. Nevertheless, it is important for us to consider what true fruitfulness is.

There are two other references this time that might encourage us. Yeshua referred to the budding of the Fig Tree when He was talking to His disciples about the signs of His return:

Now learn this lesson from the fig tree: As soon as its twigs get tender and its leaves come out, you know that summer is near. Even so, when you see all these things, you know that it is near, right at the door. (Matthew 24:32-33)

Could this be the day in which we are living? Could it be that the Fig Tree refers to a true teaching of Torah which coincides with the rebirth of Israel, relating this metaphor back to when the Fig Tree was cursed and the authority was taken from Israel's teachers of the Torah? Could it be that what was said in Isaiah's day could be true in our day?

In days to come Jacob will take root, Israel will bud and blossom and fill all the world with fruit. (Isaiah 27:6)

Once more a remnant of the house of Judah will take root below and bear fruit above. (Isaiah 37:31)

What is this fruit? If we take a warning from the parable and cursing of the Fig Tree we must beware of external show. If all our enquiry into the roots of our faith brings is a fascination for Judaism and the fruits of Judaism which led to a denial of Yeshua as

Messiah, then they are not the roots that were intended when we first began. We may adopt forms of dress and the wearing of ornaments or the putting up of Jewish symbols in our home, but if this is all, then we must question whether we have found what we were first seeking.

We remember that Yeshua's ministry was not to abolish Torah but to fulfil it. Therefore, our search for the Messianic roots of our faith, which we have also called the Jewish Roots, are concerned with the true understanding of Torah (the teaching of God) and the fruitfulness that this brings. We must, therefore, ask two questions. The first is, 'What is Torah?' The second is, 'What are the true fruits of Torah?'

Some of us began this mission desiring to follow God and to bring forth fruitfulness. We highlighted to others what we were doing as we made steps along the way. Perhaps we thought everyone would see things as we did and that we might answer our questions together. However, there are various strands developing now, and not all seem to be going down the same path. Some are more fruitful than others. If we look back and consider this we might realise that what we did not produce along the way was a clear view of what fruitfulness might be. We went along a step at a time and did not make it totally clear where we were going. There might be good reasons for this at the beginning of a walk of faith, but it may now be time to bring greater precision to this mission. It seems an appropriate time for us to draw up some lists of criteria to test our fruitfulness. Just what are the fruits of our labours, and how would they measure up to the Lord's criterion for fruitfulness? Some people may be in danger of walking off the track if this is not done.

One of the main issues that were to be addressed was the Greek philosophical influence on Christianity as contrasted with the Hebraic roots from which Christianity emerged. We were to look at the roots of our faith and find ways of deepening their penetration into the original soil. That is not to say that we were to throw off all the Church's true heritage, particularly that which was won so dearly at the Reformation. By digging around the roots, pruning here and there, softening the soil, the roots might then go down deeper causing that which was already fruitful to be more fruitful. This might be the starting point for compiling a list of objectives by which to test the fruitfulness of our movement. Thus our list of objectives might begin to read as follows:

Fruitfulness of the Movement to Restore the Roots of the Christian Faith will include:

An enriched understanding of Yeshua Hamashiach (Jesus the Messiah).
Deeper worship of God and His Son Yeshua, through deeper fellowship with the Holy Spirit.
Clearer understanding of the Torah (teaching) of God.
Clearer understanding of how to study Scripture.
Greater commitment to the study of Scripture.
A greater unity of all believers in the Faith – the Olive Tree, the one body of the redeemed throughout all history.
A greater sympathy to the role of Israel.
A deepening and refinement of Christian doctrine.
A more mature walk of Faith, in the wisdom of God.
A greater witness to our lives of Faith in family and community.
A more comprehensive view of Salvation history.
A greater impact on our nations as to the full revelation of the Gospel message and the true interpretation of Torah.
Deepening linguistic and valid cultural foundations to our Faith.
More care for the lost and commitment to the Great Commission.
More humility and covenant love.
Less worldliness and vulnerability to deception.

For Study and Meditation: In 2 Peter 3:11 there is a challenge, in the light of the times that we are in, to consider what sort of people we ought to be. What fruit should we be bearing in our lives as members of the worldwide covenant community?

Halakhah

Who are we?

Because of the way most of the Church among the nations distanced itself from the Jews over many centuries, a fresh emphasis on restoring the true roots of the Christian faith leads to many questions. How much should we be like the Jews? Which Jews? What practices? What shall we call this movement? What shall we call ourselves? A flood of questions comes with the desire to be properly rooted. As is often the case, there are not single sentence answers to such questions. Nevertheless, the answers are to be found and the answers are within our ability to understand.

A useful starting point is the plan of salvation. When Adam and Eve fell from fellowship with God there was a need for mankind to be restored to fellowship. The chief emphasis of the history of the world is this restoration process. Out of all mankind and across all history, God has been restoring a family for fellowship with Himself. The mystery of the ages was fully revealed in His Son, Yeshua HaMashiach (Jesus Christ, the Anointed Saviour). The picture of bride and bridegroom from Scripture demonstrates this relationship between Yeshua (Jesus) and those who are saved by the grace of God from the nations of the earth, and gives emphasis to the family nature of the redeemed community. Restoration into fellowship with the Father through faith in the Son is the fundamental call to those who are being saved from among the nations. This is God's priority in history, along with His teaching about the way we should live as we wait for our Saviour's return.

The history of our family is written across the pages of Scripture. Our model for faith is Abraham, our father figure concerning faith:

Therefore, the promise comes by faith, so that it may be by grace and may be guaranteed to all Abraham's offspring - not only to those who are of the law but also to those who are of the faith of Abraham. He is the father of us all. As it is written: 'I have made you a father of many nations.' He is our father in the sight of God, in whom he believed - the God who gives life to the dead and calls things that are not as though they were. Against all hope, Abraham in hope believed and so became the father of many nations, just as it had been said to him, 'So shall your offspring be.' (Romans 4:16-18)

Abraham's physical descendants through Isaac and Jacob became the particular nation (Israel) whom the Lord would use in the plan of salvation. There are those from among this nation, even before the coming of the Son of God in the flesh, who had saving faith as they looked forward in faith to His coming (there is a list in Hebrews 11, for example). These were the true Israel, who were both born of the physical line of Jacob and who had saving faith. Paul reminds us that the true Israelite was not born of the flesh alone:

For not all who are descended from Israel are Israel. Nor because they are his descendants are they all Abraham's children. On the contrary, 'It is through Isaac that your offspring will be reckoned.' In other words, it is not the natural children who are God's children, but it is the children of the promise who are regarded as Abraham's offspring. For this was how the promise was stated: 'At the appointed time I will return, and Sarah will have a son.' Not only that, but Rebekah's children had one and the same father, our father Isaac. Yet, before the twins were born or had done anything good or bad–in order that God's purpose in election might stand: not by works but by him who calls–she was told, 'The older will serve the younger.' Just as it is written: 'Jacob I loved, but Esau I hated.' (Romans 9:6-13)

Paul shows through the way Jacob was chosen and Esau was not, that physical descent is not enough, and so it is with Israel after the flesh. Faith is built in those whom God chooses as the children of promise, in the nation of Israel (and later from all nations). The history of Israel and Judah is clearly revealed in Scripture. A time came when the term Jew was used to replace Israelite as the focus of God's dealings with the children of Israel. Judaism developed from the time of Ezra and was a system of interpretation of God's Torah. Yet, when Yeshua came, there was a need for reformation in the context of fulfilment. Yeshua showed the goal of true saving faith in the context of the Judaism of His day, which had become a thing of ritual rather than saving faith of the heart. Nevertheless, the first followers of the reformed faith were all Jews, those who were called, and to whom Yeshua's Messiahship was revealed.

From Abraham to Yeshua there developed a thread of salvation history that was embedded in Torah (the teaching of God) but which required faith and that the Torah be written on the heart. True believing Israel, the saved Jews of Yeshua's day, were the first of the family to which called and saved people from all nations are joined. Those who are saved from among the nations do not replace Israel, but join the true Israel of God, that is those who have faith in Yeshua:

Therefore, remember that formerly you who are Gentiles by birth and called 'uncircumcised' by those who call themselves 'the circumcision' (that done in the body by the hands of men)– remember that at that time you were separate from Christ, excluded from citizenship in Israel and foreigners to the covenants of the promise, without hope and without God in the world. But now in Christ Jesus you who once were far away have been brought near through the blood of Christ. For he himself is our peace, who has made the two one and has destroyed the barrier, the dividing wall of hostility, by abolishing in his flesh the law with its commandments and regulations. His purpose was to create in himself one new man out of the two, thus making peace, and in this one body to reconcile both of them to God through the cross, by which he put to death their hostility. He came and preached peace to you who were far away and peace to those who were near. For through him we both have access to the Father by one Spirit. Consequently, you are no longer foreigners and aliens, but

fellow citizens with God's people and members of God's house-
hold, built on the foundation of the apostles and prophets, with
Christ Jesus himself as the chief cornerstone. (Ephesians 2:11-20)

The picture of the family of God being like a tree is often given in Scripture. Several metaphors merge together, including the vine, the olive and the fig-tree. The Olive Tree of Romans 11 is among the clearest examples to consider, though the other metaphors give certain additional emphasis. Going back deep into the soil of Yeshua are the roots of our faith, reaching down to the depth of faith shown by Abraham. Because of the choice of Israel, later focussed on the Jews, there is a sense in which we can see this as Jewish soil, particularly because Yeshua came as the King of the Jews. The nation of Israel grew as the Covenant people, but there came a time when they did not bear the right fruit (the fruit of faith, the fruit of the Holy Spirit). The tree was pruned (cut down to its stump). This did not change the nature of the family of faith. Yeshua and the first Apostles became the stump into which were grafted unnatural branches (according to the flesh) from the Gentile world, but coming in with equality, and the same saving faith. The root which once supported the tree, which was Israel, now supports us too. In the end days there will be a grafting in of many with saving faith from physical Israel itself, God's promise still standing for that nation. It is a useful aid to understanding to sketch the stages of development of this 'family tree'.

Our common characteristic is faith in Yeshua. Our heritage is the Torah of God written on our hearts, the true interpretation of the teaching of God, which was partly understood over the centuries by some of the physical descendants of Jacob (profoundly so by some, such as King David). Our heritage is not the elements of teaching and practice which went into error in some areas of rabbinical Judaism. Our heritage is the pure faith and the practices in our lives which should result. We are grafted into the family of faith in Yeshua and are to feed on the heritage given to us by our Hebrew Lord, the King of the Jews, a holy community within the communities of the world. We are grafted into the family called the Israel of God, with all its privileges and responsibilities. We have the

Torah of God to interpret in the light of this and we are not to pervert our faith through practices that are as much bondage as when taught by the rabbis in Yeshua's day, yet we are to interpret Torah and live by it in accordance with all that the historical family of faith means. We are to study Scripture, inspired and explained by the Holy Spirit, in order to determine what pleases our Father in Heaven, who gave the two great commandments, to love the Lord our God with all our heart and mind and strength, and love our neighbour as ourselves.

For Study and Meditation: Consider some of the characteristics of the whole family of faith from all nations.

Halakhah

Part 3: Character and Purpose

The Supreme Goal

The supreme goal of mankind is to know the One True God and His Son Jesus Christ (Yeshua HaMashiach). This is the purpose of all history. This is what Creation cries out to us. This is what all of the Torah (teaching) of God is for. This is the Covenant promise. This is the reason for the sacrificial death and resurrection of Yeshua.

Adam and Eve had the privilege of intimate fellowship with God, but before they were secure in their relationship they reached out for a different sort of knowledge, the knowledge of good and evil that came from the forbidden tree. Knowledge of God was replaced by knowledge of sin, and that knowledge has dominated every generation since the days of Adam and Eve. Yet, instead of the whole of God's creation being immediately destroyed, God allowed history to proceed. Instead of destroying all that lived, He established a Covenant with mankind, that there would be a restoration of lost fellowship for a remnant from every nation, who would know Him as Father. This knowledge would eventually be as intimate as the purest relationship of bride to bridegroom. A family would emerge from among the nations as a bride for His only Son. This relationship is so precious that the Son would even die for His bride, so that her sins and her sinful nature would be, one day, remembered no more.

The promise was first given to Abraham:

And I will establish my covenant between me and thee and thy seed after thee in their generations for an everlasting covenant, to be a God unto thee, and to thy seed after thee. (Genesis 17:7)

The promise was full of mystery, but held in faith. The mystery was to be revealed more fully as time went on. Jeremiah was given a clearer understanding:

And they shall teach no more every man his neighbour, and every man his brother, saying, Know the LORD: for they shall all know me, from the least of them unto the greatest of them, saith the LORD: for I will forgive their iniquity, and I will remember their sin no more. (Jeremiah 31:34)

Isaiah foresaw a wonderful day when the whole earth would be full of such knowledge:

....the earth shall be full of the knowledge of the LORD, as the waters cover the sea. (Isaiah 11:9)

Such knowledge of God was the focal point of Yeshua's High Priestly prayer just before He became the sacrifice for our sins:

These words spake Jesus, and lifted up his eyes to heaven, and said, Father, the hour is come; glorify thy Son, that thy Son also may glorify thee: As thou hast given him power over all flesh, that he should give eternal life to as many as thou hast given him. And this is life eternal, that they might know thee the only true God, and Jesus Christ, whom thou hast sent. (John 17:1-3)

What is this knowledge? How are we to achieve it? How will we know when we have achieved it? First, we must say that it is not knowledge about God that we seek. Even the demons have knowledge about God:

Thou believest that there is one God; thou doest well: the devils also believe, and tremble. (James 2:19)

There are two sorts of knowledge. There is the sort of knowledge about issues that enable us to pass examinations, win quizzes, even gain theological degrees, but this is not our Covenant inheritance. Yes, knowing God begins with knowing about Him, through His Creation, through His Works, through His written Word, and most importantly through His Son, but the objective is far more intimate. It is more intimate than any experience in this world, while remaining absolutely pure. It is more intimate than family relationships, including those between husband and wife. It is far more intimate, far more holy - and deeply spiritual. It is something that is experienced. It is practice and not just theory.

Like many important biblical concepts, there is a self-definition within Scripture. This definition is discovered in the following way. Where the concept occurs (and there are a large number of places in the Bible where the concept of knowledge is used), there is an application of the concept. Through prayerful meditation on individual uses of the concept and cross-referencing to other uses of the concept, the meaning begins to develop. However, unless there is also some deeper involvement with the concept there is only knowledge about it - we can even have knowledge about knowledge. Yet through prayer, as we study, the concept takes root in a spiritual way and we find that the Holy Spirit leads us into experiences that bear witness to the use of the concept through Scripture. Hence, the principle becomes rooted like a seed in us, which grows and gives true life. As far as knowledge of God goes, we will begin to experience the true knowledge of God, like a down-payment for the future that is in store for us when all has been accomplished in this fallen world, and we are with Him forever.

This is why Torah is deeply practical. However, if Torah becomes practices and rituals alone, we have missed the point. Furthermore, it is no use trying to re-institute what was for a previous era. For example, while we can meditate on the deep meanings that were attached to Tabernacle and Temple rituals, we should not desire to rebuild them. Yet they do convey pointers to the intimacy that true knowledge of God is meant to be for us. As close as the High Priest came to God, it is less than the intimate relationship which our Father offers to us now that the veil of the Temple has been torn in two. Yet there are practices which retain deep significance and that are opportunities for spiritual experience that is related to growth in knowledge of God. Water Baptism, for example, is both practical and spiritual, as is the sharing of Bread and Wine. One accompanies a deep immersion into the life of Yeshua, the other a feeding on Him, as well as a memory of Him. Knowing God is to be a spiritual reality, and not just a theory. This is the supreme reason for all that this groaning world represents. Are we entering fully into this inheritance, as far as is possible on this earth, or are we talking about it from a distance? Do we really know our God as intimately as He desires for us, or are we standing back from this awesome relationship?

We have quoted from Isaiah, who went on to say:

And in that day there shall be a root of Jesse, which shall stand for an ensign of the people; to it shall the Gentiles seek: and his rest shall be glorious. And it shall come to pass in that day, that the Lord shall set his hand again the second time to recover the rem-nant of his people, which shall be left, from Assyria, and from Egypt, and from Pathros, and from Cush, and from Elam, and from Shinar, and from Hamath, and from the islands of the sea. And he shall set up an ensign for the nations, and shall assemble the outcasts of Israel, and gather together the dispersed of Judah from the four corners of the earth. (Isaiah 11:10-12)

This is the day in which we live and was the reason for the beginning of a move of restoration in the Church - a fresh search for the root of our faith. It is time to search the Scriptures for our root and foundation, but as we do so, let us test it all against the supreme goal of whether we are finding ourselves drawn near to God. Are we knowing Him more? Is this our true experience in these days of restoration? It should be.

For Study and Meditation: Consider what it means to be a member of the worldwide united Covenant people of God, and consider if your priority of knowing God as a child knows a perfect father, or even as a wife knows her husband, is your own supreme goal.

Halakhah

The Ambassadors

There is a famous masterpiece by the artist Hans Holbein, hanging in the National Gallery in London. The picture is entitled *The Ambassadors*. It is a picture of two men of eminence at the time of the Renaissance, the time in history when Humanism rose up, seeking to exalt the power of men in the arts and sciences and also in religion. The two men in the picture are of high rank in society. One is the French envoy to London, the other a bishop. Both stand in a stately pose in the picture, at first sight conveying the idea of affluence and success. Between them, there are two shelves on which rest objects which represent the arts, the sciences and also the Church. Again, at first sight these seem to convey the idea of the success of man in understanding both the world around him and the God who made him. Among the objects, for instance, is a globe and other scientific instruments of the day. There are also musical instruments, representing the power of art and music, and there is a copy of a hymnbook on the lower shelf where the musical instruments are placed.

At first sight, the men are successful and the instruments a measure of the success of mankind, yet on looking closer this is seen to be a superficial point of view. The men show no joy. They are flat figures cramped in their world and the objects are a clutter rather than symbols of success. The picture conveys a message about Humanism. It has the trappings and superficiality of success, but leads to the flat two-dimensional life that Holbein succeeds in portraying in this picture. Indeed, he subtly interweaves a deeper message. There is a further image in the picture of a skull, which represents death. While the two men in the portrait are trapped, the skull has freedom, conveying the message that Humanism not only fails to give depth of meaning to this life, but has no answer to the fate of all mortals, death itself.

An even more telling message emerges regarding the Church. At the time of the rise of Humanism in the Renaissance, a Reformation of the Church occurred, to free it of both the corruption and Humanism of the Roman Catholic Church of the fifteenth and sixteenth centuries. Nevertheless, Holbein places a bishop of the Church into the picture, which is a comment on the Church in the Sixteenth Century and a challenge to the Church in our own generation. Holbein saw the Church itself as sufficiently full of Humanism as to be included in his comment on the flatness of life that it produced. He challenges us to consider our doctrines and our forms of religion and see if we are true ambassadors of Yeshua HaMashiach (Jesus the Messiah) who said of His coming:

> I am come that they might have life, and that they might have it more abundantly. (John 10:10)

This echoes the words of David:

> Thou wilt show me the path of life: in thy presence is fulness of joy; at thy right hand there are pleasures for evermore. (Psalm 16:11)

Holbein showed that the Church can be like the world in offering only an intellectual and Humanistic framework for our existence, that looks like a masterpiece, but is really like a flat and lifeless two-dimensional painting. This is what Paul warned Timothy about. He said that there would be those among believers, in the last days who would have:

> ...a form of godliness, but denying the power thereof. (2 Timothy 3:5)

Paul also wrote to the Thessalonians (as he taught elsewhere):

> For our gospel came not unto you in word only, but also in

power, and in the Holy Ghost, and in much assurance; as ye know what manner of men we were among you for your sake. And ye became followers of us, and of the Lord, having received the word in much affliction, with joy of the Holy Ghost: so that ye were ensamples to all that believe in Macedonia and Achaia. (1 Thessalonians 1:5-7)

Disciples of Yeshua HaMashiach (Jesus the Messiah) are ambassadors on this earth, but not of lifeless religion that has compromised with Humanism, resulting in a flat two-dimensional existence, but through the power of the Holy Spirit, who has come to indwell and fill every believer, a three-dimensional, full life.

Another criticism of the branches of the Church that emerged from the Reformation, that are strong on philosophy but weak on the life of the Holy Spirit, is that they emphasise individual salvation but do not build community. The missing dimension to Holbein's painting is the life of the Holy Spirit. Through the Holy Spirit, the Lord will enable individuals to live a full life and also enable families and communities of believers to live in the same power and fullness.

Holbein's picture of *The Ambassadors* conveys a challenge to the Church today as it did three hundred years ago, to walk with God as individuals, united in families and communities, by the power of the Holy Spirit, as true ambassadors of the Living God.

For Study and Meditation: Read Paul's First Letter to the Thessalonians. Consider particularly Chapter 1 Verses 5 to 7. How might your fellowship have such a commendation?

Halakhah

The Living Word

Every religion has its books. No community can survive without basic principles of law and order. Even atheistic societies have learned this, and the written words of their leaders and thinkers, considered to be the wise men and women of the society, guide others in ordering their lives. If there is no concept of a god, human philosophy alone is used to direct and order society and the ideas of men reside in the writings that are used for reference in the community. If there is a concept of a god then the writings seek to lead the community to obey that god.

Even if there is a concept of a god, however, some religions consider that this god does not lead through present-day communication, but has put all his instructions in written form.

Both Christianity and Judaism have written books and knowledge of God. Indeed, the written books (the Bible) give a true revelation of the One True God. As it is written:

There is none like unto the God of Jeshurun, who rideth upon the heaven in thy help, and in his excellency on the sky.
(Deuteronomy 33:26)

The One True God and the Bible are in complete harmony. The written Scriptures of the Bible point to Him and invite believers to fellowship with Him. These Scriptures are of infinite value. Yet, it is possible to turn the Bible into a religious book and use it as if the Living God does not have living fellowship any more with His people.

Judaism turned the Tanakh (Old Testament) and the Oral Traditions into a set of rules that lost the heart of the message of God, and resulted in dry legalism. Christianity can do the same with the Old and New Testament. If there is no fellowship with the Living God as a result of prayerful study and meditation on the Scriptures then a flat lifeless religion can result.

There is a Hebrew concept of the *Memra*. This refers to any manifestation of the Living God and this has been in a variety of ways. God has communicated to His prophets in ways that can be expressed as words in our languages, for example. He has also spoken and the universe came into existence, He has appeared to His people in various forms, and He has appeared in His Shekinah Glory. The word *Memra* refers to any manifestation of God brought to us in this physical world, whether as communication or by His presence or by His creative power. The word *Word* that we use is not sufficient to describe this, because whatever is manifested in this physical world from God began in the unseen heavenly place, and we use the word *Word* in very literal ways.

Our Bible is the most precious book in the whole universe and cannot be replaced. All else that is written is less and has error. All that the Bible has in its writings came from God as a manifestation of His communication and so is linked to this concept of *Memra*. God, from the unseen heavenly place, spoke with power and with life and a result is our record written into the Bible. Yet the written word does not replace the Living Word, but simply points to Him. There was mystery in all God spoke before He communicated to us fully and completely in Yeshua. The manifestations of the *Memra* were only complete in Yeshua.

Because the New Testament comes to us in Greek, there is a Greek term used in the Gospel of John for the Hebrew equivalent of *Memra*. The Greek word is *Logos*. Unfortunately, we can be diverted onto Greek philosophical ideas because of this, instead of a concept of the Living *Memra* made flesh in Yeshua. At worst this will be the beginning of a process whereby the Bible is read in the manner of Greek philosophy rather than living faith. The English equivalent of the Greek word *Logos* is simply the word *Word*. Thus we read John 1:1 as:

In the beginning was the Word, and the Word was with God, and the Word was God.

Because of this ambiguous word *Word*, which we also use to refer to the Bible (the Word of God), precious though the Bible is, we can replace fellowship with the Living God with intellectual study of the Bible.

This is a delicate matter to tackle! Yet, the Living God calls us into fellowship by the power of His Spirit and wants us to use the Bible for all it is worth to that end, rather than replace the Living Word with the written records which we call the Word of God.

Where the Bible says:

...the Word was made flesh, and dwelt among us. (John 1:14)

we can read,

...the Memra was made flesh, and dwelt among us.

The Apostle John points us back to the same power from heaven that was manifest at the Creation of the world and which revealed God in mysterious ways throughout the history of His people, but now we see that the power, the means of communication, revelation and creation was, and came from, the One who would come to live among us to be our Saviour and Lord.

The Bible is a manifestation of the Word (*Memra*) of God, but Yeshua is the Word of God. He is the Living Word. Now He has sent us another representation of His being, of His life, of His *Memra*. He has sent the Holy Spirit to live in us and to be with us. Judaism and Christianity must no longer be dry religions. Yes, we are 'people of the Book', but that Book is, in a sense, to be brought to spiritual life in us, who are saved by faith in Yeshua, and not left as a philosophy of the mind.

The Living Word is God Himself, who revealed Himself to us fully in His Son Yeshua and invites us to living fellowship with Him through the manifestation of His Spirit in us. To deny this is to have a form of Christian religion while denying the life of God, and a living walk with our Living God.

For Study and Meditation: Consider the working of the Holy Spirit in Genesis 1, John 1, Acts 2 and in your own life.

Halakhah

Guidance Through Scripture

When Paul taught us to live by the Spirit he did not expect us to neglect the Scriptures. When we declare that the priority of our discipleship is to seek to live in fellowship with the Living God, it is not at the expense of the proper use of the Scriptures.

It was Paul who wrote:

There is therefore now no condemnation to them which are in Christ Jesus, who walk not after the flesh, but after the Spirit. For the law of the Spirit of life in Christ Jesus hath made me free from the law of sin and death. For what the law could not do, in that it was weak through the flesh, God sending his own Son in the likeness of sinful flesh, and for sin, condemned sin in the flesh: that the righteousness of the law might be fulfilled in us, who walk not after the flesh, but after the Spirit. For they that are after the flesh do mind the things of the flesh; but they that are after the Spirit the things of the Spirit. (Romans 8:1-5)

Paul also wrote:

…continue thou in the things which thou hast learned and hast been assured of, knowing of whom thou hast learned them; and that from a child thou hast known the holy scriptures, which are able to make thee wise unto salvation through faith which is in Christ Jesus. All scripture is given by inspiration of God, and is profitable for doctrine, for reproof, for correction, for instruction in righteousness: that the man of God may be perfect, thoroughly furnished unto all good works. (2 Timothy 3:14-17)

The first quotation from his letters refers to the life of the Spirit, the second to the usefulness of Scripture. Again, he wrote:

This I say then, Walk in the Spirit, and ye shall not fulfil the lust of the flesh. (Galatians 5:16)

And:

And be not drunk with wine, wherein is excess; but be filled with the Spirit; speaking to yourselves in psalms and hymns and spiritual songs, singing and making melody in your heart to the Lord. (Ephesians 5:18-19)

But he also wrote:

Let the word of Christ dwell in you richly in all wisdom; teaching and admonishing one another in psalms and hymns and spiritual songs, singing with grace in your hearts to the Lord. (Colossians 3:16)

Much of Paul's writing was to exhort us to reject the sort of legalism that had beset the religious Jews of his day. This shows that it is possible to interpret Scripture into a framework of human philosophy quite devoid of its true heart intent and lacking the life that the Holy Spirit brings. This is a most important point because it can apply to the use of the New Testament as well as the Old Testament. However, having said that, the question concerns how we should use the Scriptures while walking with the Holy Spirit. One extreme (without the life of the Spirit of the Lord) is lifeless legalism, but another extreme can be neglect of Scripture, thinking that it is more spiritual that way. We can be sure that the Lord who inspired the writing of Scripture is not going to want us to neglect it. The Living Word inspired the written word, so to speak.

Perhaps the key is to be found in James' Epistle:

Be ye doers of the word, and not hearers only, deceiving your own selves. For if any be a hearer of the word, and not a doer, he is like unto a man beholding his natural face in a glass: for he beholdeth himself, and goeth his way, and straightway forgetteth what manner of man he was. But whoso looketh into the perfect law of liberty, and continueth therein, he being not a forgetful hearer, but a doer of the work, this man shall be blessed in his deed. (James 1:22-25)

We can be sure that James was talking of Halakhah here, the doing of what the Scriptures teach and not just the thinking about them. If we read this with the true intent that Halakhah is a walk with the Spirit of the Lord, we can see that James was confident to expose those who had a kind of philosophy as a substitute for the true faith given by the Holy Spirit. If, further, we allow 'perfect law of liberty' to mean the whole Torah (teaching) of God, just as is implied by the use of 'word' earlier in the passage, then we see that the Holy Spirit will use the whole of Scripture as a mirror to our life. In the history of all God's dealings with mankind, set before us in Scripture in its various ways, we have reflections of His dealing with us and His expectation of us. Hence, through the various patterns and principles of Scripture, the Holy Spirit will speak to us of His work in our lives and of our walk with Him.

Thus, just as we use a mirror to see our face, we can expect the Holy Spirit to use Scripture. It is a 'mirror' that He designed. This is why we will find ourselves close to the Lord as we take up our Bibles expectantly, but it is in fellowship with Him that the Bible should be read and then we can talk to Him about how to understand what we read in the context of our lives and the lives of our families and communities. Without Him, we will end up in philosophy and legalism. With Him beside us and living in us, we can know His life and walk as we ought.

For Study and Meditation: Choose one of the 'heroes of faith' from Hebrews 11 and then read the whole Scriptural account of their life and ministry. Consider how your own life reflects some of the principles of their life.

Halakhah

Would God that all the LORD'S people were prophets, and that the LORD would put his spirit upon them! (Numbers 11:29)

Above all people Moses experienced a close walk with the Lord by the power of His Spirit. He knew of the wisdom of God to lead the people, yet there were so many people to lead and among whom he had to administer justice that Moses was glad when the Holy Spirit came to rest on seventy elders of Israel. He knew the blessing and privilege of a close walk with God and would have wanted all of the Lord's people to know this. It would be both for personal blessing and blessing of the community, as responsibilities were shared.

Centuries later, Joel prophesied that Moses' desire would come true one day, when the Lord would restore His people:

...ye shall know that I am in the midst of Israel, and that I am the LORD your God, and none else: and my people shall never be ashamed. And it shall come to pass afterward, that I will pour out my spirit upon all flesh; and your sons and your daughters shall prophesy, your old men shall dream dreams, your young men shall see visions: and also upon the servants and upon the hand-maids in those days will I pour out my spirit. (Joel 2:27-29)

This was the Lord's promise, so there should be no surprise that Yeshua announced the coming of the Holy Spirit:

And I will pray the Father, and he shall give you another Comforter, that he may abide with you for ever; even the Spirit of truth; whom the world cannot receive, because it seeth him not, neither knoweth him: but ye know him; for he dwelleth with you, and shall be in you. I will not leave you comfortless: I will come to you. (John 14:16-18)

Howbeit when he, the Spirit of truth, is come, he will guide you into all truth: for he shall not speak of himself; but whatsoever he shall hear, that shall he speak: and he will show you things to come. He shall glorify me: for he shall receive of mine, and shall show it unto you. (John 16:13-14)

The same Holy Spirit who guided Moses and the elders would eventually come to all believers to continue the purposes of guiding and teaching the Lord's people. This fulfilment began when Peter preached on the day of Shavuot following the Lord's Ascension.

And when the day of Pentecost was fully come, they were all with one accord in one place. And suddenly there came a sound from heaven as of a rushing mighty wind, and it filled all the house where they were sitting. And there appeared unto them cloven tongues like as of fire, and it sat upon each of them. And they were all filled with the Holy Ghost, and began to speak with other tongues, as the Spirit gave them utterance. And there were dwelling at Jerusalem Jews, devout men, out of every nation under heaven. Now when this was noised abroad, the multitude came together, and were confounded, because that every man heard them speak in his own language........Peter, standing up with the eleven, lifted up his voice, and said unto them, Ye men of Judaea, and all ye that dwell at Jerusalem, be this known unto you, and hearken to my words: for these are not drunken, as ye suppose, seeing it is but the third hour of the day. But this is that which was spoken by the prophet Joel; and it shall come to pass in the last days, saith God, I will pour out of my Spirit upon all flesh: and your sons and your daughters shall prophesy, and your young men shall see visions, and your old men shall dream dreams: and on my servants and on my handmaidens I will pour out in those days of my Spirit; and they shall prophesy. (Acts 2:1-18)

Until this time even the close disciples of Yeshua lacked the power to fulfil the Great Commission, but afterwards through the empowering of the Holy Spirit the Gospel message went out across the whole world and the community of believers has grown in power since that day. This has gone on until today and will proceed to the end of time. All that the Holy Spirit speaks is in a general sense prophetic. He speaks into and through men to give revelation, teaching, healing, encouragement, hospitality, love, faith and all the other manifestations of His creative power. Paul showed that through the Holy Spirit's working in us we would build up the family of God:

Now concerning spiritual gifts, brethren, I would not have you ignorant. Ye know that ye were Gentiles, carried away unto these dumb idols, even as ye were led. Wherefore I give you to understand, that no man speaking by the Spirit of God calleth Jesus accursed: and that no man can say that Jesus is the Lord, but by the Holy Ghost. Now there are diversities of gifts, but the same Spirit. And there are differences of administrations, but the same Lord. And there are diversities of operations, but it is the same God which worketh all in all. But the manifestation of the Spirit is given to every man to profit withal. For to one is given by the Spirit the word of wisdom; to another the word of knowledge by the same Spirit; to another faith by the same Spirit; to another the gifts of healing by the same Spirit; to another the working of miracles; to another prophecy; to another discerning of spirits; to another divers kinds of tongues; to another the interpretation of tongues: but all these worketh that one and the selfsame Spirit, dividing to every man severally as he will. For as the body is one, and hath many members, and all the members of that one body, being many, are one body: so also is Christ. (1 Corinthians 12:1-12)

And he gave some, apostles; and some, prophets; and some, evangelists; and some, pastors and teachers; for the perfecting of the saints, for the work of the ministry, for the edifying of the body of Christ: till we all come in the unity of the faith, and of the knowledge of the Son of God, unto a perfect man, unto the measure of the stature of the fulness of Christ. (Ephesians 4:11-13)

Moses' desire and Joel's prophecy have been fulfilled through the prayer of Yeshua. All His disciples should be encouraged to become prophetic in some sense, receiving the creative Words of the Holy Spirit for the purpose that they are placed into the Lord's people. Together we journey through life in a way that was symbolised in the day of Moses, and together we need the same Holy Spirit for the purposes of God in our day. It is not that we should receive a once-and-for-all blessing of the Holy Spirit, but that through our ongoing walk with Him, like Moses in one sense and Yeshua in a fuller sense, that we will serve the people of God together as we go step by step with Him. This is according to the purposes and leading of the Holy Spirit, in whatever way He chooses to lead us and fulfil the Lord's purposes. This partnership of ministry within the body of believers will be totally servant-like and ordered if His people learn obedience. In the end, it will result in a united body (the Bride) in unity with the Holy Spirit, fulfilling the final purpose of God. Moses' desire will be fully accomplished when a united voice calls on the Lord to return:

And the Spirit and the bride say, Come. And let him that heareth say, Come. And let him that is athirst come. (Revelation 22:17)

Let us be glad and rejoice, and give honour to him: for the marriage of the Lamb is come, and his wife hath made herself ready. (Revelation 19:7)

In the meanwhile, on our walk as aliens and pilgrims, we must learn to fulfil our prophetic calling, by the power of the Holy Spirit, who works in us and through us in many ways.

For Study and Meditation: Compare the choosing of 70 men by Moses (Numbers 11:16-17) to the sending out of 70 men by Yeshua (Luke 10:1-17). Is Yeshua's ministry through the 70 to be fulfilled in us through what Paul taught in Ephesians 4:1-13?

Halakhah

When ye come together...

When Paul wrote to the Corinthians he assumed that everyone had something that was inspired by the Holy Spirit already prepared for them to share:

When ye come together, every one of you hath a psalm, hath a doctrine, hath a tongue, hath a revelation, hath an interpretation. (1 Corinthians 14:26)

The implication bears out our experience that, as each of us seeks to walk closely with the Lord, we will be inspired in various ways. When we are preparing to meet together, we will discover that among the spiritual words that the Lord gives us, whether for revelation, proclamation, worship, healing, encouragement or any other of the many ways in which the Lord works among us, we can all receive something for sharing and edifying the body of believers when we meet. There are a number of things to consider.

First, every one of the Lord's disciples should expect to be inspired not only for himself but for the edification (building up) of others, whether in our family meetings or in our wider community. There should not be an expectation that any one person will have all the revelation from the Lord. This has major implications for the world-wide body of believers and for the local body. There is no place for papal decrees or central control, but there must be an interacting living body of believers all over the world, most strongly expressed in the local community. This does not deny the fact that the Lord raises up some people to minister (serve) in a general sense, but emphasises that within the exercising of these general ministries we should expect the Lord to use each believer to

contribute to the spiritual life of others.

Secondly, this has a bearing on how community meetings can be conducted. There are priestly functions within the body of believers, such as the receiving of tithes and the pronouncement of blessings, but we are a Royal Priesthood together (1 Peter 2:9). Every word that is given by the Holy Spirit to minister, to whoever it is given, puts that person into a priestly role, as a representative of God. This can be a holy calling to both men and women. This is why, for example, Paul instructs women to cover their heads when praying or prophesying, on account of the angels (messengers of God) (1 Corinthians 11:10). It is to encourage them to minister God's Word within the submissive attitude they have to their husbands, while being separated to the Lord for service to the body. With an attitude of submission they can be purer channels for the Lord's ministry and the whole body can benefit. It is the same holy position that each person takes when ministering in the Lord's Name in any way, whether men or women.

There is no place for one person to expect to be the sole administrator of the Lord's ministries within the body. If a person sets himself up as a priest or "vicar of Christ" then he is likely to deny others the service of what the Lord has given, and so deny the working of the Holy Spirit in various ways. Even a pastor, with all good intent, can mistakenly set himself up in a priestly role if he takes too much upon himself. Thus, meetings should be arranged with sharing of ministry in mind. The home is the place where this can begin and small groups in study and prayer together can be particularly blessed because of the way each person can be involved.

Thirdly, there is the assumption that believers will meet together. This reflects what the writer to the Hebrews said, and what we read of the disciples in the Book of Acts:

And let us consider one another to provoke unto love and to good works: not forsaking the assembling of ourselves together, as the manner of some is; but exhorting one another: and so much the more, as ye see the day approaching. (Hebrews 10:24-25)

And they, continuing daily with one accord in the temple, and breaking bread from house to house, did eat their meat with glad-ness and singleness of heart, praising God, and having favour with all the people. And the Lord added to the church daily such as should be saved. (Acts 2:46-47)

Fourthly, the One who created the universe and sent His Torah has shown Himself to be perfectly disciplined and ordered in all that He does. If there is disorder in our lives it is because we have not learned to walk closely to the Lord individually or together. Therefore, even though we all may have something special to share from the Lord when we meet together, we must also expect an order to our meetings. Some have denied the full life of the Holy Spirit and quenched the interaction that might have otherwise taken place in believers' meetings, because of the disorder that can come from immaturity. This is why Paul wrote so strongly to the Corinthian believers. Something that we should learn together is how to value the contributions of others while learning how to serve the body with what the Lord has given to us.

We must seek to live a full and shared life with all of God's spiritual gifts and blessings among us, while living within the order and discipline of the Lord in all things. Each person is needed and the Lord will not leave any willing disciple to be a spectator of His work among us.

For Study and Meditation: Read the First Letter to the Corinthians.

Halakhah

Battles

It sounds easy! Once we have seen it, once we have believed it, once we have freed ourselves from the misconceptions of others, all we need to do is walk with God! What a wonderful vision! What freedom! What power! The problem is that this cannot happen in a moment. We come out of a fallen and sinful world and we will not reach maturity in one moment.

One of the battles we face is against our natural personality, our fallen nature. Paul expressed it clearly, by describing the battles that he himself seemed to have to face, as he learned to live in the victory of Yeshua and learned to walk in the the Spirit:

For we know that the law is spiritual: but I am carnal, sold under sin. For that which I do I allow not: for what I would, that do I not; but what I hate, that do I. If then I do that which I would not, I consent unto the law that it is good. Now then it is no more I that do it, but sin that dwelleth in me. For I know that in me (that is, in my flesh,) dwelleth no good thing: for to will is present with me; but how to perform that which is good I find not. For the good that I would I do not: but the evil which I would not, that I do. Now if I do that I would not, it is no more I that do it, but sin that dwelleth in me. I find then a law, that, when I would do good, evil is present with me. For I delight in the law of God after the inward man: but I see another law in my members, warring against the law of my mind, and bringing me into captivity to the law of sin which is in my members. O wretched man that I am! who shall deliver me from the body of this death? I thank God through Jesus Christ our Lord. So then with the mind I myself serve the law of God; but with the flesh the law of sin. (Romans 7:1-25)

Paul's teaching in this section leads up to our goal of the life of the Spirit. This is in Romans 8, but he highlights clearly in Romans 7 the battle that rages against the things of God in our fallen flesh. Yeshua HaMashiach freed us from the power of sin which condemns because of the weakness of our flesh, but nevertheless our walk is a walk of learning, of discipleship. We begin with saving faith and commitment to discipleship, and then we go out on a path whereby we are free to learn. However, like every child we will not learn every lesson that is relevant to our personal Halakhah in one moment.

If we are not conscious of this very real aspect of discipleship, we will overstep the mark many times. The Lord will give us inspiration and ministry, like any teacher, according to our stage of learning and according to His plans for us and those around us. Above all we must be teachable and gradually learn how to resist the sinful and ambitious flesh so that our spiritual walk may be matured day by day. We must test everything to ensure that we don't mistake the desires of our flesh for the call of God. We must help one another in this.

If one battle is against the flesh another is against Satan. As Peter taught:

Be sober, be vigilant; because your adversary the devil, as a roaring lion, walketh about, seeking whom he may devour: whom resist stedfast in the faith, knowing that the same afflictions are accomplished in your brethren that are in the world. (1 Peter 5:7-9)

Peter would know as well as anyone the reality of what he wrote. Before giving into the weakness of his flesh and the power of temptation in denying our very Lord and Master, with whom he had walked so closely, Yeshua told him:

Simon, Simon, behold, Satan hath desired to have you, that he may sift you as wheat: but I have prayed for thee, that thy faith

fail not: and when thou art converted, strengthen thy brethren.
(Luke 22:31-32)

The Lord knew Simon Peter better than he knew himself. Peter said that he was ready to go to prison and even death for the Lord, but the Lord knew he would deny him first.

And he said unto him, Lord, I am ready to go with thee, both into prison, and to death. And he said, I tell thee, Peter, the cock shall not crow this day, before that thou shalt thrice deny that thou knowest me. (Luke 22:33-34)

Indeed, tradition has it that Peter did die a martyr's death, but he was not ready for that death until much later. We would be wise to realise that our battles will also be against the power of Satan at times:

For we wrestle not against flesh and blood, but against principalities, against powers, against the rulers of the darkness of this world, against spiritual wickedness in high places. (Ephesians 6:12)

If we take our model from the Lord's dealings with Peter, we will realise that temptations will come, which we must overcome, and that through overcoming we will grow in maturity and availability for service. We can rely on the Lord's intercessions for us as with Peter. As Paul taught:

God is faithful, who will not suffer you to be tempted above that ye are able; but will with the temptation also make a way to escape, that ye may be able to bear it. (1 Corinthians 10:13)

Whether our battles are against the flesh or the devil we can be sure that our path of discipleship will require our refinement and we are intended to come out as changed and refined people, prepared for service and worthy of the Lord at His coming:

Blessed be the God and Father of our Lord Jesus Christ, which according to his abundant mercy hath begotten us again unto a lively hope by the resurrection of Jesus Christ from the dead, to an inheritance incorruptible, and undefiled, and that fadeth not away, reserved in heaven for you, who are kept by the power of God through faith unto salvation ready to be revealed in the last time. Wherein ye greatly rejoice, though now for a season, if need be, ye are in heaviness through manifold temptations: what the trial of your faith, being much more precious than of gold that perisheth, though it be tried with fire, might be found unto praise and honour and glory at the appearing of Jesus Christ. (1 Peter 1:3-7)

Let us not be among those who treat our Halakhah lightly. Let us not be presumptuous in our fellowship with God. Yes, it is a glorious walk with the Spirit of God who will lead us into spiritual ministry, but it is also a path of discipleship and refinement. We will meet trials and testing and we must learn how to go through such trials in faith, expecting to grow in maturity through them. The disciple will be an overcomer of things of this world and of the devil. Not immediately, but step by step, progress in ministry and in maturity will result, in preparation, not only for this world, but also for the Kingdom to come.

For Study and Meditation: Read the Book of Job. Consider the trials of the nation of Israel. Consider Peter's testing and temptation. Consider even the Lord's confrontation with Satan after His baptism (Luke 4:1-13). Read Hebrews 12 and then assess the reality of the battles of discipleship we face while still living by the power of the Holy Spirit in personal life and ministry.

Halakhah

Vision and Purpose

A verse from Proverbs carries a profound truth:

Where there is no vision, the people perish: but he that keepeth the law, happy is he. (Proverbs 29:18)

The Lord knows that the people He has made need constant encouragement and an objective in life. In the Torah (law) of God are many goals for our lives. Indeed, one of our goals is to understand Torah! If we set this verse from Torah alongside our invitation to walk with the Holy Spirit then He will establish the goals of our lives with us. Our life will be full of purpose.

Within our purpose come our personal desires to serve the purposes of the Lord. Again, it is the Lord Himself who will envision us. Psalm 20 reflects a blessing that we all want in our lives:

The LORD hear thee in the day of trouble; the name of the God of Jacob defend thee; send thee help from the sanctuary, and strengthen thee out of Zion; remember all thy offerings, and accept thy burnt sacrifice; grant thee according to thine own heart, and fulfil all thy counsel. We will rejoice in thy salvation, and in the name of our God we will set up our banners: the LORD fulfil all thy petitions. (Psalm 20:1-5)

The Lord places vision in us and then fulfils that vision in our lives. Sometimes vision is given mysteriously, prophetically and pictorially, according to the prophecy of Joel:

And it shall come to pass afterward, that I will pour out my spirit upon all flesh; and your sons and your daughters shall prophesy, your old men shall dream dreams, your young men shall see visions. (Joel 2:28)

Desire rises in us to serve the Lord and He may set a vision before us, a goal to achieve. How, then should we expect Him to fulfil that vision? First, we must state that the Lord knows us through and through, better than we know ourselves. He knows how impatient we are to see a promise fulfilled, yet He also knows how much we need a time of preparation. Hence, He may give us a goal or purpose to be fulfilled that will take many years to come about.

Secondly, it is His vision and not ours. At the end we will say:

We are unprofitable servants: we have done that which was our duty to do. (Luke 17:10)

Indeed, once the promise is spoken it will come about:

Heaven and earth shall pass away: but my words shall not pass away. (Luke 21:33)

Despite this, we will have our self-doubts. We will wonder if we have fully understood what the Lord promised, and we may find that there were some elements of misunderstanding as to how the Lord would achieve His purposes through us. Nevertheless, once the vision is given, if it is from the Lord it will increase in us as if it is our own possession, and as years go by we will find that the Lord breaks us of our fleshly response to His promises, so that we come into willing obedience for His purposes. There may be painful days of preparation before what the Lord promised in our lives comes about.

We would be advised, therefore, to seek the Lord for vision and purpose, as part of our heritage in Him, for indeed we are all called to serve the purposes of His Kingdom. Then, we must let Him teach us patience and we must realise that though we own the vision, we must see ourselves as servants and not masters. In the end, the promise for our lives will be fulfilled exactly on time, according to the plans of the Lord. In giving us a vision He also allows Himself time to get us to the point that is required before the vision can be fulfilled. When we think that the vision is late or forgotten, we must tell ourselves that while we may think this, it is only that we ourselves have not reached the point of readiness in our lives. It is God's work in us that must be completed. Yet, there is the confidence that the Lord will not easily take away from us what He promised, despite the battles that must be fought along the way of our discipleship. It will be for us as it was for Habakkuk who, through perplexing times was told:

> Write the vision, and make it plain upon tables, that he may run that readeth it. For the vision is yet for an appointed time, but at the end it shall speak, and not lie: though it tarry, wait for it; because it will surely come, it will not tarry. (Habbakuk 2:2-3)

At the deepest level, when we consider our works of service for the Kingdom, whatever they are, they are all within the general purpose of the Lord to fulfil the Covenant He made with Abraham, to build a family from all nations to meet the Lord at His return, and be one with Him. Thus, the prime example for the way vision is given and fulfilled is in the life of Abraham. It was a long way from his first steps out of Ur to laying down the vision that depended on Isaac on the altar at Mount Moriah. The promise was certain, but it was also mysterious and would be fulfilled a long time afterwards, through Yeshua, and a long time after Abraham's death. Abraham had his doubts and made his mistakes, but the promise was not taken away. Abraham is our model and we should study him and see a reflection of ourselves. Indeed, we will realise that it is not so much vision as faith that the Lord will increase in us, just as He did for Abraham. Indeed, we may see our vision fulfilled or die in faith for the vision that the Lord gives us, just as Abraham and many of us who went before us have done:

> These all died in faith, not having received the promises, but having seen them afar off, and were persuaded of them, and embraced them, and confessed that they were strangers and pilgrims on the earth. (Hebrews 11:13)

For Study and Meditation: Has the Lord given you a vision for your part in the Great Commission? Study the life of Abraham and read Hebrews 10 to 12 to see how well your own life is paralleled in Scripture.

Halakhah

Authority of Yeshua

There are some key words in Scripture that can have several meanings. It all depends on the way that we read them – on our way of thinking. We can have dictionary definitions of words that are good for everyday use and that apply to situations in our human experience. In general terms these serve us well. Nevertheless, much of our human way of thinking is based on human philosophy rather than on higher understanding. James showed us this in relation to wisdom:

Who is a wise man and endued with knowledge among you? let him show out of a good conversation his works with meekness of wisdom. But if ye have bitter envying and strife in your hearts, glory not, and lie not against the truth. This wisdom descendeth not from above, but is earthly, sensual, devilish. For where envying and strife is, there is confusion and every evil work. But the wisdom that is from above is first pure, then peaceable, gentle, and easy to be entreated, full of mercy and good fruits, without partiality, and without hypocrisy. (James 3:13-17)

The wisdom that is from above is what Solomon asked for in order to govern Israel. (2 Chronicles 1:8-12) It is the wisdom that James told us all to ask God for. (James 1:5).

Wisdom is justified of her children. (Matthew 11:19)

True wisdom, that which motivates our decisions and actions in life, bears the fruit of the Holy Spirit. It is given from God and has spiritual life. Thus, there is a definition of wisdom that is verified by its fruit. This is directly linked to our Halakhah, for there can be no true Halakhah without the spiritual gift of wisdom. The Book of Proverbs can only be read correctly with this in mind. Similarly, knowledge, understanding, faith and love are among the words and concepts which are defined by their fruit according to a heavenly/spiritual definition rather than the philosophical definition of Humanism. These are all gifts from above.

Similarly, the concept of authority is to be understood in this way. The dictionary definition relating to delegated power to rule and enforce authority is only a beginning to understanding of the spiritual manifestation of authority. It was said of Yeshua:

The people were astonished at his doctrine: for he taught them as one having authority, and not as the scribes. (Matthew 7:28-29)

This means far more than that Yeshua gave the right interpretation of Scripture, which of course He did. His teaching moved His hearers spiritually too. The scribes had turned the teaching of the Bible into ritual and philosophy of men that had an influence on the way people lived but lacked joy and lacked life. It was said of Yeshua, following His teaching:

When he was come down from the mountain, great multitudes followed him. And, behold, there came a leper and worshipped him, saying, Lord, if thou wilt, thou canst make me clean. And Jesus put forth his hand, and touched him, saying, I will; be thou clean. And immediately his leprosy was cleansed. (Matthew 8:1-3)

The authority to teach and to perform miracles did not come as theory, but with spiritual life and power. This power transformed lives and compelled people to change their lives and follow Him.

Authority is spiritual when it is sent from above, and bears the fruit of the Holy Spirit in its outworking. Human definitions of authority involve control and dominance. The authority given to Yeshua by the Father was to bring freedom in the Holy Spirit, to restore, to bring order among God's people and build them up according to the purposes of God. Like wisdom, the authority of

Yeshua is defined by its fruit. The word is defined by the way Yeshua ministered. All that the Father intends for His people is to come through the ministry of Yeshua. No human being can reach up to heaven and grasp the authority that is given to Yeshua. It can be given according to the Lord's will, but we would be wise to seek a true definition of what this authority is through studying the life and ministry of Yeshua, before we make the mistake of putting earthly definitions on a heavenly concept.

For Study and Meditation: Read one of the Gospel accounts. Consider from the way Yeshua taught and ministered in the power of the Holy Spirit, how we might define true authority.

Halakhah

All Authority

Using His total authority, Yeshua gave the Great Commission:

*All power is given unto me in heaven and in earth. Go ye there-
fore, and teach all nations, baptizing them in the name of the
Father, and of the Son, and of the Holy Ghost: teaching them to
observe all things whatsoever I have commanded you: and, lo, I
am with you alway, even unto the end of the world. (Matthew
28:18-20)*

He gave responsibility to His disciples to go into the entire world
just as He had once sent them out two by two to minister in the
towns and cities of Israel and Judah. Just as He delegated some of
His power and authority to His disciples in those days in order to
accomplish the Great Commission, He does so today:

*And he gave some, apostles; and some, prophets; and some,
evangelists; and some, pastors and teachers; for the perfecting of
the saints, for the work of the ministry, for the edifying of the
body of Christ: till we all come in the unity of the faith, and of the
knowledge of the Son of God, unto a perfect man, unto the
measure of the stature of the fulness of Christ. (Ephesians 4:11-
13)*

*Now concerning spiritual gifts, brethren, I would not have you
ignorant. Ye know that ye were Gentiles, carried away unto these
dumb idols, even as ye were led. Wherefore I give you to understand, that no man speaking by the Spirit of God calleth Jesus
accursed: and that no man can say that Jesus is the Lord, but by
the Holy Ghost. Now there are diversities of gifts, but the same*

Spirit. And there are differences of administrations, but the same Lord. And there are diversities of operations, but it is the same God which worketh all in all. But the manifestation of the Spirit is given to every man to profit withal. For to one is given by the Spirit the word of wisdom; to another the word of knowledge by the same Spirit; to another faith by the same Spirit; to another the gifts of healing by the same Spirit; to another the working of miracles; to another prophecy; to another discerning of spirits; to another divers kinds of tongues; to another the interpretation of tongues: but all these worketh that one and the selfsame Spirit, dividing to every man severally as he will. (1 Corinthians 12:1-11)

The Great Commission is concerned with the fulfilment of the Covenant Promise made with Abraham, and will result in some from every nation being gathered into one body, the family of God, united as a Bride in preparation for the return of the Messiah.

The One with all authority is Yeshua and He is our Head:

The head of every man is Christ. (1 Corinthians 11:3)

We can expect Him to give us authority in the area of His choosing if He has called us to be disciples. This authority will be God's power to minister in the area He has chosen for us to serve. Such authority is not carnal and we must learn to obey the prompting of the Spirit of God who works through us. We must serve in the way that the Lord Himself served, who said of Himself:

I do nothing of myself; but as my Father hath taught me, I speak these things. And he that sent me is with me: the Father hath not left me alone; for I do always those things that please him. (John 8:28-29)

If we are to serve the purposes of God's Kingdom, it is a mistake to think that God grants His power and authority for us to serve according to our own strategy. If we try to exercise our ministry in this way, it will be carnal and lifeless, but if we seek to walk with Him and listen to His promptings, speaking and doing what He gives us to speak and do, then we will have power and authority for our ministry. We must learn to make this a full part of our Halakhah, our walk in the Spirit.

There is a difference between preaching according to the rhetoric of the Greek philosophers and according to the power of the Holy Spirit. There is persuasion and control in the former, but conviction and edification in the latter. There is a difference between pastoring according to the strategies of human counsellors, based on human psychology, and that which is motivated by the power of the Holy Spirit. The former is logical and humanistic but the latter is uplifting and full of the love of God. There is a difference between evangelism according to human campaigns and methods and evangelism in the power of the Holy Spirit. The former promotes Christian religion and the latter convicts of sin and brings repentance and conversion of the inner man. So it is with all the spiritual manifestations of the Lord, born out of His authority working in and through us.

Spiritual gifts are given by God alone and not through the will of man. They are living words abiding in us to be administered according to His guidance for the purposes they were given. We can learn how to obey the Lord in the ministries that He has given us, remembering that *all* authority is given to Yeshua. He has promised to be with us in all that we do in His Name, just as the Father was always with Him. We can learn to discern the difference between spiritual authority and human motivation, a most important issue in our Halakhah.

For Study and Meditation: Read Matthew 4:18 and Ephesians 5:18 where we read of the anointing and filling of the Holy Spirit. Look up other references to these manifestations of the Holy Spirit and ask the Lord to teach you how these things apply to you in your service within the family of God.

Halakhah

Boundary Stones

There is a Halakhah principle in the curses that were spoken over the Children of Israel from Mount Ebal. This principle can be applied to ministry in the body of believers today:

Cursed be he that removeth his neighbour's landmark. And all the people shall say, Amen. (Deuteronomy 27:17)

In other translations, we read that the curse was to be upon those who moved the boundary stones that divided a person's land from his neighbour's. If a stone were moved, it would have the effect of enlarging one person's possession and decreasing that of the other. This is clearly theft.

If we generalise the principle, we can see how it might apply to ministry. When a group of people are in fellowship and serving together, jealousies can develop and human competitiveness may develop to cause one person to desire to serve in the manner of another. In the day of expectation of the fulfilment when we will serve the Lord, shoulder to shoulder according to Zephaniah 3:9, the parallel is strong and clear.

If we were free to choose our area of ministry, before the revelation of the Lord as to what this might be, many of us would answer carnally, according to our human desires and possibly according to the idols that we had established for ourselves as we considered the ministries of others. This same carnal motive can drive some people to copy others and even attempt to 'move the boundary stone' marking off their inheritance in ministry. This may be out of mistaken intent, but it nevertheless causes confusion and tension within the body of believers.

There are some powerful examples in the Scriptures to show that this principle is serious in the Lord's eyes. The ministry of the Kingdom and of the Temple required careful lines of service to be drawn up. For example, the roles of the King and of the Priests were clearly defined. When Saul made a sacrifice that was the responsibility of Samuel, he lost his kingdom. His heart had been exposed and he was not worthy or trustworthy for leadership of the kingdom. A judgement relating to Deuteronomy 17 was spoken by Samuel:

> Samuel said to Saul, Thou hast done foolishly: thou hast not kept the commandment of the LORD thy God, which he commanded thee: for now would the LORD have established thy kingdom upon Israel for ever. But now thy kingdom shall not continue: the LORD hath sought him a man after his own heart, and the LORD hath commanded him to be captain over his people, because thou hast not kept that which the LORD commanded thee. (1 Samuel 13:13-14)

Another example is where Uzza tried to steady the Ark of the Covenant when it was falling off the cart on its way back to Jerusalem. He was not among those anointed for the service of the Ark:

> Uzza put forth his hand to hold the ark; for the oxen stumbled. And the anger of the LORD was kindled against Uzza, and he smote him, because he put his hand to the ark: and there he died before God. (1 Chronicles 13:9-10)

Both Saul and Uzza, in human eyes, were trying to further the work of God, but neither of them had a concept of the boundary of their ministry and the way God orders His work through different ministries. Such people are not safe. They tend to react out of human impulsion and are not able to hear and obey the Lord. Such people cannot be trusted to work in a team that is responsible together to the Lord. They will cause offence to others and deprive themselves of the ministry that might otherwise be defined within the bounds of their own service.

By way of contrast, David, though tempted to usurp Saul's authority as King, resisted twice (1 Samuel 24 and 26). This was even though he knew that he himself was to become King and that Saul was not a good King. Indeed, David's lament for the death of Saul (2 Samuel 1) increases our understanding of the heart of David to acknowledge the anointing of the Lord and to stay within the bounds of one's own anointing.

Harmony in the family of believers is according to the principles taught by Paul:

For the body is not one member, but many. If the foot shall say, Because I am not the hand, I am not of the body; is it therefore not of the body? And if the ear shall say, Because I am not the eye, I am not of the body; is it therefore not of the body? If the whole body were an eye, where were the hearing? If the whole were hearing, where were the smelling? But now hath God set the members every one of them in the body, as it hath pleased him. (1 Corinthians 12:14-18)

The Lord Yeshua removed the curse of the law, so we may not lose our lives like Uzza for tampering with the order of the Lord's ministries, but the ordering of His ministries is still as important as it always was. We will not find our own ordained area of service and we will disrupt the service of others if we do not know where our boundary stones are placed. When we do remain within our own boundaries of ministry, we will find that our anointing from the Holy Spirit will be according to the measure we need to complete our service, and this will also be the place of peace and joy.

For Study and Meditation: Read the accounts of Saul in 1 Samuel 13, of Uzza in 1 Chronicles 13 and David in 1 Samuel 24 to 2 Samuel 1. Having reflected on the importance of knowing ones own area of ministry, read 1 Corinthians 12 and ask the Lord to show you step by step the boundaries of your own service and also the boundaries of the service of others.

Halakhah

Under Grace

Much can be written about law and grace. One of the fundamental principles taught by Paul on this subject affects our approach to Halakhah. He wrote:

For sin shall not have dominion over you: for ye are not under the law, but under grace. (Romans 6:14)

In this passage, Paul was developing his teaching towards the main thrust of his message in Romans 8:

There is therefore now no condemnation to them which are in Christ Jesus, who walk not after the flesh, but after the Spirit. For the law of the Spirit of life in Christ Jesus hath made me free from the law of sin and death. (Romans 8:1-2)

If we add two other passages of Scripture, we are in a position to understand this important aspect of Halakhah:

Let not him that eateth despise him that eateth not; and let not him which eateth not judge him that eateth: for God hath received him. Who art thou that judgest another man's servant? to his own master he standeth or falleth. Yea, he shall be holden up: for God is able to make him stand. One man esteemeth one day above another: another esteemeth every day alike. Let every man be fully persuaded in his own mind. (Romans 14:3-5)

Christ hath redeemed us from the curse of the law, being made a curse for us: for it is written, Cursed is every one that hangeth on a tree: that the blessing of Abraham might come on the Gentiles

through Jesus Christ; that we might receive the promise of the Spirit through faith. (Galatians 3:13-14)

The key to our Halakhah is a walk with the Spirit. It is only in regard to this principle that we can fully understand the balance of law and grace. Before this walk with the Spirit was possible, the Lord's people were to tread carefully, mindful of the principles of the written Torah (law). In general, the way to know right from wrong was through ritual observance. If we walk with the Holy Spirit, the one through whom the Torah was given, we will not expect Him to lead us against the principles of Torah, but lead us into them and enable us to live by them. The same principles apply, but we learn to live in obedience to the Living Word in the light of the written word, rather than by the written words of Scripture alone.

This is why a principal of our walk is that each man should be persuaded of the things of the Torah in his own mind, as the Holy Spirit leads us to the relevant principals for our own path of discipleship. There are community aspects to this, of course, as we learn together, but it is to the teaching of the Holy Spirit that we are freed.

The freedom that we have if we walk according to the Holy Spirit's leading is that we are free from the condemnation of the Torah (law). We are free to learn God's ways. Without this freedom, we live under the condemnation of the curses of the law - the punishments for disobedience. This is the curse of the law that Paul wrote about in Galatians 3. It is not that the law is a curse. Far from it - it is holy. But, because of our inability to obey without the help of the Holy Spirit, by trying to obey the law in our own strength, we fail and come under the law's punishment. This is the curse of the law - reflected in the curses that were spoken over Israel at Mount Ebal. We are not free of the law, but free to learn by the power of the Holy Spirit and free of the punishment for our failures as we seek to learn.

As the Lord's disciples, we come under the grace of His forgiveness bought by His own blood on the Cross, as we live by the grace of the Holy Spirit. This is what it means to be under grace and not law. It means to be led by the Holy Spirit, free of condemnation. This applies only to those who are led this way, because this is a path of discipleship, a path for those whose heart and mind are set on obeying the teaching of the Lord, whose positive teaching is still to be found in the pages of Torah.

Perhaps this positive view of our discipleship can be seen in the contrast between the teaching of Hillel, a Rabbi living around the time of Yeshua, and the teaching of Yeshua. When asked to sum up the Torah in one command, Hillel said, 'What is hateful to yourself do not do to your fellowman. That is the whole of Torah.' This could reflect the negative approach to Torah when one is conscious of the punishments for transgression. It can be seen as a set of don'ts and not as a set of dos. While there are both positive and negative aspects to Torah, of course, there is a distinct emphasis in Yeshua's answer that is different to that of Hillel. Yeshua's answer seemed almost the same, but it was different in that He spoke positively, about what to do, rather than negatively about what not to do:

Therefore all things whatsoever ye would that men should do to you, do ye even so to them: for this is the law and the prophets. (Matthew 7:12)

The Holy Spirit echoes the positive approach of Yeshua, to go out and do the things of God under His guidance, confident in the grace given to learn, as opposed to learning through fear of the punishment of failure. By this means, we will achieve more of the positive results of Torah and with the sense of joy of discipleship, rather than the doubts about failure and punishment.

For Study and Meditation: Read Romans 1 to 8 and consider how we have been freed to learn, providing we seek to walk with the Holy Spirit as our teacher, allowing Him to empower us for obedience and service.

Halakhah

Clothes to Wear: Inner Character

The Torah contains many rules of practical application. Even the clothes that the Lord's people were to wear are given some attention. For example, the clothes that were to be worn by the Priests are described in great detail in the Book of Exodus.

Since the Torah is also to be written on the heart, we can expect to find meanings that typify the character of the Lord's people as well as the way they look. Indeed, it is apparent that the garments that people wear often reflect something of their character. We might study all that the Scripture teaches about clothing and find an extensive study of the expected character of the Lord's people.

Paul gives a hint to us about the truth of this in his teaching about godly women:

> In like manner also, that women adorn themselves in modest apparel, with shamefacedness and sobriety; not with broided hair, or gold, or pearls, or costly array; but (which becometh women professing godliness) with good works. (1 Timothy 2:9-10)

Paul shows us that while there may be a tendency for us to concentrate on the superficial appearance that clothing gives, the deeper principle of heart character which results in good works (worn like a garment) is a higher priority. Presumably, part of the purpose of wearing clothes that reflect our occupation or ministry (like the Priests) was to cultivate the habit of thinking about the characteristics that these clothes symbolised, and thereby acquiring such inner characteristics. This applied, similarly to the wearing of tzit-tzit, the tassles to be worn on the fringes of the garment, according to Deuteronomy 22:12. They were as a reminder to obey all of the Torah, which was eventually, however, to become an inner characteristic of the heart, according to Jeremiah 31:31-33. Indeed, the symbolism of wearing the Torah like a garment was eventually to be fulfilled at its highest level by Paul's teaching:

For as many of you as have been baptized into Christ have put on Christ. (Galatians 3:27)

We can assume that the practices of Torah, including wearing the appropriate and prescribed clothes, while useful of itself, was also a reminder of spiritual truths and was intended to point to the spiritual manifestations that are now given by the Holy Spirit. Nevertheless, Torah is still a mirror to our inward condition, and as we reflect on the practices of Torah, we can ask ourselves if we are indeed fulfilling their deeper intent.

Take, for example, Deuteronomy 22:11:

Thou shalt not wear a garment of divers sorts, as of woollen and linen together.

There is a good practical reason for this. Two fibres of different strength and character will not usually weave together well. Yet, what is the heart intent of this mitzvah? Meditation upon the fact that this speaks of an inner character of mankind leads to the realisation that this speaks of a single-minded character. At the deepest level, there must be single-mindedness in our service of the Lord (no idolatry or worldliness). Within this principle, we must be undivided in our motivations in all things. We must have no 'hidden agendas' in our dealings with one another. We must concentrate on being straightforward, without mixed motives, in all that we do. Otherwise, we will cause inner tension as one motive does not harmonise with another. Indeed, if this is our inner character, it will soon be perceived by those around us. We could sometimes appear insincere, suspicious or untrustworthy, if this inner character is discerned, rather than honest, straight and true. With the inner tension of different motivations, we could also be weak in ministry, possibly with divided loyalties, even committing the sin that Yeshua condemned:

> *No man can serve two masters: for either he will hate the one, and love the other; or else he will hold to the one, and despise the other. Ye cannot serve God and mammon. (Matthew 6:24)*

Consideration of this very simple practice of not wearing a garment made of two fibres can be a point of meditation for a deep issue of character, and through that meditation, we can see ourselves as in a mirror.

For Study and Meditation: Meditate upon the meaning of Deuteronomy 22:11 and see if it reveals anything about your own character.

Halakhah

Food to Eat: Inner Character

Just as the clothes we wear can be a symbol or point of reflection on our inner character, so can the food that we eat. Eating food and wearing clothes are two practical issues, that are part of our everyday life and so are appropriate points for our teaching.

Among the mitzvot concerning food are those concerning clean and unclean animals:

Ye shall therefore put difference between clean beasts and unclean, and between unclean fowls and clean: and ye shall not make your souls abominable by beast, or by fowl, or by any manner of living thing that creepeth on the ground, which I have separated from you as unclean. (Leviticus 20:25)

The kosher laws for animals have been carefully observed for centuries by the Jews. There is certainly practical value in eating only food that is healthy for the body, carrying no impurities, like the scavenger fish and birds. Yet there must also be a heart intent behind this. Indeed, this is expressed in Leviticus 20:26 as a literary parallelism:

And ye shall be holy unto me: for I the LORD am holy, and have severed you from other people, that ye should be mine. (Leviticus 20:26)

There is holiness in obeying God's commandments at their face value, but there is also holiness in many other things that are implied by the more general point that is being made. Kosher eating is a pointer to the inner character of purity and holiness that is expected of God's people, and the eating of clean foods is intended to be a constant reminder of this.

As the Lord's people, we are intended to feed on Him:

I am the living bread which came down from heaven: if any man eat of this bread, he shall live for ever: and the bread that I will give is my flesh, which I will give for the life of the world. (John 6:51)

We can assume that the kosher rules were in preparation for the coming of the Lord, when we would realise that there is only one true source of life and purity. We must learn to feed on Him by imbibing the truths of the Scriptures, made alive by the Holy Spirit living in us. Thus the kosher rules pointed specifically to inner character. The Lord Himself made this clear:

And he saith unto them, Are ye so without understanding also? Do ye not perceive, that whatsoever thing from without entereth into the man, it cannot defile him; because it entereth not into his heart, but into the belly, and goeth out into the draught, purging all meats? And he said, That which cometh out of the man, that defileth the man. For from within, out of the heart of men, proceed evil thoughts, adulteries, fornications, murders, thefts, covetousness, wickedness, deceit, lasciviousness, an evil eye, blasphemy, pride, foolishness: all these evil things come from within, and defile the man. (Mark 7:18-23)

When we look at the list of unclean animals in Leviticus 11, we see animals that have characteristics that we should not desire - scavengers, wild beasts and so on - as well as animals that are unhealthy to eat. This is another point for meditation and was intended to be so.

There may still be good health reasons for eating only animals that are declared to be clean, but we can be sure that the Holy Spirit has been sent to impart the deeper truths that these foods were meant to teach us. We must also know that salvation does not come through the food we eat. Nevertheless, we can be conscious of the witness that we give to the world both by the food that we eat and the clothes that we wear, and in this we should be careful.

At the deeper level, neither eating nor not eating is the question, as Paul pointed out:

For the kingdom of God is not meat and drink; but righteousness, and peace, and joy in the Holy Ghost. (Romans 14:17)

We must be concerned to drain the blood from our meat. That was a commandment going right back to Noah and also enforced at the Council of Jerusalem, but that was for a different reason.

Concerning kosher foods, however, there is an interesting question. As with all practical issues of Torah, this is a mirror to our inner condition. We sometimes assume that we will achieve that inner condition without any self-discipline, yet the question is whether we do achieve this, for we have a tendency not only to neglect the practices of Torah, but also the principle that was behind the teaching. It may be that on our individual Halakhah, we will sense the Holy Spirit's prompting to consider certain of the practical kosher rules as right for us to observe, as a witness to our holy lifestyle, as a teaching point as it was originally intended, so that we will seek inner holiness. If this is so, we must remember that this is not a criterion for salvation and is within the principle of Romans 14:5:

Let every man be fully persuaded in his own mind.

For Study and Meditation: Consider the kosher laws of Leviticus 11 and assess your growth in the characteristics of holiness that they represent.

Halakhah

Part 4: Be Filled with the Holy Spirit

The Lord is King

When Israel conquered Canaan, unlike all the other nations they were not to have an earthly king. God Himself was to be King. He would rule His people through chosen leaders. Moses was the first judge of the people and then later, responsibility for minor decisions was delegated to other elders of the community (Exodus 18:25-26). The judge also had a prophetic role, in that he was to consult with the Lord Himself on behalf of the people. Later the role of the Levitical Priesthood also developed, but on no account were the people intended to have a king like the nations around them.

Among the Judges of Israel when they occupied the Promised Land, there were few if any of the stature of Samuel. In his old age he was able to stand openly before all Israel and say:

'I am old and grayheaded; and, behold, my sons are with you: and I have walked before you from my childhood unto this day. Behold, here I am: witness against me before the LORD, and before his anointed: whose ox have I taken? or whose ass have I taken? or whom have I defrauded? whom have I oppressed? or of whose hand have I received any bribe to blind mine eyes therewith? and I will restore it you.' And they said, 'Thou hast not defrauded us, nor oppressed us, neither hast thou taken ought of any man's hand.' And he said unto them, 'The LORD is witness against you, and his anointed is witness this day, that ye have not found ought in my hand.' And they answered, 'He is witness.' (1 Samuel 12:2-5)

Yet, when Samuel was old, the Children of Israel wanted to be like the other nations and they asked for a king:

Then all the elders of Israel gathered themselves together, and came to Samuel unto Ramah, and said unto him, Behold, thou art old, and thy sons walk not in thy ways: now make us a king to judge us like all the nations. (1 Samuel 8:4-5)

Samuel was downcast, but he himself was only a servant of the Lord. It was not Samuel but the Lord Himself who was being rejected. In seeking to have a king, the people were seeking to follow a man and not the Lord:

But the thing displeased Samuel, when they said, Give us a king to judge us. And Samuel prayed unto the LORD. And the LORD said unto Samuel, Hearken unto the voice of the people in all that they say unto thee: for they have not rejected thee, but they have rejected me, that I should not reign over them. (1Samuel 8:6-7)

Indeed, the Lord through Samuel told the people exactly what would happen if they chose to follow a king instead of the Lord:

And he said, This will be the manner of the king that shall reign over you: He will take your sons, and appoint them for himself, for his chariots, and to be his horsemen; and some shall run before his chariots. And he will appoint him captains over thousands, and captains over fifties; and will set them to ear his ground, and to reap his harvest, and to make his instruments of war, and instruments of his chariots. And he will take your daughters to be confectionaries, and to be cooks, and to be bakers. And he will take your fields, and your vineyards, and your oliveyards, even the best of them, and give them to his servants. And he will take the tenth of your seed, and of your vineyards, and give to his officers, and to his servants. And he will take your menservants, and your maidservants, and your goodliest young men, and your asses, and put them to his work. He will take the tenth of your sheep: and ye shall be his servants. And ye shall cry out in that day because of your king which ye shall have chosen you; and the LORD will not hear you in that day. (1 Samuel 8:11-18)

The Bible contains the history of the Children of Israel under their kings. All that the Lord said happened. Israel has not ceased to be the covenant nation, yet it has suffered through not allowing the Lord to be King - it has suffered from that day to this. Because God made an unbreakable Oath to Israel there is a golden thread of His keeping them through their history, nevertheless. We see a type of Messiah in David, the man after God's own heart and we see the way Solomon could rule with heavenly wisdom. There were times of seeking God afresh, such as at the time of Josiah and Hezekiah but on the whole, Israel was not led in God's ways even to the point where God sent them into exile.

Despite Israel's rebellion the Covenant stands, and so even if the Lord has allowed the Kingdom to be put into the hands of earthly kings who did not seek Him for wisdom, this situation cannot last forever, and the Kingdom will be returned fully to Him. Indeed, this is to be fulfilled through Yeshua HaMashiach, His Son.

Then cometh the end, when he shall have delivered up the kingdom to God, even the Father; when he shall have put down all rule and all authority and power. For he must reign, till he hath put all enemies under his feet. The last enemy that shall be destroyed is death. For he hath put all things under his feet. But when he saith all things are put under him, it is manifest that he is excepted, which did put all things under him. And when all things shall be subdued unto him, then shall the Son also himself be subject unto him that put all things under him, that God may be all in all. (1 Corinthians 15:24-28)

Psalm 2 shows that it is the Lord who appoints the rulers over His people:

I set my king upon my holy hill of Zion. (Psalm 2:6)

This Psalm points to the Kingship of Yeshua HaMashiach, who confirmed this to Pilate:

And Pilate asked him, saying, 'Art thou the King of the Jews?' And

he answered him and said, 'Thou sayest it.' (Luke 23:3)
This was also confirmed through the writing on the Cross:

And a superscription also was written over him in letters of Greek, and Latin, and Hebrew, THIS IS THE KING OF THE JEWS. (Luke 23:38)

Through Yeshua HaMashiach, God is restoring the Kingdom to Himself, as it was intended at the beginning. Indeed, for those of us who believe in Yeshua for salvation, we have already acknowledged Him as King. For us, it should be as it was intended before Israel asked for a king like the other nations. We should be living under the Lord's direct rulership. Indeed, Yeshua said that He would rule from the heavenly place:

My kingdom is not of this world: if my kingdom were of this world, then would my servants fight, that I should not be delivered to the Jews: but now is my kingdom not from hence. (John 18:36)

The Lord has given us the Torah (His teaching) and the whole of Scripture and He appoints those in His Kingdom who are to be responsible to Him for day to day judgements and leadership, those who can seek Him and hear Him and lead the people to obey Him. It is like it was at the time of Moses, except that Moses is replaced by Yeshua and rules from the heavenly place:

And thou shalt teach them ordinances and laws, and shalt show them the way wherein they must walk, and the work that they must do. Moreover thou shalt provide out of all the people able men, such as fear God, men of truth, hating covetousness; and place such over them, to be rulers of thousands, and rulers of hundreds, rulers of fifties, and rulers of tens: and let them judge the people at all seasons: and it shall be, that every great matter they shall bring unto thee, but every small matter they shall judge: so shall it be easier for thyself, and they shall bear the burden with thee. If thou shalt do this thing, and God command thee so, then thou shalt be able to endure, and all this people shall also go to

their place in peace. (Exodus 18:20-23)

The difference is that the Holy Spirit has also been sent to all God's people, so that together we are a Royal Priesthood (1 Peter 2:9). We all have a part to play within the Kingdom purposes of God. Nevertheless, there is order in His Kingdom and boundaries of anointed ministries.

We are not left alone. God Himself is King and it is to Him that we are directly responsible. We must seek Him in all things, not allowing ourselves to be led in the ways of the world. One day all the struggles will be over and the Lord will indeed reign. There is a type and shadow of this in the Second Book of Samuel. David had ruled in Hebron as King over Judah for seven and a half years and then all Israel came to proclaim him King, recognising that he was the anointed of the Lord. This points to the time when the whole world will proclaim Yeshua as King. Indeed, the fulfilment will be infinitely more marvellous than the types and shadows of Scripture.

And the seventh angel sounded; and there were great voices in heaven, saying, The kingdoms of this world are become the kingdoms of our Lord, and of his Christ; and he shall reign for ever and ever. (Revelation 11:15)

For Study and Meditation: Read 1 Samuel 8-12 and Ephesians 4, and consider how the Lord is ordering His Kingdom today so that we are led by Him directly as His people. Consider whether it is possible for men to try to assert their leadership among the people of God and try to rule independently of Him.

Halakhah

Bet Din

The Torah (teaching) of God was intended to cover, in general terms, all aspects of life. If we study the first five books of the Bible, which are called the Books of Moses, we find the foundations of all that God wants to teach us. These books encompass the life of faith as well as the legal requirements of a holy community. They cover all the basic principles of personal, family and community life for God's people. There is much to discover about the deeper intent of Torah and the way Torah was eventually to be fulfilled through Yeshua, and then through the heart response to the workings of the Holy Spirit in God's people. Nevertheless, the principles of Torah begin in these five books.

While the general principles are clearly written, the particular application of God's teaching requires interpretation into daily life. Over the centuries, the Jews developed the Bet Din, or House of Judgement, as the place where judgements and interpretations of the laws of God would be decided. This tradition goes back to the time of Moses, when (Exodus 18) elders were appointed to make day-to-day judgements on all matters relating to community life.

The principal of the Bet Din can be considered as the foundation of the Ecclesiastical Court of the Church. However, in both the Bet Din and the Ecclesiastical Court, it is possible that judgements can be made based on dry human logic, turning the Bible into a religious book of rules. In this way, decisions can be made devoid of the inspiration of God, based on the philosophies of men alone. This happened both in the nation of Israel and in the Church. Indeed, at the time of Yeshua, the religious leaders came under His criticism very heavily.

Yet, the need to have a group of leaders who are able to manage community affairs in the light of Scripture still exists. The transition point for the Lord's community was at the Council of Jerusalem (Acts 15). Here were the first rulings for the worldwide community of believers, which included believers from the Gentile world. The essential principle of 'it seems good to the Holy Spirit and us' should be the hallmark of all community decisions, in the same way concerning all judgements among the people of God.

Leadership of the community of believers is delegated to local elders in a parallel way to the delegation of the elders at the time of Moses. The requirements of elders today are similar to those at the time of Moses. The requirements of elders are that they should be:

....able men, such as fear God, men of truth, hating covetousness. (Exodus 18:21)

.....wise men, and understanding, and known among your tribes. (Deuteronomy 1:13)

Those who:

....judge righteously between every man and his brother, and the stranger that is with him.

And who

...do not respect persons in judgment; but hear the small as well as the great; not being afraid of the face of man; for the judgment is God's. (Deuteronomy 1:16-17)

They

...must be blameless, the husband of one wife, vigilant, sober, of good behaviour, given to hospitality, apt to teach; not given to wine, no striker, not greedy of filthy lucre; but patient, not a brawler, not covetous; one that ruleth well his own house, having

his children in subjection with all gravity; (For if a man know not how to rule his own house, how shall he take care of the church of God?) Not a novice, lest being lifted up with pride he fall into the condemnation of the devil. Moreover he must have a good report of them which are without; lest he fall into reproach and the snare of the devil. (1 Timothy 3:2-7)

The conditions for elders as given by Paul in the letter to Timothy is in accord with those given by Moses concerning elders in his day. Indeed, the command to establish elders in every city given by Paul to Titus was a continuation of that given by Moses:

Judges and officers shalt thou make thee in all thy gates, which the LORD thy God giveth thee, throughout thy tribes: and they shall judge the people with just judgment. (Deuteronomy 16:18)

…ordain elders in every city. (Titus 1:5)

In short, it is God's way to have a group of men of suitable character to take up the office of eldership, working with Him to judge and order the community, in every town. The principle of eldership is that a group of representatives of the Lord are to seek Him together on general community matters and on particular areas of dispute or need for clarification among the families of the community, not lording it over the people, but supporting the authority of each home, the building block of the Lord's community. They are not to enforce rules and interpretations of Scripture according to the philosophies of men, but to sit together before the Lord on behalf of the community and be the agents of the Lord's judgements and wisdom. As it says in Deuteronomy 1:17:

….for the judgment is God's.

For Study and Meditation: Read the qualifications of an Elder in Titus 1:6-9, and in the verses quoted above. Reread Acts 15, recognising it to be the first Messianic Bet Din. Consider how local eldership should function as a group of men living under the inspiration of the Holy Spirit.

Halakhah

Wisdom

Wisdom is different from understanding, and understanding is different from knowledge. These three concepts are linked and are behind much that is said in the Bible, particularly in the book of Proverbs. True wisdom is the ultimate goal. This is the inner motivating power that directs us to a right course in life.

Knowledge is what we acquire through observation and experience, and understanding is to do with the way relationships are formed between areas of knowledge, while wisdom is the application of our knowledge and understanding to the way we live our lives.

There are both carnal and spiritual meanings to all these words, and regarding wisdom, James warns us about the difference and that we should seek the wisdom that is from above:

Doth a fountain send forth at the same place sweet water and bitter? Can the fig tree, my brethren, bear olive berries? either a vine, figs? so can no fountain both yield salt water and fresh. Who is a wise man and endued with knowledge among you? let him show out of a good conversation his works with meekness of wisdom. But if ye have bitter envying and strife in your hearts, glory not, and lie not against the truth. This wisdom descendeth not from above, but is earthly, sensual, devilish. For where envying and strife is, there is confusion and every evil work. But the wisdom that is from above is first pure, then peaceable, gentle, and easy to be entreated, full of mercy and good fruits, without partiality, and without hypocrisy. And the fruit of righteousness is sown in peace of them that make peace. (James 3:11-19)

Yeshua spoke of the fruits of true wisdom:

But wisdom is justified of all her children. (Luke 7:35)

Paul taught about the importance of and the fruits of true wisdom:

For this cause we also, since the day we heard it, do not cease to pray for you, and to desire that ye might be filled with the knowledge of his will in all wisdom and spiritual understanding; that ye might walk worthy of the Lord unto all pleasing, being fruitful in every good work, and increasing in the knowledge of God. (Colossians 1:9-10)

Now we have received, not the spirit of the world, but the spirit which is of God; that we might know the things that are freely given to us of God. Which things also we speak, not in the words which man's wisdom teacheth, but which the Holy Ghost teacheth; comparing spiritual things with spiritual. But the natural man receiveth not the things of the Spirit of God: for they are foolishness unto him: neither can he know them, because they are spiritually discerned. (1Corinthians 2:12-14)

That your faith should not stand in the wisdom of men, but in the power of God. Howbeit we speak wisdom among them that are perfect: yet not the wisdom of this world, nor of the princes of this world, that come to nought: but we speak the wisdom of God in a mystery, even the hidden wisdom, which God ordained before the world unto our glory. (1Corinthians 2:5-7)

That the God of our Lord Jesus Christ, the Father of glory, may give unto you the spirit of wisdom and revelation in the knowledge of him: the eyes of your understanding being enlightened; that ye may know what is the hope of his calling, and what the riches of the glory of his inheritance in the saints..... (Ephesians 1:17-18)

In all that we do in life, disciples of the Lord Jesus are to seek the

wisdom that comes from above. There is no true Halakhah independent of this wisdom. This is the wisdom that heads of homes are to seek on behalf of their family and the wisdom that elders of communities are to seek together. This wisdom is spiritual and is a gift from God. The wisdom of God is in accord with all the teaching of the Bible. The wisdom of God causes us to hear Him and obey Him with the Scriptures as a mirror to His Living Word within us. We must seek heavenly wisdom and resist earthly philosophy, and such wisdom will only come out of relationship with God through prayer.

The Book of Proverbs is based on the wisdom given to Solomon. The first chapters personify wisdom:

> *She crieth in the chief place of concourse, in the openings of the gates: in the city she uttereth her words, saying, how long, ye simple ones, will ye love simplicity? and the scorners delight in their scorning, and fools hate knowledge? (Proverbs 1:21-22)*

Wisdom is considered the highest thing to gain:

> *She is more precious than rubies: and all the things thou canst desire are not to be compared unto her. Length of days is in her right hand; and in her left hand riches and honour. Her ways are ways of pleasantness, and all her paths are peace. She is a tree of life to them that lay hold upon her: and happy is every one that retaineth her. (Proverbs 3:15-18)*

Indeed, the more we study the importance and nature of heavenly wisdom, the more we see that wisdom is associated with the gift of the Holy Spirit:

> *Wisdom crieth without; she uttereth her voice in the streets....*
> *.....Turn you at my reproof: behold, I will pour out my spirit unto you, I will make known my words unto you. (Proverbs 1:20-23)*

The gift of wisdom is a manifestation of the gift of the Holy Spirit and comes to believers as a fulfilment of the prophecy of Joel:

And it shall come to pass afterward, that I will pour out my spirit upon all flesh. (Joel 2:28)

James assures us that those who ask God for wisdom in faith will receive this gift:

If any of you lack wisdom, let him ask of God, that giveth to all men liberally, and upbraideth not; and it shall be given him. But let him ask in faith, nothing wavering. For he that wavereth is like a wave of the sea driven with the wind and tossed. For let not that man think that he shall receive any thing of the Lord. (James 1:5-7)

For all aspects of our Halakhah, whether at a personal level, for our family life or for the general direction of our community life, we, or those responsible for particular aspects of leadership in the community, must turn to the Lord in faith and He will answer our prayers, and give us guidance. All this is within our fellowship and walk with the Holy Spirit. If we ask for wisdom, we are asking for the Holy Spirit, and there is no other way for the true Halakhah to be discovered.

For Study and Meditation: Using a Bible dictionary, make a study of the references to wisdom in the Bible and consider how believers should live their life in fellowship with the Holy Spirit, who gives this wisdom.

Halakhah

Bet Midrash

To fulfil their call to live according to the teaching of God, the Jewish people established synagogues for meeting together and for performing various community functions. Here the elders could sit in 'Moses' seat' relating to judgements. In addition, it was the place where the Torah was expounded and studied. As to study, it was a tradition that Esau and Jacob attended the bet ha-sefer (literally, the house of the book, a primary school) until the age of 13. After this, Esau wasted his time while Jacob attended the bet ha-midrash, the house of study. Similarly, it is considered that it is a high and important calling for Jews to study in the bet midrash, the study centre associated with the synagogue. It is taught that those who go straight from the synagogue service to the bet midrash are deemed worthy of the Divine Presence, and of entry into the study centres in the world to come.

For the Jew, study is considered a higher priority than prayer, and though we would be unwise to raise study higher than prayer among disciples of the Lord, we should nevertheless make it a high priority in the local community. Just as we have developed buildings for the local believing community to meet in the manner of the synagogue, so study should be a priority for the community of believers, as a function within these buildings. It is not the buildings that are important, of course, but the activity, so in both our homes and our study centres we should encourage the study of Scripture.

Because faith has been replaced by philosophy for many believers, study of the Scriptures can become an intellectual exercise and, as such, put into the area of special expertise gained by those who go away to university or college for special qualifications. While there is some need for special preparation for some in ministry, this should not replace the general call on every believer to have access to facilities for study. What was true for Timothy is true for us all:

Study to show thyself approved unto God, a workman that needeth not to be ashamed, rightly dividing the word of truth. (2 Timothy 2:15)

Every believing community should have facilities and programmes for all believers to become mature in the study of the Scriptures. Primarily, every believing home should be orientated to such study. There can be central resources for the community to share, and study should be the natural consequence of discipleship.

There is a difference between listening to lectures or sermons and participation in discussion and study. While exposition of the Scriptures by a mature believer has a valid part to play, there should also be an emphasis on sharing, discussing and debating, where all believers are involved in discovering the relevant truths of Scripture.

We have much to learn from the Jewish Yeshiva, where a lively discussion is expected, and where questions can be as powerful as answers, where topic after topic can be studied together under the general guidance of a mature teacher of the Bible, but where active participation by all is the key.

The Lord said:

For where two or three are gathered together in my name, there am I in the midst of them. (Matthew 18:20)

Yeshua indicated that, unlike the synagogues who require a minimum of ten men to be present for the meeting to be official (a minyan), the Lord would be with any small group who gathered for His purposes. There is a refreshing sense of informality in the Lord's meetings with His people. This should not be a licence for presumption, of course, but it does mean that when small groups of

His disciples gather together for study and discussion, with their Bibles and study materials in front of them, and with their questions and discussions brought to the meeting, He will be there too. This means that, in addition to the discussions being free and lively, all disciples should learn to hear the Lord's interventions with heavenly wisdom, knowledge and understanding. His presence with them can be very real.

The times of study are also times of prayer, in this sense, and times of fellowship with the Lord Himself. These should be very special times for the believing community. What a privilege we have and this privilege is for all, in the order of the Lord's body!

For Study and Meditation: Consider Paul's exhortation to Timothy (2 Timothy 2:15) and prayerfully consider how a believing community should be organised to make study a priority.

Halakhah

A House of Prayer

We must always be careful to distinguish between a physical building and people. In the Scriptures there are many types and shadows that start in the physical realm and find their fulfilment in the spiritual realm. One important example is the Temple. Glorious as the Temple was, it pointed ultimately to the people of God:

> *Ye also, as lively stones, are built up a spiritual house, an holy priesthood, to offer up spiritual sacrifices, acceptable to God by Jesus Christ. Wherefore also it is contained in the scripture, Behold, I lay in Sion a chief corner stone, elect, precious: and he that believeth on him shall not be confounded. Unto you therefore which believe he is precious: but unto them which be disobedient, the stone which the builders disallowed, the same is made the head of the corner, and a stone of stumbling, and a rock of offence, even to them which stumble at the word, being disobedient: whereunto also they were appointed. But ye are a chosen generation, a royal priesthood, an holy nation, a peculiar people; that ye should show forth the praises of him who hath called you out of darkness into his marvellous light: which in time past were not a people, but are now the people of God: which had not obtained mercy, but now have obtained mercy. (1 Peter 2:5-10)*

Peter used the image of a spiritual house, of which the Temple, with its priesthood and all its activities, was a central example of all Scripture, and blended this with the picture of the people of God, demonstrating how the fulfilment of the Temple should be understood. A house is a people before it is the place where they meet. The Lord is interested in us rather than in where we meet.

The facilities for our meeting are only for the purposes of what He is doing in us. Indeed, all the functions of the Temple, reflected in the purposes of both the synagogue and the Church building, are to be understood as spiritual ministries within the Lord's people as individuals and together.

The Lord Yeshua spoke of His house being a house of prayer:

My house shall be called the house of prayer. (Matthew 21:13)

He was referring to the prophecy of Isaiah:

Also the sons of the stranger, that join themselves to the LORD, to serve him, and to love the name of the LORD, to be his servants, every one that keepeth the sabbath from polluting it, and taketh hold of my covenant; even them will I bring to my holy mountain, and make them joyful in my house of prayer: their burnt offerings and their sacrifices shall be accepted upon mine altar; for mine house shall be called an house of prayer for all people. (Isaiah 56:6-7)

The Temple, the synagogue, the Church building, and anywhere the people of God meet has a primary function. It has many functions, such as the bet din and the bet midrash, but it's primary function is as a place for prayer and is to be known by all people as a place of prayer. However, the meeting place is also secondary to the people, who themselves are being built into the Lord's household - His living Temple. Since we are the Lord's people, we should have the special characteristic, known through our good reputation, to all people, that we are always full of prayer. We should be known primarily as a people of prayer.

When we understand that the spiritual functions normally considered to go on in the meeting place of believers are really intended to apply to the spiritual life that is within us, we begin to understand that all of our Halakhah results from an overflow of this prayerful walk with God. Everything that we do should result from the prayer that is alive in us, whether we are alone or together.

Prayer itself is a manifestation of the Holy Spirit within us:

Likewise the Spirit also helpeth our infirmities: for we know not what we should pray for as we ought: but the Spirit itself maketh intercession for us with groanings which cannot be uttered. And he that searcheth the hearts knoweth what is the mind of the Spirit, because he maketh intercession for the saints according to the will of God. (Romans 8:26-27)

We are the Lord's house of prayer and it is necessary for His people to grow out of the traditions of attending prayer meetings as if they were the place where duty begins and ends, and rather for us all to learn what the Apostle Paul meant when he said that believers should:

Pray without ceasing. (1 Thessalonians 5:17)

For Study and Meditation: Read 1 Thessalonians 5 and Matthew 26:41. Consider the importance of the Lord's people (His house) being a house of prayer and how this might be fulfilled in your own life.

Halakhah

A Living Temple

In a limited sense individual believers, and in a corporate sense all of the Lord's disciples, are characterised by the Temple. In terms of service, they are like the Priesthood. The Priesthood had a ministry to the Lord and to the world. They were to go in to the Altar of Incense to hear the Lord on behalf of the people and then out to the people to teach God's ways. They ministered between the Altar of Sacrifice and the Altar of Incense, in the abiding place of the Temple. This can be seen from the commitment of Ezra:

For Ezra had prepared his heart to seek the law of the LORD, and to do it, and to teach in Israel statutes and judgments. (Ezra 7:10)

This reflects the priestly duties outlined elsewhere, for example in Ezekiel:

They shall enter into my sanctuary, and they shall come near to my table, to minister unto me, and they shall keep my charge. And they shall teach my people the difference between the holy and profane, and cause them to discern between the unclean and the clean. (Ezekiel 44:16-23)

The Royal Priesthood, of which all of Yeshua's disciples are members, has parallel ministries to the Priests of the Temple. They must live holy (separate) lives, coming into the presence of God with spiritual offerings and going out to declare the praises of God, within the call to distinguish between the holy and profane:

Ye also, as lively stones, are built up a spiritual house, an holy priesthood, to offer up spiritual sacrifices, acceptable to God by

Jesus Christ....But ye are a chosen generation, a royal priesthood, an holy nation, a peculiar people; that ye should show forth the praises of him who hath called you out of darkness into his marvellous light. (1 Peter 2:5-9)

Just as we can see that the Priesthood is to be fulfilled in us (according to the model of the Temple applied to the order of Melchizedek) we can discover that there is a fulfilment of all the types of the Temple that must contribute to the life within us.

The Altar of Sacrifice is fulfilled in the sacrifice of Yeshua. As we go forward into the presence of God we are always to be conscious of the Lord's sacrifice for our sin. We approach God in a repentant attitude and also in a humble attitude as we are full of joy and thankfulness.

The Laver is the washing of His Word (sanctification by the power of the Holy Spirit). As we approach the Lord we will find limits on fellowship if we are not sanctified by faith in the power of His blood. Our sins are revealed by the truth of the Scriptures, and our holiness is made perfect through faith in the Lord.

There are many other symbols of the inner life we must live, including representations of the Lord's community in the Menorah and the Table of Shewbread. Just as God is ever conscious of His people, so the life of the Holy Spirit in us as we approach, as it were, the presence of God, makes us conscious of the Lord's people – of community.

The Altar of Incense is the place of intercession. As a Royal Priesthood of the New Covenant we are to live with all the spiritual realities of the Temple within us. Our spiritual life must encompass them all simultaneously, and we must not remain in just one place. To stay at the place of the Cross is to remain at the place of salvation, and not going forward to maturity and priestly service. To meditate upon the Word of God for sanctification alone, though supremely important, is to proceed only so far, and to fall short of full fellowship with God. Mature believers fulfilling their priestly role are always conscious of the Cross behind them, and of inner sanctification, as they are also constantly in the place of intercession for the Lord's people, and in close fellowship with the Lord. The place of intercession is the place of bringing the needs of others to the Lord, in terms of the whole of the Great Commission. All of the many types of the Temple and its priestly service are to be constantiy at work in a member of the Royal Priesthood, in the right way and in the right balance.

The life of the Holy Spirit within us is manifested through fulfilment of the types and shadows of the Tabernacle and Temple. Imperfect though we may be, this is our inheritance in the abiding place with the Lord, in whom these types were perfectly fulfilled in the High Priestly sense.

For Study and Meditation: Read the account of the construction of the Tabernacle in Exodus 25-40. Prayerfully consider how these are types of spiritual realities to be fulfilled simultaneously in disciples of the Lord, and consider if you are growing in all of these areas of fellowship and ministry, particularly the ministry of intercession.

Halakhah

Praise

Let every thing that hath breath praise the LORD. (Psalm 150:6)

Praise is a conscious response to the Lord God. It is to be distinguished from worship, which at its most profound level is a totally spiritual inner offering to God and possibly most intense when the human body is completely submitted to the power of the Spirit within. Praise, on the other hand, has an element of human intent, a mental and logical appreciation of an offering to God.

The one who praises God has had a revelation of the perfection of God and, by contrast, who we are as fallen, yet redeemed, human beings. Without the sacrifice of Yeshua there can be no true and living fellowship with the Living God, who is who is totally holy and pure that He is unapproachable unless we have a covering for our sin.

To know God's holiness is to be able to contrast it with the sinfulness and uncleanness of this fallen world. Of course, there is the residue of God's image placed in mankind, and the residue of the perfection of His creation around us. However, everything in this world is so far from the holy condition and abiding place of God that there is no possibility of our having fellowship with God except through the intercessions of Yeshua and the forgiveness that the Lord bestows. Everything that we touch and are, in the natural sense, is tarnished. Our praise begins with the knowledge of renewed fellowship, the understanding of the place from which we are lifted and the place to which we will be lifted one day.

There is a passage in Isaiah 44 that represents quite the

opposite to praise:

> *He heweth him down cedars, and taketh the cypress and the oak, which he strengtheneth for himself among the trees of the forest: he planteth an ash, and the rain doth nourish it. Then shall it be for a man to burn: for he will take thereof, and warm himself; yea, he kindleth it, and baketh bread; yea, he maketh a god, and worshippeth it; he maketh it a graven image, and falleth down thereto. He burneth part thereof in the fire; with part thereof he eateth flesh; he roasteth roast, and is satisfied: yea, he warmeth himself, and saith, Aha, I am warm, I have seen the fire: and the residue thereof he maketh a god, even his graven image: he falleth down unto it, and worshippeth it, and prayeth unto it, and saith, Deliver me; for thou art my god. (Isaiah 44:14-17)*

This speaks of a human being quite blind to his fallen condition, cutting a piece of wood. With some of the wood he cooks a meal and with the rest he makes an idol and worships it. When, however, we are conscious of our true position and also have a knowledge of the True and Living God, we *may* nevertheless want to take something of this world, but instead of making an idol, we want to offer it to Him as a symbol of praise, as we also lift our hearts to Him in praise, acknowledging who He is, what He has done, with our hearts and minds recognising and speaking about His glory.

Instead of taking something of this world and treating it as if it were a god, we must recognise the limits of this world and all that is in it. We recognise that we do live within these limits, and that it is from here that we must present something to God. We take something and fashion it in the best way that we can and we raise it heavenwards in praise of God. The symbol of our praise can be many different things. An obvious example is a piece of wood, but instead of making an idol, we might fashion a musical instrument and compose a hymn of praise to God. Our instrument is played in a way that represents the hymn of our heart to God. Or we can compose a prayer, to speak out to Him. Or we can take the natural skill that has been given us in any way and make or do something that represents our desire to speak the praises of God from our lives and our hearts, something from this physical world, lifted to God as our symbol of praise, echoing the praise of our hearts and minds. Whatever comes to our hands from this natural world can be used as a symbol of our best attempt to lift praise to God. Like a child, we might offer something that we have made or done, as a symbol of our very best intent to offer Him praise for what He has done. Of course, His gifts to us are so much more than our offerings to Him, but as our perfect Father, He will accept the offering of our hearts.

Such praise offerings are acceptable to God. In the Temple, the offering of the best from the flock was acceptable, providing it was accompanied by a true heart intent. This sort of offering is no longer necessary, though we might find benefit in the exercise of using something physical to express the desire of our heart to lift spiritual praise from the fallen situation of this world to the throne of God. We might simply beat a tambourine, or lift our hands high to express this reaching out of our heart from Earth to Heaven, if there is nothing else in our hands to raise, offer or play.

Through these offerings of praise in which we might take the best we can make or do and raise something heavenward to God from this fallen world, we can move on. Through the service of our heart that this brings, we can experience a more constant expression of praise that comes from all of our life as we live it day by day, where everything that we do can be like a praise offering to God.

Praise starts with recognition of who we are and who God is. Praise can be accompanied and aided by something of this fallen world fashioned with the intent of making a physical expression of lifting an offering to God. There are many ways in which this can happen, including the expression of praise on beautifully made and played musical instruments that we commonly use in our meetings. Through practice or meditation upon this principle, we may also begin to recognise that all of our actions in life can be an expression of praise to God. Through our desire to offer God something holy from this fallen world, we also learn to offer our best in everything and come to realise that our best is acceptable though still tarnished, and we can be at peace with our life on this earth, too.

This will come when our praise is full of faith in our Saviour who has prepared a place for us when this world comes to an end, and when we will abide in the pure holy place where He is now.

> *Praise ye the LORD. Praise God in his sanctuary:*
> *Praise him in the firmament of his power.*
> *Praise him for his mighty acts:*
> *Praise him according to his excellent greatness.*
> *Praise him with the sound of the trumpet:*
> *Praise him with the psaltery and harp.*
> *Praise him with the timbrel and dance:*
> *Praise him with stringed instruments and organs.*
> *Praise him upon the loud cymbals:*
> *Praise him upon the high sounding cymbals.*
> *Let every thing that hath breath praise the LORD.*
> *Praise ye the LORD. (Psalm 150)*

> *But ye are a chosen generation, a royal priesthood, an holy nation, a peculiar people; that ye should show forth the praises of him who hath called you out of darkness into his marvellous light. (1 Peter 2:9)*

For Study and Meditation: Read Isaiah 40 to 44. Consider the holiness of God and the situation of this earth from which we are redeemed. In what way does this lead you to want to take something from this fallen world and lift it to heaven in praise of God, because this is the way He has lifted us from this fallen world, preparing us for the perfection of Heaven? As you go about your daily life, take something precious and with which you have taken some special care, or something that your natural eyes or other senses find beautiful, and use it as a means of offering praise to God.

Halakhah

Intercession

There is a ministry at the heart of all we do as a Royal Priesthood. It is a general calling to all and a special responsibility for some. It is a ministry that is, more than any, a ministry of the Holy Spirit within us. It is a mysterious ministry, but there is little point in asking why it is a necessary ministry. It is simply God's way. It is the ministry of intercession.

The theme of intercession occurs throughout the Scriptures. Intercession is linked closely to faith. The ministry is associated with prayer, but it is not prayer alone, even intense prayer. An intercessor is a broken person. He or she will have been moulded by the Lord for this specific calling, probably over many years. The biggest inhibition to intercession is the flesh of man. The flesh wars against the Spirit of God and must be broken. Personal ambition, desire for recognition, and plans and motives that originate in the human mind all have to submitted to the will of God. It is a process of inner crucifixion that brings a person to the point where intercession is real. The intercessor through faith submits to the will of the Spirit and so intercession can rise to the throne of God like the incense that once rose up in the Holy Place of the Temple.

In intercession, a person is ministering on behalf of the people of this fallen world to the Lord Himself. The intercessor is standing in the gap between Earth and Heaven expressing through the spiritual outpouring that comes from the Holy Spirit the needs of the people in this world whom the Lord would help. The intercessions are directed by the Lord and so are in accord with His own strategy. It would be an error to try to turn the ministry of intercession into something that we can fully understand through human philosophy,

but it is clear that the intercessor is conscious more of the sovereign purposes of God than of the free will of man to pray on behalf of man.

Intercession is likely to be a more hidden ministry than most, and is typified by the ministry of the Priests in the Temple at the Altar of Incense, hidden away from the world in the Holy Place. The Holy Place of the Temple was only a physical representation of an inner relationship, whereby, in a spiritual sense, a person draws near to the Lord. There is no Temple now, except that the Lord's people are a living Temple, where the Spirit of God abides. Thus, the physical surroundings are secondary to the spiritual reality. One can be in intercession, at the call of God, anywhere. It is He that decides the times and places where He will use a person's body as a channel for intercession, powerfully overwhelming the person at times as He ministers through them. Nevertheless, these times are times of separation. They can be outside in the countryside or in the inner room of a building, but they will be times of separation from the world.

When a person is being prepared and used in intercession, it is likely that he or she will be deeply involved in the concerns that are the objects of intercession. The ministry of intercession may be preceded by, or may accompany, practical ministry. Examples of this are ministry to families, ministry to prisoners, the poor or the sick or ministry in a particular country of missionary service, perhaps ministry to Israel. Through practical involvement in an area of service, a person's heart is moved to care for the wider needs of people in this area of service. The person may have immense experiences of God's interventions in this area of ministry, and faith grows for God's work to be multiplied. Then there may come a time when the practical ministry is restricted by the Lord, perhaps even taken away. At this time the person turns to God in faith for the greater manifestation of his or her area of prior service, and practical activity is replaced by intercession by the power of the Holy Spirit. The intercessor now believes in the fuller realisation of ministry through the lives of others. This is the way of the Torah of God, that through practical experience a spiritual ministry grows.

Indeed, it is in accordance with the principal of intercession that a person is to be completely identified with the people for whom he or she is interceding. The ministry of intercession for some people, may continue to be paralleled through practical service. For others, the practical service will give way more fully to the spiritual ministry. The Lord Himself has individual callings for individual people.

There will be times when the intercessor feels that he or she is wrestling with God on an issue, even though inspired to the intercessions by the Lord Himself. At a certain point, peace comes and it is as if a victory is won. At that point, faith grows for that particular work of God, in a general sense, and the victory need not be won in the same way again. The ministry of God may then be multiplied time and again in that area of ministry where the victory of faith was first won.

All leaders of the people of God should manifest the ministry of intercession to some degree. We find many examples in the Scriptures. Moses, for example, interceded for the people whom the Lord was going to destroy on account of the golden calf:

And Moses returned unto the LORD, and said, Oh, this people have sinned a great sin, and have made them gods of gold. Yet now, if thou wilt forgive their sin– and if not, blot me, I pray thee, out of thy book which thou hast written. (Exodus 32:31-32)

God is always looking for an intercessor in relation to the needs of the world:

And I sought for a man among them, that should make up the hedge, and stand in the gap before me for the land, that I should not destroy it: but I found none. Therefore have I poured out mine indignation upon them; I have consumed them with the fire of my wrath: their own way have I recompensed upon their heads, saith the Lord GOD. (Ezekiel 22:30-31)

An intercessor knows God. He knows His character and has the boldness to come close to Him, though this boldness is not based on reckless and fleshly behaviour, but on commitment to holiness, which can only come through breaking and after deep discipleship training under the Lord Himself. The intercessor is so taken up with the needs of other people that he himself would have the Lord attend to the needs of these people, even at the expense of his own life. This was seen in the life of Moses and also in the life of Paul who said concerning his own people of Israel:

> For I could wish that myself were accursed from Christ for my brethren, my kinsmen according to the flesh. (Romans 9:3)

The highest example of all is Yeshua Himself. He is our High Priest. The High Priest of the Levitical Priesthood went into the Holy of Holies to the place of deep intercession just once a year, on the Day of Atonement (Yom Kippur). But Yeshua, of the order of Melchizedek:

> ...is able also to save them to the uttermost that come unto God by him, seeing he ever liveth to make intercession for them. For such an high priest became us, who is holy, harmless, undefiled, separate from sinners, and made higher than the heavens. (Hebrews 7:25-26)

His High Priestly intercession from the Cross is being answered from generation to generation:

> Father, forgive them; for they know not what they do. (Luke 23:34)

Intercessions from those called to the ministry today are within the intercessions of the Lord. The Holy Place in the Temple is replaced by the abiding place in Him, in a spiritual way, from where the intercessions rise. This is the place of fulfilment of the promise of Yeshua:

> If ye abide in me, and my words abide in you, ye shall ask what ye will, and it shall be done unto you. (John 15:7)

In this abiding place, the will of the intercessor is given over to the will of God and so what is asked is according to His will. It is a costly ministry and there will be times of groaning in the Spirit:

> *Likewise the Spirit also helpeth our infirmities: for we know not what we should pray for as we ought: but the Spirit itself maketh intercession for us with groanings which cannot be uttered. (Romans 8:26)*

The sufferings that we experience as intercessors are the sufferings of the Lord Himself, and intercessors will discover what Paul discovered in his own ministry:

> *I Paul am made a minister; who now rejoice in my sufferings for you, and fill up that which is behind of the afflictions of Christ in my flesh for his body's sake, which is the church. (Colossians 1:23-24)*

For Study and Meditation: Study Abraham's intercession for Sodom (Genesis 18), Moses' intercession for the Children of Israel (Exodus 32) and Yeshua's intercession for all believers (John 17, Luke 22-23). Ask the Lord if you are being called to intercession in some way.

Halakhah

Obedience

As we consider our Halakhah, our walk with God, our highest call is to walk as Yeshua walked. John said this clearly:

He that saith he abideth in him ought himself also so to walk, even as he walked. (1 John 2:6)

As we consider this, we might study all the Scriptures and make a list of the things that Yeshua did and then try to do the same sorts of things. However, this is most likely to be a work of the flesh, and could be dangerous if we try to exercise spiritual ministries in a carnal way.

Sin came into this world due to disobedience in the Garden of Eden. This was disobedience to the direct word of God given to Adam and Eve. All sin is disobedience to the teaching of God in some way. This is the reason for the sacrifices. What did Samuel say to Saul, however, when Saul had disobeyed God?

And Samuel said, Hath the LORD as great delight in burnt offerings and sacrifices, as in obeying the voice of the LORD? Behold, to obey is better than sacrifice, and to hearken than the fat of rams. (1 Samuel 15:22)

Sacrifices were given for the covering of disobedience, but it was better to obey than to have need for such sacrifice. Ultimately, it was the Lord's own Sacrifice that was given for the disobedience of us all. Better it would have been that we had obeyed than that He should have been sacrificed - if this were possible. Indeed, if we are looking for the quality of the Lord that we should attempt to acquire

in order to be like Him, it is the quality of obedience:

> *Though he were a Son, yet learned he obedience by the things which he suffered; and being made perfect, he became the author of eternal salvation unto all them that obey him. (Hebrews 5:8-9)*

> *And being found in fashion as a man, he humbled himself, and became obedient unto death, even the death of the cross. (Philippians 2:8)*

If we can learn the chief characteristic of Yeshua, to be obedient to God, then the rest will follow. John wrote of Him:

> *Then answered Jesus and said unto them, Verily, verily, I say unto you, The Son can do nothing of himself, but what he seeth the Father do: for what things soever he doeth, these also doeth the Son likewise. For the Father loveth the Son, and showeth him all things that himself doeth: and he will show him greater works than these, that ye may marvel. (John 5:19-20)*

> *Jesus saith unto them, My meat is to do the will of him that sent me, and to finish his work. (John 4:34)*

> *I can of mine own self do nothing: as I hear, I judge: and my judgment is just; because I seek not mine own will, but the will of the Father which hath sent me. (John 5:30)*

> *Jesus answered them, and said, My doctrine is not mine, but his that sent me. If any man will do his will, he shall know of the doctrine, whether it be of God, or whether I speak of myself. He that speaketh of himself seeketh his own glory: but he that seeketh his glory that sent him, the same is true, and no unrighteousness is in him. (John 7:16-18)*

The key to being like Yeshua and walking as He did is to seek to do the will of the Father, to know what the Father is doing and obey Him in what He is asking us to do. This is the true Halakhah of ministry, and God has redeemed us from the curse that Adam brought through disobedience, so that we might learn again what it is to obey Him in all things. This is more than a life governed by biblical principles, it is a life lived in fellowship with and prayerful communication with the Living God. Indeed, it is a life where the power of the Holy Spirit is at work in us to do the will of the Father.

> *I beseech you therefore, brethren, by the mercies of God, that ye present your bodies a living sacrifice, holy, acceptable unto God, which is your reasonable service. And be not conformed to this world: but be ye transformed by the renewing of your mind, that ye may prove what is that good, and acceptable, and perfect, will of God. (Romans 12:1-2)*

For Study and Meditation: Read again the Bible references given in this section. Read the story of David in 2 Samuel 5, where on two occasions he sought God for guidance and different guidance was given each time for a similar circumstance. Prayerfully consider whether you are seeking to obey God in your own life and ministry.

Halakhah

Rivers of Living Water

There is no doubt that the Scriptures use the image of water as a symbol of the Holy Spirit. For example, we read:

For I will pour water upon him that is thirsty, and floods upon the dry ground: I will pour my spirit upon thy seed, and my blessing upon thine offspring: and they shall spring up as among the grass, as willows by the water courses. (Isaiah 44:3-4)

This is written in a poetic style where the familiar thought of refreshing water is used to build the expectation of the refreshment that will come when the Holy Spirit is given to the Lord's people. A reason for the physical parallels is that we cannot see into the spiritual world and so we can be helped through the use of familiar concepts from our experiences of this world.

Just as we cannot see the way the Holy Spirit works in us, so we cannot see the spiritual part of our own character where the Holy Spirit comes to dwell. The Scriptures call this inner part our *heart* or in some of the older translations our *belly*, because of the sense we have that when the Holy Spirit is working in us there is some relationship with this part of our anatomy. This spiritual centre of our existence, our heart, is such an important and familiar concept in Scripture that it is found over eight hundred times and in most of the books of the Bible.

We should not consider the concept of the *heart* as a metaphor alone, as if the physical part of our body were the only part of us. Our spiritual heart is a real part of us - indeed, the most important part of us.

The fulfilment of the Scriptures, which pointed to the coming of the Holy Spirit, was through Yeshua. On the last day of the Feast of Tabernacles, where water was poured symbolically by the Priests, there was a remembrance of the promises that the Holy Spirit would come, for example:

Ho, every one that thirsteth, come ye to the waters, and he that hath no money; come ye, buy, and eat; yea, come, buy wine and milk without money and without price. (Isaiah 55:1)

And in that day thou shalt say, O LORD, I will praise thee: though thou wast angry with me, thine anger is turned away, and thou comfortedst me. Behold, God is my salvation; I will trust, and not be afraid: for the LORD JEHOVAH is my strength and my song; he also is become my salvation. Therefore with joy shall ye draw water out of the wells of salvation. And in that day shall ye say, Praise the LORD, call upon his name, declare his doings among the people, make mention that his name is exalted. Sing unto the LORD; for he hath done excellent things: this is known in all the earth. Cry out and shout, thou inhabitant of Zion: for great is the Holy One of Israel in the midst of thee. (Isaiah 12:1-6)

Yeshua stood up at that Feast and announced the fulfilment of the promise:

In the last day, that great day of the feast, Jesus stood and cried, saying, If any man thirst, let him come unto me, and drink. He that believeth on me, as the scripture hath said, out of his belly shall flow rivers of living water. (John 7:37-38)

John explains this in the next verse of this chapter:

But this spake he of the Spirit, which they that believe on him should receive: for the Holy Ghost was not yet given; because that Jesus was not yet glorified. (John 7:38)

Thus, from the risen Lord comes the gift of the Holy Spirit to live in the centre of the being of all believers - in their very heart. One reason for the gift of the Holy Spirit is for spiritual ministries. All of the ministries of the Church are spiritual and it should be the expectation of both ministers and those to whom ministry is given that there will be a fulfilment of what Yeshua said:

> ....*out of his belly shall flow rivers of living water.*

In the ministries of the Church, there should be an experience of the Holy Spirit ministering one to another according to the call and gifting that God Himself gives.

There are counterfeits to the ministries of the Holy Spirit based on human strategies, where human philosophies and psychologies take the place of spiritual ministry. Whenever spiritual ministry is being exercised, it should be our expectation that there will be a sense of the power and working of the Holy Spirit from believer to believer, which can be likened to water flowing from out of the innermost being of the person who is the Lord's vessel for ministry. Always we should experience a measure of this and there may be times when the flow of the Holy Spirit's life will be almost overwhelming as the Lord's love is made manifest in the lives of believers in special ways. Where there is a sense of dryness in our ministries we should ask whether we are truly fulfilling the promise that the Lord made when He stood and spoke in the Temple precincts on the day of fulfilment of the promise of the years, at the Feast of Tabernacles. Are we vessels through whom flows the life of the Holy Spirit, like living water to a thirsty land?

For Study and Meditation: Read 1 Corinthians 12, and prayerfully review your expectation of the working of the Holy Spirit among believers, of which you are a part.

Halakhah

Halakhah for Jews and Halakhah for non-Jews

There is one worldwide body of believers spanning many centuries, made up of Jews and non-Jews. In the one body there is equality and unity:

There is neither Jew nor Greek, there is neither bond nor free, there is neither male nor female: for ye are all one in Christ Jesus. (Galatians 3:28)

Thus, there is a sense in which we are all the same. Certainly this applies to all having equal standing before God, but does it apply to every aspect of our Halakhah? Clearly, there are some instructions for women that do not apply to men, such as in the order of authority in the home. Thus, there must be scope in the Lord's Torah for unity in diversity. Particularly in this generation of restoration of the people of Israel, there are questions concerning how Halakhah is to be understood for Jews and non-Jews. Are there some things that apply differently to these groups of believers? Are there certain obligations for Jews that are not obligations for non-Jews?

The Covenant Promise was given to Abraham. Torah was given at Mount Sinai to the physical descendants of Israel. There was only one group of people - the physical descendants of Abraham to whom the Torah came directly. It is wise to consider whether some of the things that originated in those days concerning the physical descendants of Israel alone, still only apply to the physical descendants in that way and whether they were for all time, or until

Messiah was revealed. We can consider some examples.

One of God's promises is that the Land of Israel would remain a possession of the physical descendants of Israel forever:

> *And the LORD said unto Abram, after that Lot was separated from him, Lift up now thine eyes, and look from the place where thou art northward, and southward, and eastward, and westward: for all the land which thou seest, to thee will I give it, and to thy seed for ever. (Genesis 13:14-15)*

Another example is the Sabbath Day, where it is a clear obligation on Israel, but possibly not on other people:

> *Six days may work be done; but in the seventh is the sabbath of rest, holy to the LORD: whosoever doeth any work in the sabbath day, he shall surely be put to death. Wherefore the children of Israel shall keep the sabbath, to observe the sabbath throughout their generations, for a perpetual covenant. (Exodus 13:16-17)*

There is also an example in the Book of Esther, which brought an obligation on Jews in every age to celebrate Purim:

> *Wherefore they called these days Purim after the name of Pur. Therefore for all the words of this letter, and of that which they had seen concerning this matter, and which had come unto them, the Jews ordained, and took upon them, and upon their seed, and upon all such as joined themselves unto them, so as it should not fail, that they would keep these two days according to their writing, and according to their appointed time every year; and that these days should be remembered and kept throughout every generation, every family, every province, and every city; and that these days of Purim should not fail from among the Jews, nor the memorial of them perish from their seed. (Esther 9:26-28)*

These are three different examples. The first is a physical promise to the physical descendants of the nation of Israel, that their land will always belong to them (even, presumably, when they are in exile). The second example concerns an extremely important aspect of the Torah of God, one of the Ten Commandments, the keeping of the Sabbath Day. The third is a Jewish custom. Of these three examples, the second is possibly the most relevant example for non-Jews to consider regarding personal Halakhah. Non-Jews who come to faith in Yeshua, according to Ephesians 2, become fellow citizens with all the saints in the commonwealth of Israel. They thus need to discover whether they are obliged to follow Torah in the manner of the Jews. For example, is the Sabbath Day an obligation?

The key may lie within the term *obligation*. If we were to use the term *privilege* or *wise teaching*, then we would approach the subject in a different way. If it is an obligation to obey certain aspects of Torah, including the Sabbath, then we sin if we do not observe it in the way the Children of Israel were expected to do, and in which, from the Scriptures, it appears they must make every effort to do for all time. If non-Jews start with the principle that the Sabbath is a gift from God and that it is a wise thing to adopt it, then we are free to learn the benefits of the Sabbath according to the leading of the Lord, but this is different from being obliged to celebrate it. Both Jews and non-Jews may celebrate the Sabbath, but are they to come to it from a different perspective?

This seems to have been the attitude of the Council of Jerusalem (Acts 15). Here the central question was whether new male converts from the Gentile world had to be circumcised. The general principle regarding Halakhah, however, that came as the conclusion to the meeting was that there was not to be an obligation for believers from the Gentile world to follow Torah in the manner of Jewish custom, but within a freedom to learn as led by the Holy Spirit. The principle given in Paul's teaching was in line with this:

One man esteemeth one day above another: another esteemeth every day alike. Let every man be fully persuaded in his own mind. He that regardeth the day, regardeth it unto the Lord; and he that regardeth not the day, to the Lord he doth not regard it. He that eateth, eateth to the Lord, for he giveth God thanks; and he that eateth not, to the Lord he eateth not, and giveth God thanks. (Romans 14:5-6)

Indeed, we can read from Scripture that the curse (punishments for transgression) of the law was removed so that Gentiles might be saved.

Christ hath redeemed us from the curse of the law, being made a curse for us: for it is written, Cursed is every one that hangeth on a tree: that the blessing of Abraham might come on the Gentiles through Jesus Christ; that we might receive the promise of the Spirit through faith. (Galatians 3:13-14)

We must consider the situation in the world when the Gospel first went out among the Gentiles. Though it had been possible for the Law of Moses to be heard from synagogues around the world, not all Gentiles were god-fearers - those who sought to live by these laws and serve the God of the Jews. Many Gentiles, though they may have had a desire to know the true God, would come from backgrounds of pagan practices. To impose the Laws of Moses, which Jews knew from birth, in some ritualistic way would have made it difficult for them to enter the covenant community. Instead, they were given the Holy Spirit to lead them into all truth and the main teaching was to live by the Spirit and not the works of the Law (though we would not expect the Holy Spirit to teach anything outside of the Laws of God).

Thus in Paul's day, there was a clear distinction between those from a Jewish background and those from a non-Jewish background in their starting point in the life of faith in Yeshua. Indeed, we find that Paul recognised this and was careful not to offend the Jews in regard to traditions whilst, nevertheless, ministering to the Gentiles by the power of the Holy Spirit.

This picture inclines us to think that there are indeed differences in Halakhah for Jews and for non-Jews. However, we might also consider that as time went on, the practices of Jews and non-Jews might have come closer together. Unfortunately, the antiSemitism in the Church and the teaching that the Gentile Church has replaced Israel in the purposes of God has caused a number of generations of the Church not to treat Halakhah as carefully in relation to Jewish and non-Jewish characteristics as we otherwise might have done.

While it does seem that some of God's teaching puts specific requirements on every generation of the physical descendants of Israel, in order that they remain a distinct people on whom He can show mercy through the atoning blood of Yeshua HaMashiach, it is surely time for us to consider what these distinctions ought to be, if indeed there are any. In Romans 3:30 we have interesting terminology, whereby Jews are saved *by* faith and Gentiles *through* the same faith, possibly indicating that there is a different starting point on certain aspects of the obligation to obey the Law of Moses. Jews, by failing through falling short of certain obligations, are saved by faith in Yeshua. Gentiles, who have fallen short of the Law, which they did not know as the Jews did, are saved through the same faith in Yeshua. Both are saved because of their faith, and regenerated by the power of the Holy Spirit and both have a living Halakhah in terms of their walk in the Spirit, but there may be some ways (for example, regarding observance of the Sabbath) where there is a different way of looking at obligation to obedience of Torah. Torah is high and holy for both Jews and Gentiles and a perfect manifestation of the loving heart of God within His covenant community, nevertheless.

When we look into the Book of Revelation, we see the picture of the Tribes of Israel, and also those from every other tribe in the world, around the throne of God (Revelation 7). We can suppose that there will remain a distinctiveness among believers from the tribes of the earth even in Heaven.

We would be wise to (at least) begin a mature study of what aspects of Halakhah are obligations to Jews on account of their specific place in the Covenant plans of God, but which are not obligations, in the same sense, to non-Jews. Clearly the physical descendants of Israel have some specific characteristics, such as having possession of the Land of Israel forever, and may be required by the Lord to have other characteristics that the world will see. They have some traditions that come from the agreement within the Tribes of Israel, like the celebration of Purim, which is also part of that distinctiveness. Then there are some elements of the Law of Moses which might be approached in a different way. In all of this, both Jews and Gentiles are to seek to walk with the Spirit of God, and remain members of the Covenant people only on account of faith in Yeshua, of course.

For Study and Meditation: Make a study of places in the Torah where it seems to indicate that the physical descendants of Israel have an everlasting obligation. Prayerfully consider how both Jews and non-Jews should approach such obligations. Should non-Jews value all of Torah, but see some things (including perhaps the Sabbath) as a goal, but not an obligation? Make sure that you study the whole of Scripture to confirm or contradict your ideas. Raise these things up in discussion with others. Could it be said, however, that the prime obligation on all believers, whether from a Jewish or Gentile background, is to seek to walk in obedience to the Holy Spirit? In this walk with the Holy Spirit, according to Romans 14:5 and 1 Corinthians 6:12, could it be said that at any one time there will be differences in the priorities of Halakhah for many of the Lord's people whether Jew or non-Jew?

Halakhah

Self-righteousness

It is possible to start in the Spirit and go on in the flesh. The Galatians found this and received a stern rebuke from the Apostle Paul:

> *O foolish Galatians, who hath bewitched you, that ye should not obey the truth, before whose eyes Jesus Christ hath been evidently set forth, crucified among you? This only would I learn of you, Received ye the Spirit by the works of the law, or by the hearing of faith? Are ye so foolish? having begun in the Spirit, are ye now made perfect by the flesh? (Galatians 3:1-3)*

It is apparent that after Paul's teaching about the true Halakhah of the life of the Spirit, there came teachers among them who diverted them to ritual observance of aspects of the law, and they considered this to be a truer path to holiness.

We might feel that after all the years since then, this is not such a problem. However, it is not only the Jewish leaders of Yeshua's day who could interpret the Torah of God into a series of man-made philosophies and rules. Despite the fact that the Jews were largely ignored by the Church in the Gentile world for nearly two thousand years, there have been many legalistic sects in the Church, and it is possible to turn the New Testament into a set of rules just as much as the Old Testament. Indeed, anything born of the flesh and not of the Spirit is likely to be legalistic in one form or another, and the Church has not always been full of the Holy Spirit.

In these days of the restoration of Israel, perhaps we will see various approaches to Torah and Halakhah promoted around the world, just as in Paul's day, so there may be an added possibility for believers to be seduced into works of the flesh, just as the Galatians were.

For many of us, it is a challenging and refreshing time to contemplate the restoration of the whole body of believers in this day of the restoration of Israel. Yet in our zeal, we may want to go ahead of the Holy Spirit's teaching in our lives and so we will become vulnerable to taking on practices of Torah or Jewish tradition that simply fascinate us in a fleshly way. We can soon leave behind the fellowship of the Spirit of God and live in a ritualistic way. Indeed, there can be many persuasive arguments that would incline the believer to accept a ritualistic, prescriptive Halakhah. One of the sins of the flesh that will contribute to this is the desire to be seen by men to be obeying a form of Halakhah that makes them appear to be knowledgeable and pious. This is the sort of desire that caused some of the teachers of the Torah to wear wide phylacteries and be seen praying in public in Yeshua's day.

It is a short route from fleshly observance of the law to self-righteousness and sham. This is quite the opposite to the humility that comes as a fruit of the Holy Spirit. Self-righteousness comes from the lie that we can tell ourselves that we can be saved by our own efforts, and live out our Halakhah without a daily walk and relationship with the Holy Spirit. Humility tells us that we need Him in every area of our lives and that we are lost if we rely on our own efforts to please God.

In the coming days, there will be a breaking-off of proud branches of the Church, just as Paul warned:

And if some of the branches be broken off, and thou, being a wild olive tree, wert grafted in among them, and with them partakest of the root and fatness of the olive tree; boast not against the branches. But if thou boast, thou bearest not the root, but the root thee. Thou wilt say then, The branches were broken off, that I might be grafted in. Well; because of unbelief they were broken off, and thou standest by faith. Be not highminded, but fear: for if

God spared not the natural branches, take heed lest he also spare not thee. Behold therefore the goodness and severity of God: on them which fell, severity; but toward thee, goodness, if thou continue in his goodness: otherwise thou also shalt be cut off. (Romans 11:17-22)

In restoring the true Halakhah of God, which is a daily walk with the Holy Spirit, with a consciousness of the times we are in and the whole Torah of God, we must maintain a steady and humble walk. We must not boast on account of the fact that we stand by faith while the Jews were sent to exile, nor adopt a self-righteous attitude to Torah that would both deprive us of our inheritance and provoke the Jews to anger. Not by external forms of religion nor by internal philosophies of man should we seek to walk, but only by the humility that comes from the daily Halakhah with the Holy Spirit.

Wherewith shall I come before the LORD, and bow myself before the high God? shall I come before him with burnt offerings, with calves of a year old? Will the LORD be pleased with thousands of rams, or with ten thousands of rivers of oil? shall I give my firstborn for my transgression, the fruit of my body for the sin of my soul? He hath showed thee, O man, what is good; and what doth the LORD require of thee, but to do justly, and to love mercy, and to walk humbly with thy God? (Micah 6:6-8)

For Study and Meditation: Read Paul's Epistle to the Galatians and consider the difference between a Judaising approach to Halakhah and a walk with the Holy Spirit.

Halakhah

Grace to Learn

When all has been considered, we have the privilege beyond measure of the gift of God's Holy Spirit, who will come to us, dwell in us and be our personal teacher regarding the ways of God. He will show us the true meaning and intent of Torah and He will teach us as no other teacher can:

> But this shall be the covenant that I will make with the house of Israel; After those days, saith the LORD, I will put my law in their inward parts, and write it in their hearts; and will be their God, and they shall be my people. And they shall teach no more every man his neighbour, and every man his brother, saying, Know the LORD: for they shall all know me, from the least of them unto the greatest of them, saith the LORD: for I will forgive their iniquity, and I will remember their sin no more. (Jeremiah 31:33-34)

There is an individual relationship with the Lord through fellowship with His Spirit, and there is a community Halakhah that we learn as the family of God together.

When we begin to understand that our true Halakhah is a walk with the Holy Spirit, and not ritual observance of the Torah, we also, however, can become open to an error. If we have the tendency to be hard to teach in the natural world, we will probably be hard to teach in the spiritual world. A disciple is one who has the desire to learn and is teachable. One error is that we can try to go too quickly and end up in ritualism, having started well with the Spirit of God but then leaving Him behind. Another error results from the same tendency, but has a different consequence. It is the tendency to leave a disciplined approach to learning behind and try to run ahead in spiritual matters.

Far from being what some have called super-spiritual in behaviour, those who seek to manifest spiritual behaviour that is not a result of the guiding of the Holy Spirit can go into fanciful expectation or spiritual deception. They try to live on a higher spiritual plane than is the Lord's intent for them, so leaving the true Spirit of God out of their lives in the end.

For some, who are spiritually immature in this way, the next step is the almost total neglect of the Torah of God. They obey the law of God neither ritually nor in obedience to the Spirit of God. Feeling free of the constraints of the law they think that they are not able to sin now, because they think that they live by the Spirit and under the atoning blood of Yeshua. They fall into the category that Paul warned about, which is to live with a false concept of grace and sin as if grace came in such abundant measure that they need not even be conscious of what sin is. They leave the true Holy Spirit out of their lives in this way and are open to deception and reaction from human emotion, believing either of these things to be a prompting of the Holy Spirit.

The walk of discipleship is a walk of learning and one on which the road narrows and does not get wider. Holiness is still determined by the principles of Torah, yet grace covers the sins of those who fall short of the full measure as they are willing to learn through their walk with the Spirit of God, who will take them to fulfilment of the deeper principles of Torah, not by ritual, but through a closer walk with Him. It is this true walk with Him that is our walk in grace. Grace has been given that we might learn.

Thus our Halakhah should involve daily disciplines of prayer and study and we should not think that we would be so spiritual as to leave these disciplines behind. While it is the Living Word who is our guide, we will find that in His teaching programme He will build in safeguards to ensure that we maintain a disciplined path of discipleship. For example, though He could teach us everything that is in the Scriptures without our need to read them for ourselves, He will probably ensure that our inspiration begins through our daily ordered and disciplined reading. He will begin to teach us as we study and pray according to the Scriptures that He has inspired us to read, taking the written themes and relating them to our lives. There can also be specific ways that He will guide us, but if we follow Him in all things, we will find ourselves on a safe and disciplined path of discipleship. Similarly, the Lord is able to take away all our difficulties and diseases, but it is often a better path of discipleship for the Lord to teach us, guide us and be with us through some of these difficulties than to remove them all.

We thank God that because of the gift of His Spirit, our Halakhah is deep and spiritual and comes out of our living relationship with Him, but let us also remember always to be disciplined disciples as the Torah of God is being gradually written on our hearts. Let us seek to grow day by day in the freedom and grace that has been given to us, but also in the discipline of the Lord. We will have grace in times of need, grace to help us persevere and grow in faith and obedience. We must test all things spiritual, and in all things seek to follow the path that the Lord sets before us.

Study to show thyself approved unto God, a workman that needeth not to be ashamed, rightly dividing the word of truth. (2 Timothy 2:15)

Fathers, provoke not your children to wrath: but bring them up in the nurture and admonition of the Lord. (Ephesians 6:4)

The end of all things is at hand: be ye therefore sober, and watch unto prayer. (1Peter 4:7)

…but ye are washed, but ye are sanctified, but ye are justified in the name of the Lord Jesus, and by the Spirit of our God. All things are lawful unto me, but all things are not expedient: all things are lawful for me, but I will not be brought under the power of any. (1 Corinthians 6:11-12)

One man esteemeth one day above another: another esteemeth every day alike. Let every man be fully persuaded in his own mind. He that regardeth the day, regardeth it unto the Lord; and he that regardeth not the day, to the Lord he doth not regard it. He that eateth, eateth to the Lord, for he giveth God thanks; and he that eateth not, to the Lord he eateth not, and giveth God thanks. (Romans 16:5-6)

For Study and Meditation: Study Romans 1 to 8 and ensure you have understood the balance of Paul's message regarding the life of the Spirit and observance of the Torah of God.

Appendix

What's in a name?

**Articles previously published in Prophecy Today Vol 16
Numbers 4 (July/August 2000)
and 5 (September/October 2000)**

When the Gospel went out to the Greek speaking world our Saviour was called Jesus. This is a modification of Yeshua, the Hebraic form of his name. A growing number of believers are using the name Yeshua again. This is linked to the growth of a movement to restore the Hebraic foundations of the Christian faith. The name is rich in meaning, being associated with the Hebrew word for salvation. Indeed, if we look closely at the Hebrew letters which make up the name, we will discover even greater significance.

The name Yeshua is made up of four consonents, ישוע. Reading from right to left these are *yud, shin, vav, ayin.* It is interesting to compare the letters which form the word with the letters, יהוה known as the tetragrammaton, which make up the name of Yahweh, God the Father. These are *yud, hay, vav, hay.* If we put the letters for the Son's name under the letters for the Father's name, we can compare them more easily:

Yahweh	יהוה
Yeshua	ישוע

Both names have yud (י) and vav (ו). There are meanings attached to Hebrew letters. To some extent they are like hieroglyphics, conveying meaning through pictures. One Jewish tradition is that the vav(ו) symbolises the power that binds together the souls of Israel. We will return to this point later. The hay (ה) is symbolic of a window. It looks as though the Son's name is derived from the Father's name by changing the two symbols of the window for the shin (ש) and ayin (ע). Perhaps something happened when the windows of heaven opened to reveal the Son. Obviously we can stretch these ideas too far, but there would seem to be something important to consider if we go a little further.

First, we can consider the yud (י) and the vav (ו) which are in both the names of the Father and the Son. The letter yud (י) is the symbol for hand - the Hebrew word for hand, yad, comes from this. The letter vav (ו) is the symbol for a nail or a hook and the word vav itself is the Hebrew for the kind of nail that is used to pin something down while it is being stretched. Now we can see the power of the message behind the letters. The hands (yud) of Yeshua (Jesus) were pierced by nails (vav) as his body was stretched on the cross. This was the means by which those saved from Israel may be bound together with the Father, fulfilling the Jewish tradition in a remarkable way. It cannot be by chance that the names of the Father and the Son both contain the symbols of the suffering that took place for the salvation of Israel.

Now we should look at the other two letters that make up the name of Yeshua. These also have clear meaning. The shin (ש) is the symbol of teeth, and the word shin also means tooth in Hebrew. The ayin (ע) is the symbol of eyes, and the word ayin also means eyes in Hebrew. This is a mystery until we read the messianic promise given by Jacob to Judah in Genesis 49:8-12 where there is reference to the eyes and teeth of the Messiah. Among the things that were said, we have, "His *eyes* shall be red with wine and his *teeth* white with milk." But what else does the symbolism of eyes and teeth mean? If we put the ayin with the shin, we form the word שע, which is associated with the word delight. But what of this delight? Like the psalmist, surely *Yeshua* delighted in the Torah (law) of God. Indeed, this is so when we recall that eyes and teeth are symbolic of the righteousness of the justice of God, eye for eye and tooth for tooth (Exodus 21:24).

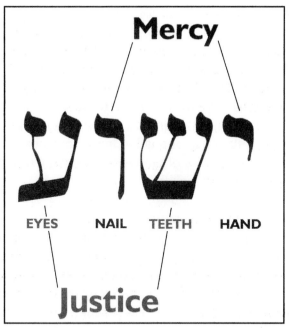

In the name of Yeshua (which means salvation)
Justice and Mercy meet in perfect balance.

The name Yeshua contains justice and mercy in perfect balance. While ayin (ע) and shin (ש) symbolise justice of the law of God, yud (י) and vav (ו) symbolise the extent of God's mercy. There is a way of restoration for those who have broken the laws of God whatever they have done, and this principle is all bound up into the name of Yeshua, which means salvation. Those who believe in Him can be saved from their sins, whatever they have done. It is important to remember this when we consider the next point, which is deeply relevant to millions of people today.

We should go back to the passage from Exodus 21 from which <u>the principle eye for eye and tooth for tooth comes. This principle of justice is associated with harm that is done to an unborn child.</u> If someone damages the eye or tooth of an unborn child, they will have the equivalent penalty. God cares for the poor and oppressed and expresses this by applying the principles of His righteousness to the most defenceless of our society, our unborn children. Indeed, not only is the penalty for damaging an unborn child eye for eye and tooth for tooth, it is also life for life. What then of abortion? Surely we must infer eye for eye, tooth for tooth and death for death. Those who have taken the life of an unborn child have the curse of death hanging over them. Indeed, the blood of murder calls for justice in the whole of our nation. We thank God that the name of Yeshua contains mercy (the symbols of *his* death - the nail pierced hands) which shows that our death penalty can be taken by him. The time has come for repentance in our nation from those who have, in their ignorance, broken the laws of God even in such extreme ways as taking the lives of unborn children.

We praise God that He has made provision through his Son for all our needs when we turn to him for forgiveness, and we rejoice that he has sealed up these truths before the beginning of time when he designed the Hebrew language in a way that could demonstrate the great truths of perfectly balanced justice and mercy in the very letters of the name Yeshua. *'And you shall call his name Yeshua because he shall save his people from their sins.'* Matthew 1:21).

What is in a name? When that name is that of the Son of God, the answer is, very much. Even those who have committed the sin of abortion can be restored to fellowship with God through faith in Him. He took their sins upon Himself when His nail pierced hands pinned Him to the cross. In Him, as shown even in His Name, was mercy and justice in perfect balance, but through Him, mercy triumphs over judgement for all who repent of their sins through faith in Him.

There is even more to see. For example, we can consider how the prophecy over Judah (Genesis 49:8-12) pointed to the perfect righteousness of the coming Messiah: His eyes shall be red with wine and his teeth white with milk. Yet even in the symbols of the eyes and teeth pointing to the outworking of 'eye for eye and tooth for tooth', we can also consider a wonderful picture of mercy triumphing over justice. If the repentant sinner were to look into the face of the Messiah, he or she would see not a frown of judgement, but a smile of friendship, love and mercy. The love of God shines out from Yeshua's smile and loving eyes. Indeed, those teeth and eyes are as much a sign of love as judgement when the repentant sinner turns to the Messiah for forgiveness.

There is yet another important insight. We recall that the Hebraic form of the name Jesus is Yeshua, which is made up of four Hebrew letters, ישוע. Many Jews rejected Yeshua as Messiah and for centuries they have sought to profane his name. In shortening the name to Yeshu, as many religious Jews do, they declare 'May his name be profaned'. Let us consider how this act accompanies justice according to the principle of 'an eye for an eye'. The Hebrew for Yeshu is ישו the same as the Hebrew for Yeshua except that the letter ayin, ע, has been removed from the end. If we recall that the letter ayin means 'eyes' then we can understand the link with what Paul said in 2 Corinthians 3:14-16.

EYES   NAIL   TEETH   HAND

To this day the same veil remains when the old covenant is read. It has not been removed, because only in Christ is it taken away. Even to this day when Moses is read, a veil covers their hearts. But whenever anyone turns to the Lord, the veil is taken away.

No other name

There is no other name except Yeshua through whom anyone can be saved. Those who profane his name have brought judgement on themselves, leaving a partial blindness to this day. With the removal of the letter that symbolises eyes from the name of Yeshua (Jesus) a partial blindness came to those who read the

Torah but fail to see that it points to Him. We look forward to the day when repentance will sweep through Israel, when the ayin will be recovered into the name of Yeshua, resulting in the opening of eyes of understanding of who he really is. Then He will be worshipped instead of profaned, as those who have rejected him will see love in his beautiful smiling face rather than the judgement that they brought upon themselves. We have this promise within the prophecy of Paul contained in Romans 11, when the whole company of God's people will be gathered into the one Israel of God in the last days.

Back Issues of the Journal Tishrei and other papers published by Tishrei International, relating to the restoration of the biblical foundations of the Christian faith, are available. These publications emphasise the need to reconsider the Jewish and Hebraic roots of the Bible and of the Christian faith. These principles must be at the foundation of true unity of the Church, and are relevant to the mission of the Church in these last days of human history.

Cambrian Bible College offers correspondence courses to Certificate, Diploma and Degree level. The correspondence courses help to build an understanding of the Torah foundation of Scripture and application to personal life. The courses can also support preparation for ministry in Church and mission.

By arrangement seminars can be offered to local congregations who wish to explore some of the issues raised by *The Covenant People of God*.

For a list of publications, details of correspondence courses and enquiries relating to itinerant ministry write, enclosing a stamped addressed envelope with your letter, to Dr Clifford Denton, C/O The Orchard, 5 The Street, Gillingham, Beccles, Suffolk, England NR34 OLH, or e-mail at fcjdenton@aol.com

Notes

Notes

Notes

Notes